LARRY BUTTROSE was born on the very edge of the world, in Adelaide, South Australia. He began writing poetry in his teens, and co-edited two long-running alternative literary magazines during the 1970s. He moved to Sydney in the early 1980s as a singer with a cabaret group called Quietly Confident. Since then he has continued to write poetry (though not, fortunately, to sing) and has in more recent years branched out into play and screen writing, as well as satisfying his ever-present itch to travel.

Larry Buttrose

the Blue Man

Tales of Travel, Love & Coffee

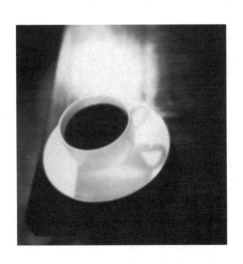

LONELY PLANET PUBLICATIONS
Melbourne · Oakland · London · Paris

The Blue Man: Tales of Travel, Love & Coffee

Published by Lonely Planet Publications
    Head Office: PO Box 617, Hawthorn, Vic 3122, Australia
    Branches: 150 Linden Street, Oakland, CA 94607, USA
                 10a Spring Place, London NW5 3BH, UK
                 1 rue Dahomey, 75011, Paris, France

First published in Australia by HarperCollins*Publishers* Pty Limited, 1997
This edition published by Lonely Planet Publications, 1999

Printed by The Bookmaker Pty Ltd
Printed in China

National Library of Australia Cataloguing in Publication Data

Buttrose, Larry, 1952- .
The blue man: tales of travel, love & coffee.

ISBN 1 86450 000 X.

1. Buttrose, Larry, 1952- – Travel. 2. Authors, Australian –
20th century – Travel – Biography. 3. Poets, Australian –
20th century – Travel – Biography. 4. Restaurants – Anecdotes.
I. Title.

910.4

Text © Larry Buttrose 1997, 1999
Map © Lonely Planet 1999

For my mother, my father,
my sister Mary-Anne

– and for Kathryn

Contents

Café Royale

The Pearl of the Orient

The Air Bar

Acknowledgements

The author wishes to thank Jane Britten, Gabrielle Haumesser, Clare Forster, Lisa Mills, Rachel Skinner, Clive Dawkins and Stephen Measday for their invaluable assistance with the journeys and the writing of this book. Thanks also to Maureen Wheeler, Susan Keogh and Janet Austin.

Apologies to my various family members for the utterly appropriate comments on golf. Let's discuss at the 19th hole.

London Paris
Athens
Casablanca
Dakar Timbuktu
Ouagadougou
Accra
Cochin Pondi-
cherry
To
Sydne

The Blue Man

Café Royale

Desert

Martinis

I was indignantly painting my bedroom ceiling, duck-egg blue. I was renting out my house, leaving Australia to live in Los Angeles. I was getting out of Sydney because I hadn't made it as a playwright. My most recent work – an adaptation of Conrad's *Heart of Darkness*, with a dash of *Nostromo* mixed in – had gone on in an old inner-city church hall thanks to the efforts of a dedicated bunch of actors, director, designers, ticket sellers and cheap claret pourers. It did well enough. The reviews were good. The houses were good too, at first, then fell off, then built up again. Inevitably there was the packed final night. Cheering, bows, hugs, vows. Most of the actors got other work from it, one or two of them new, improved agents. But most of the co-operative, myself included, got little more than our split of the takings – a few hundred dollars. It had taken me three years to write, develop and workshop that play, and now it was over it felt like it was all for nothing. There was some interest in further productions, including one major theatre company interstate, but over the next year or so it all drifted away. In effect, the theatre community had collectively smiled, patted me on the head and said, 'Thank you for that,' and wandered off to its post-show suppers saying, 'The poor dear silly boy – can't he *tell*?'

Up a ladder, I painted hard. I'd had it with Sydney, its craven hierarchy and petty cliquery. I was going to America, to the level playing fields of opportunity. But even in this heightened condition I wondered what it might be like to be yet another unemployed screenwriter in a condo down at Santa Monica. With the state of LA's beaches, you couldn't even paddle.

There was a knock at the front door. It was my friend Eamon from down the street. He was a stage designer. Among other things, he designed shows for David Atkins, the famous dancer. He said David was having troubles with the book (the stage dialogue, as opposed to the song lyrics) for a new musical he was opening. Would I come to a meeting? I knew very little about musicals, but was curious to find out what was involved. I got down off my ladder, changed out of my painting things, cleaned myself up and drove over to the meeting.

We met at the Chianti Restaurant, a chromium and steel Italian place, its post-modern metal chic affirmed by the steady flow of clientele from the Australian Opera next door. I had never met David before. He was open and direct and I liked him straight away. He had been rehearsing tap routines all day and was hungry: he ordered a big plate of antipasto – three slices of frittata, wafers of cheese, prosciutto and salami, tongues of baked orange capsicum. The rapidity of the words that came between mouthfuls underlined the urgency of the task at hand.

'It's a tap dancing musical. Like all those Broadway musicals from the thirties and forties. We need a writer who understands classic musical comedy.' I shifted in my chair but said nothing. 'Someone who can write stuff like the Marx Brothers,' David went on. 'You know, snappy gags, fast paced.'

'How much have you got so far?' I asked.

Eamon looked down into his coffee.

'We've got character outlines, and a story,' David said. 'And there's a few pages of dialogue. I've been trying to write it in my breaks.'

'And when do you need it by?'

'We start rehearsals on Monday. We open in a month.'

This was Friday. Afternoon. Late afternoon. There was also the small matter of my ticket to Los Angeles, paid for, irredeemably. Leaving in ten days' time. Could I write a Marx Brothers show in ten days? I couldn't even really get my head around the style of the thing. The only 'classic' dance musical I could recall right then was *Singin' in the Rain* – and of that just the scene where Gene Kelly splashes through puddles, singing out with mad glee.

I cleared my throat. 'I have to be honest with you – I've never written anything like this before.'

'What sort of thing do you usually write?' David asked.

'My last play was based on *Heart of Darkness*.' Eamon looked down again. 'I like Conrad, very much . . .' David cut another piece of spinach frittata. 'Look,' I said, 'I'm probably not the right person for you to talk to about this. I really don't know if I could do it. And you don't seem to have time for any hitches. I know a couple of other people who might be able to help though.' I gave David the names and got up to go. We shook hands. Almost as an afterthought I added, 'I'll give it some more thought tonight. Can I call you if I have any ideas?'

He gave me his card. 'I'll be at the dance studio. Thanks for coming.'

I could tell he was worried. And why wouldn't he be? Opening night was just a month away. The show was cast. The music, standards from the thirties and forties, was chosen. The routines were choreographed. The big torch songs were scored. Costumes were being sewn, new tap shoes awaited in boxes. A show was about to be born – but there was no book, no lines. I put the outlines and the pages of dialogue in my briefcase, and Eamon walked me out into the street.

'You could do this,' he urged. 'It's easy.'

'Eamon, Marx Brothers is not easy. Particularly with no time. How many other writers have tried to write it?'

'A couple, I think.'

I started walking away. 'By the way, what's the name of the show?'

'*Hot Shoe Shuffle*,' he said.

I did think about it, all the way home. As Eamon had said, surely it couldn't be so hard. But to write the Marx Brothers? Those inspired, lunatic routines and gags? Then I remembered Kathryn had performed musical comedy, back in drama school. She could even tap dance, had done the odd shuffle in the kitchen at parties. Perhaps she could work on it with me.

She had just begun making dinner when I got home. I sliced onions while she read the material David had given me.

'Well?'

'I know this,' she said. 'We can do this.'

She went upstairs and wrote an early scene of the showbiz fairytale, about how the seven Tap Brothers, a troupe of struggling tap dancers, get word they are to inherit a fortune in their ne'er-do-well father's will. I worked over it, then we re-worked it together. By nine o'clock we had it on the fax to David. He rang minutes later. He liked it. We worked on Act One throughout the weekend and had it ready for a first read-through with the assembled cast by Tuesday morning. Co-star Rhonda Burchmore – cast in the role of April, the flatfooted sister (or is she?) of the Tap Brothers – arrived, larger than life with an infectious toon-town grin; Jack Webster, a seasoned pro playing the Tap Brothers' father Dexter, entered with Top Cat's swagger; and then came the Tap Brothers themselves, all so very young, eager and gangly. We were extremely nervous, but the reading went well. David smiled relief.

We finished writing Act Two the day before I flew to Los Angeles. I was determined to relocate there – but I wasn't sure if Kathryn would want to come. We would have to talk that through, in the event. I had been to Los Angeles a number of times before and almost liked it. Appositely, the in-flight movie as the plane neared the California coast was *The Player*.

That weekend I drove with friends into the Mojave Desert. They knew two English girls living in a 'trailer' out there. We found them mixing sunset cocktails in the company of a crewcut Marine from a nearby base. The English girls were upper crust, plummy. They were being paid three hundred dollars a week by a notorious Hollywood producer to write porno flicks. Out here in the desert they churned out the scripts – hayseed pool cleaners and Rodeo Drive divorcees, body-sculpted gardeners and horny housewives in Pacific Pallisades, S&M sorority girls and rampant sex blobs from Mars.

The girls mixed Desert Martinis – a chilli pepper standing in for the olive. After a couple of these we all climbed the big boulder hills and sang in the moonlight. We watched as the Marine, high on martinis and whatever, leapt from boulder to boulder, hilltop to hilltop, a-whoopin' and a-hollerin' in the moonlight.

'I wouldn't recommend LA as a career move,' one of the girls said, watching him through the bottom of her martini glass. 'Not unless you have a burning desire to live in a shooting gallery on a fault line.'

Eyes and Teeth

I left Los Angeles unsure about moving there. My round-the-world ticket took me on to London where I stayed with my friend Dirk in Highgate for a week or so. Dirk was a painter. A prominent Australian artist was helping him out with a little patronage. He'd given Dirk a stipend, and a place to live in his old Georgian terrace. Jeannette Winterson lived next door. Her garden looked nice.

On the flight home I still did not know where I should live, nor what the source of my next dollar would be. When I landed in Sydney, I discovered it was opening night of *Hot Shoe Shuffle*. Kathryn and I drove miles out through the suburbs to a brick barn where the backers' season was being staged. This was the season to try the show out – and if it worked, get some serious financing involved.

I was badly jet-lagged, and the experience took on a dream-like quality. Fortunately, it was a good dream-like quality. The set and costumes were bright and fun, the tap dancing was brilliant, and the audience even laughed at the jokes. It wasn't Marx Brothers, but it was funny enough for people to feel, 'Yes, I'm sitting here watching dancing, listening to music, laughing . . . This is musical comedy.' At the urinal during intermission I heard one putative investor mutter to another mid-stream, 'Show's a hit.'

He was right. The following year it went on to play sold-out seasons all over the country. Although our royalty wasn't huge, it was a very nice thing when the cheques arrived. One day Eamon told me a London season was being talked about.

'My god, the West End. I can't believe it.'

'That's how it looks,' he said.

'Do you think it'll work there?'

'Who knows? London is different. It's political, you know.'

I had been a cold-shouldered, patronised colonial often enough in London to know exactly what he meant.

Six months later I was being flown there for our opening at the Queen's Theatre in Shaftesbury Avenue. It was going to be the full thing: the gala opening, the press hounds, the party at the Café Royal. But I sat more uncomfortably than usual in my airline seat. Kathryn had been away studying in Paris for three months, all summer – and I had gotten involved with someone else.

Kathryn and I had been together for seven years, and we had the itch. We had both seen the occasional other, but this felt different. I knew that when I saw Kathryn, I would have to tell her that I loved another woman. Would that mean the end for us? Given the history of human relationships up to this point, it should do. So could I admit to myself that it was over, and that when I returned to Australia it would be to someone else? How did I feel about that? I wasn't sure: god, to be someone who was sure about such things. The situation was further complicated by the fact that we had written a treatment for the film version of *Hot Shoe Shuffle*, and were to meet a producer in London about writing the script. We had discussed going to Morocco to write it, in the month before the show opened in March.

A sparkling, blue-skied Saturday dawned as I exited the tube at Piccadilly Circus. The temperature was near freezing point, and I had just come from an Australian summer, but I didn't feel in the least cold as I made my way up Shaftesbury Avenue. I was excited. I wanted to see the Queen's Theatre for myself, see a poster out front, a sign of some sort that this wasn't all just a fantasy. There was another show still playing, quotes from the critics emblazoned across the theatre, giant photographs of the West End stars captured mid witty line, all eyes and teeth. But there, on a rotating stand in the locked box office, was a full colour leaflet advertising our show. In fact there were dozens of the leaflets in the stand. So, I realised finally, the show really is going on.

It was still very early, much too early to ring Dirk. He kept very odd hours anyway. He was most probably just about to go to bed after another night's painting in his bunker flat. But he had just started up a new relationship, so his hours may have altered somewhat. I had an awful breakfast on Charing Cross Road, a typical English breakfast of hormone-enhanced egg, pulp-paper toast, butter mountain butter and coffee they wouldn't put in the Café Bar machine of the Engineering Department at South Sydney Council.

I greeted Dirk with a bag of Portuguese peaches at nine – a decent enough hour, I hoped. Unfortunately, he had just gone to bed. He had painted all night, then stayed up waiting for me to arrive. Sally, his new girlfriend, had gone to bed hours before. He took me up five flights of steps to the garret room he had allocated me this time. As we spoke, Jeannette Winterson popped her head through the window and handed him back something she had borrowed. She stood on the ledge between the two houses, four floors up. Dirk introduced us, and we shook hands. Then she was gone.

I met Kathryn at Heathrow that night. It being the weekend, the Arrivals lounge was crowded with family greeting family, lovers kissing lovers. The Air France flight from Paris was running late, which was lucky because so too was my tube train from Central London. I had only just reached Arrivals when passengers emerged clutching overcoats and briefcases. Kathryn appeared in a fifties-style mustard overcoat, black tights and ankle boots. She was so dark, lips cardinal-red, eyes leaf-green, dark brown hair cut straight to her shoulders. I experienced her exotic beauty all over again. That night, as we lay in bed up in the garret, she asked me if I had slept with anyone while we were apart, and I replied that yes, I had – and that I loved that other person. She said she had been seeing someone else too, a Greek composer living in Paris.

'So what now?' she asked.

'I don't know.'

'You always say that.'

'I know.'

I looked out the window and saw that it had begun to snow, big flakes fluttering down like moths out of the night sky. We got out of bed and went to the window. The slate roofs of Highgate were already a thick fairytale white.

Inhuman

But it was still snowing the next day, and by then it was not so beautiful, the streets an icy slushpit. The mercury hovered around freezing point. We shivered in our attic.

'We've got to get out of here,' Kathryn said. 'I hate London. The people are so stuck up. The streets are dirty. And it's so cold. Paris wasn't like this. It never got this cold there. This is *inhuman*.'

'We could still go to Morocco,' I suggested. 'We've got a whole month before everyone else arrives for the show. It'll be warm there.'

'Will it?' she said. 'I don't know anything about Morocco.'

'It'll be warm. It's so far south. It's *Africa* for god's sake. It's got to be warm.'

We trudged through the slush and bought our tickets from a West End bucket shop. That night at a farewell dinner with Dirk and Sally, an old friend of Dirk's, Saul, warned us that the month of Ramadan was coming. It might not be such a good time to visit Morocco.

'That's when the Muslims fast, isn't it?' I said, with the ignorance of the utterly under-researched. We had managed to get a guidebook, but had not as yet even opened it. 'You could say they fast,' Saul said. 'You could also say that no one is allowed to eat, drink, smoke, fuck or even think about sex from sunup to sundown. Not a crumb of bread, not a drop of water. By mid-afternoon they're all potential killers. And Morocco is virtually one hundred per cent Muslim. So during Ramadan it can actually be hard to find anything to eat all day.'

'Perhaps we should fly further south into Africa,' Kathryn suggested up in our garret that night.

'But I've always wanted to see Morocco.'

'But this Ramadan thing . . . maybe Saul's right.'

'No,' I said, 'he just hates Arabs – he's Jewish.' Kathryn looked at me sceptically. 'They speak French there,' I cajoled. This was a bonafide bargaining chip, as she had begun learning French during her stint in Paris and was very keen to continue with it. 'Besides, we've already got our tickets. We fly out of the snow and into Casablanca tomorrow night. Isn't that wonderful? To have Casablanca as the destination on a ticket?'

'Wonderful provided there's sunshine and we can get something to eat,' Kathryn said.

'Of course we'll be able to eat. They always provide for tourists. Don't worry.'

The Royal Air Maroc 737 was on its final approach to Tangier Airport, the stopover on the Casablanca route. 'I don't know what I'm doing sitting here,' Kathryn was saying. 'You've told me you love another woman, and yet here we are flying into Morocco together. And we're not just doing it because we're writing a film together, we haven't even signed any contract yet, and . . .'

She was cut off by a molar-jarring crash of landing gear onto tarmac as the pilot executed what could only be described as a 'hard landing'. So hard was it that I still do not understand why the wheels didn't buckle, the bottom of the plane get ripped out and all of us end up running down the runway like The Flintstones.

We were still shaking, tightly clutching each other when the doors were opened and icy air blew in. We watched the departing passengers scurry away heads down across the tarmac in driving rain.

'Don't worry,' I said, 'Casablanca's much further south.'

'That's exactly what does worry me,' Kathryn rejoined. 'We're flying there in this.'

I awoke at seven o'clock next morning in a gloomy hotel in the Ville Nouvelle of Casablanca. The guidebook had recommended the place: I couldn't for the life of me work out why. The staff were surly, the lift was hit and miss, and a group of men had decided to assemble outside our door and tell highly amusing stories in voluble Arabic all night.

Out on the street, Casablanca felt like a down-at-heel quarter of Paris, grey blocks shuttered tight in chilly morning drizzle. There were few people about, one or two female office workers in grey headscarves, the occasional moustached man mooching along in *djellabah*, that all-enclosing gown with the pointed, medieval-like hood.

The drizzle strengthened to steady rain. It was cold. I passed dim shopfronts, and peering in saw what looked like bodies scattered everywhere on tables. They were indeed bodies: sleeping ones. These men – they were all men – had stayed up until 4.30 a.m., eaten 'dinner', and were now experiencing Rapid Eye Movement in the deep sleep zone. All the restaurants and cafés were shut. I couldn't even find a cup of coffee. Eventually I discovered a booth selling matches and combs, and bought a chocolate bar. I didn't eat it right away – eating in public was probably taboo even for foreigners during Ramadan. And this was obviously Ramadan.

Returning to the hotel, the desk clerk confirmed that they would not be serving us any breakfast. '*Parce que la Ramadan,*' he said. ('Because of Ramadan.') It was a phrase oft repeated to us all through Morocco.

I went upstairs and woke Kathryn. From our room the city looked like Beirut without the bullet holes. I gave her the bad news about breakfast and we shared the chocolate bar staring out at the rain.

'This must just be Casablanca,' I said. 'It'll be better further south.'

'How far south?'

'The Sahara starts not too far down from here. It can't be raining there. It's a *desert* for Christ's sake.'

She got out of bed and pulled on my leather jacket.

It was at this point I realised just how light we were travelling. I had brought a few things, but Kathryn had come without even a change of clothes, only underwear and toiletries.

'You didn't bring anything warm at all?'

'I was planning to buy all the summer skirts and T-shirts I needed when I got here,' she said pointedly. 'We've got to get out of Casablanca,' she shivered. 'It's *inhuman.*'

Morocco has more 'guides' – hustlers and pesterers – than any country I have visited. These touts adhere themselves to you and will not let go. Often they make it impossible for the visitor simply to appreciate their country. Saul back in London had warned us about this too. 'You haven't experienced harassment until you've experienced it Moroccan-style.'

I told him we had travelled through India and many other developing countries, and we knew what we were doing.

'Don't say I didn't warn you,' he said.

Our first tout had red hair, green eyes and yellow teeth. He engaged us in a word or two of conversation while we were crossing a street in Casablanca. After five minutes he was earnestly relating tales about his French father and Moroccan mother. He was still with us eight hours later, at a bus interchange in some remote village hundreds of kilometres to the south, rain still coming down.

He was young, short, dressed in a brown *djellabah*. His fast-mumbled French was incomprehensible. But he understood us. He saw we were hungry, cold and wet. He knew where we could find an umbrella (in our haste to leave London we had neglected to pack even these!). He knew where we could eat. Over strawberry and yoghurt crêpes in a Wendy's-style plastic and primary coloured café reserved for foreigners – its existence a secret apparently confined to the touts – we told him we wanted to get out of Casablanca as soon as possible. The buses and trains were unreliable, he warned. Getting out of Casablanca today might be *difficile*. He said, however, he himself could arrange transport. It would cost a little, of course. Where did we want to go? We tossed up Marrakesh and Essaouira. Marco Moretti, a friend from Turin, a travel writer who had travelled very extensively – he had even written an Italian Lonely Planet-type guide to Australia – had recommended Essaouira as one of the most pleasant places in Morocco, a coastal fortress town, fishing port, historical site. Orson Welles had shot his version of *Othello* there. On the other hand, Marrakesh had that Crosby, Stills, Nash and Young refrain – 'all aboard that train'. But our tout gave us a warning, 'Don't go Marrakesh, too many touts,' his implication being, 'I am a good tout, all others are bad touts.' There may be a 'good tout' in Morocco. There may be, somewhere . . .

In the end we found ourselves in a Mercedes *grand taxi* driven by our tout's uncle. *Grands taxis* are for long trips; *petits taxis* run around the towns. The journey was not cheap. (We were soon to learn that Morocco is not a 'cheap' country.) Also, the driver did not take us to the destination we had negotiated. Instead we ended up being dumped in a nondescript town midway on the trip south, freezing in the wind, then jammed into another *grand taxi* shared with around twelve other people (our tout still with us, apologising all the way), then dumped again at some muddy village in the middle of nowhere, night falling, temperature falling, rain still falling. We were determined to take a bus south from there, but as our bones slowly froze, our resolve faltered. Our tout regarded us with a green, professional eye. When we cracked, he had yet another *grand taxi* pull up before us. As he waved us goodbye, he called to us that the driver was a 'good man, an honest man'. Along the way the driver gave us the choice of paying yet more, or being dropped off in the darkness. We arrived in Essaouira just before midnight, both asneeze with nascent colds. All in all it had been an instructive, if not entirely encouraging, first day in Morocco.

The Splatter Painter

Essaouira's stout white walls rise sheer from the black rocks of the sea. From the ramparts, rows of iron cannons thrust out at the blustery Atlantic. The turreted red mud inner wall of the old *medina* encloses a maze of crumbling houses, bazaars, mosques, darkened alleys and subterranean worlds. The *muezzin*'s wail wafts in on the ocean wind. But despite its seductive, brooding atmosphere, its lack of hustlers and picture-postcard beauty, somehow lucky Essaouira had remained off the package tourist track. Most European visitors to Morocco only get to see it as the backdrop for a TV commercial back home. Art directors love it.

We stayed at the Hotel Sahara, a rambling, airy old two-star. Days here were slow and quiet. *Warm.* A daily pattern soon established itself. I woke first, usually just before nine, and drew back the curtains on another clear winter's day. I read in bed a few minutes – Paul Bowles' *Days*, snippets and snapshots of his ongoing Camelot in Tangier . . . acerbic, crotchety, shrewd.

Then we rose, dressed, and walked through a misty blue morning down earthen alleyways pungent with spices, oil and fish guts. We treated our colds with herbs from a pharmacy stall in the *souks*, as prescribed by a young pharmacist, a chameleon clutched to his sleeve (we were told this was traditional for pharmacists). His stall was heaped with indigo and frankincense, with cloves for toothache and dried ginger for influenza. Kathryn bought a couple of extra outfits from a clothing stall, warm ones, for the Atlas Mountains.

Restaurant menus were somewhat limited – the Moroccan staples of *tajine*, a customised stew of meat, fish or chick-pea; and *couscous*, same again but with couscous – but the food was good and not too expensive. We found a breakfast place, the Darbaba Café on the Rue de Paris, the *medina*'s main alley. The café was run by three vivacious gays from Sicily, its signboard a grinning camel in a fez chewing a mouthful of spaghetti. Essaouira's scattering of foreigners convened daily at the tables out front for a morning coffee and orange juice. Donkeys wheezed by laden with flour sacks to jazz from a ghetto blaster in the kitchen. Women in black veils moved slowly, sunshine sleepwalkers. Grinning ancients with missing teeth drifted past hand-in-hand.

The foreigners were German, French or American for the most part. There was the pair of serious Italian girls in tassels, with shaved heads and ear, lip and nose rings, nouveau-hippies smoking roll-your-owns with silent intent. A Moroccan man was in the same corner each morning, hair straggly and dirty, dope victim, lost it long ago, the sixties in Paris, quietly cursing. A tall German in surf shorts patted his designer pony-tail over a pocket edition Thomas Mann. Aziz the waiter was polite, discreet, with a hint of humour. He brought breakfast – a baguette with homemade goat cheese, the crust very crispy, the cheese nicely sharp. Here I discovered *ns ns* (pronounced as it is spelled), a *grand café* 50/50 milk and coffee. Two of them proved an optimum morning dosage of caffeine.

The morning sun climbed quickly, slanting strongly down the dusty alley. A garbage truck, one of the few motor vehicles allowed in the old *medina*, rumbled by, a net pulled over its brimming tray of blue mineral water empties. The hooded collector sprawled on the pile of bottles, casting the foreign women a cheeky grin. He would not be eating, smoking, or drinking until the 6.30 p.m. siren. Yet he was smiling a smile that drifted on into the dusty blue of the Rue de Paris.

We liked to spend the afternoons poking about the Portuguese port. It resounded to frenetic human activity, the beating of hammers on wood, the shouts of men building skiffs with their hands, the spines set up on stone blocks like fish skeletons, the boats coming to life plank by plank. Bigger, ocean-going fishing boats busied back and forth through the oily green–black waters while others were drawn up on the slipways having their hulls careened. Fish, lobster and giant orange crabs were laid out in piles on the sand for an ad hoc market, surrounded by men and cats and swooping gulls.

One day we walked through the stiff Atlantic wind out to the end of the rocky breakwater, then back to sit in the sun on the slipway. 'You realise, of course, that if you keep seeing this woman when we get back to Australia, I'll have to stop seeing you,' Kathryn said, watching a fishing smack nose in past the breakwater.

'I suppose so, yes.'

'What do you mean, you *suppose* so? She wouldn't accept it either, would she, you seeing both of us.'

'No, she wouldn't.'

'What do you expect us to be anyway, a harem?'

'No.'

'What's her name?'

'Susan,' I said. 'What about you, and the bloke you met in Paris, the Greek composer . . . what's his name?'

She watched a threadbare black kitten scuttle off with a sardine thrashing in its teeth.

'Manolis,' she said.

We met a group of locals. It began when a woman in a robe and headscarf offered us a sprig from a bunch of mint she was buying on the street. Her name was Fatima, and she invited us back to her house for 'Moroccan whisky' – mint tea. We followed her through a hatch-like entranceway into a labyrinth of tunnels beneath the town. Along the way we caught glimpses of people's lives in this underworld, torch-lit biblical tableaux: families gathered around glowing braziers, bakers paddling rough loaves from wood-fired ovens, giant mudcrabs on hot coals, artisans in neat rows carving aromatic *thuya* wood into piled up chessboards, salad bowls, pencil cases.

Fatima's house was two rooms and a kitchen, small and dark. She seated us in the living room, then vanished. The room was bare except for cushion-covered bench seats around the walls, a low central table, a portable black and white TV and a stereo. When she came back in, she had performed a remarkable striptease, discarding her all-encompassing grey sack and revealing, almost indecently to eyes already accustomed to the Islamic mode, tight blue jeans and filmy lace blouse beneath.

'You like jazz?' She dropped a needle onto a record, and sax steamed into the little room. Over tea she told us about her husband's work. Hussein was an artist, she said, pulling out two or three canvasses – imitation Jackson Pollock, forty years on.

People began drifting in for the evening's meal – Ali the blue-robed Tuareg, the Algerian drifter-artist Muhammed, dreadlocked Hassan with his spiky blonde Swiss girlfriend Clementine. A Japanese tourist who spoke no Arabic or French and just a few words of English turned up too – how she found her way here through the maze, I had no idea. As the clock crawled towards the 6.30 p.m. siren, we all watched an Egyptian soap opera on TV. It was addictively bad, probably scheduled to take people's minds off their hunger in that last awful half-hour before they could eat. Fatima came and went from the kitchen, piling the low table with food. As the siren sounded, an inaudible sigh was heaved. Our hosts broke their fast with dates and bowls of spicy chick-pea Harira soup. The men lit strong cigarettes and relaxed back into their cushions. Later came breads, pastries, *tajine*, couscous, coffee.

After the meal the TV was switched off and several bongo-like hand drums were produced, along with hashish pipes. The drums and pipes were passed around, everyone smoking and slapping the skins for hours in this nightly jam, the drummers literally conversing through the syncopation of beats and rhythms.

After this, our presence was always requested for tea, or dinner. Even though this was not always convenient, it felt beyond our power to dissent politely. Before long, time spent alone was at a premium, and we felt less than free to enjoy being in Essaouira. We found ourselves shopping in the markets with our new friends, buying the night's food, meeting their families, being conducted to shops to look at brasswork, fabric, *thuya* handicrafts, *killim* carpets from the Middle Atlas. We were gently but insistently encouraged to buy. In the end, we did.

'We shouldn't worry about the money,' we agreed back in our room. 'They're fine people. They're being so hospitable.' But still there was an odd feeling about it all. Our time no longer felt ours. We were enmeshed in manners and obligations to which we were unused. We did not know the ground rules.

I detected Hussein's interest in Kathryn fairly early on. At first I thought I was inventing it – pandering to a racist stereotype, the lascivious Arab. But over the course of nights, the undulation of his eye over her body became obvious, to me at least. Fatima seemed to notice it too, or was I imagining that as well?

When the time came for us to move further south, Hussein mentioned he had been planning a trip down to the desert himself, to see old friends. He would come with us, as far as the oasis of Tafraoute. Again it was difficult to demur without impoliteness. He eyed Kathryn again, as if in anticipation. Or was he looking past her, at Ali, or Clementine? I wasn't sure. But Fatima wore a long-suffering look as she cleared away the dirty dishes that night. I felt uneasy.

'Don't be absurd,' Kathryn laughed, back at the hotel. 'Hussein's alright. He just wants to be friends.'

'With that glint in his eye when he looks at you?'

'Glint? What glint? He doesn't have a glint.'

'He's a bad artist,' I said.

'So?'

'You can't trust a bad artist.'

She switched off the bedside lamp. 'Don't be so judgemental. You're just being paranoid.'

'Perhaps. Or perhaps you just haven't noticed the glint.'

The next day, our last in Essaouira, Hussein accompanied us to the post office in the Ville Nouvelle to help us sea-freight home the carpets we had bought. He ran a tight operation, marshalling us around the various weighing scales and counters, whispering the amount required for each bribe as it came. In the end we paid out more on bribes than postage.

After the post office, he organised a taxi to take us to a friend's place, where he had to pick something up. It was about 10 a.m. when we arrived. The five men living in the flat were sitting around the table, groggy from the drums and hashish of the night before. They were drinking coffee, smoking cigarettes, eating a little bread . . .

'Do you think it's only the women who actually observe Ramadan?' I asked Kathryn later.

'Probably. They seem to do everything else for the men. By the way, who do you think got all our money at the post office?'

'I don't know. It was moving too fast for me to keep track. Hussein seemed to be bribing just about everyone in the place.'

'I just hope the carpets arrive back in Sydney.'

'I just hope Hussein doesn't turn up at the bus station tomorrow.'

But he did, two minutes before the bus departed. He was withdrawn and intense. We found two seats together and he sat on the other side of the aisle. 'My friends in Tafraoute have camels,' Hussein muttered to Kathryn, easing himself into his seat. 'We can ride out into the desert together.'

'That sounds wonderful,' she said.

'*Excusez-moi*,' he said, and drifted into a deep sleep as the bus hurtled through the heat of the day down the ocean road, south towards Agadir.

We argued in whispers.

'And I don't like this about the camels,' I said.

'Why not?'

'I just don't like it.'

'Why not?'

'We don't know him well enough for one thing.'

'Oh, I see, you think you're going to end up with a knife in your back in the desert, and me raped on top of a sandhill? Is that it? You're really paranoid, you know that? He's not crazy. He's an artist. And you've been watching too many trashy movies.'

But somehow, somewhere along that road I did manage to convince Kathryn that perhaps we should be a little cautious. In many ways I was sorry to do so – I knew I was probably wrong. But there were already things about Morocco I found unsettling, and the Mills & Boon stare of this ramrod-backed, steely-eyed, moustached splatter painter was one of them.

As our bus pulled into Agadir I woke Hussein and told him we were tired, would stay the night there and come on to Tafraoute the next day. He didn't like the idea of separating – particularly as he had been expecting us to pay for the *grand taxi* on the last four-hour leg down to Tafraoute. He had no money for a hotel room, or to hire a taxi himself. I gave him the taxi fare and said we would meet him the following day.

It was the last we saw of Hussein. The next morning I left a note in schoolboy French for him at the hotel desk as we checked out:

Atlantic Hotel
Agadir
Chambre 317

Si un Monsieur Hussein téléphone pour Mlle Kathryn ou M. Larry, s'il vous plaît lui dites que nous avons changé notre programme. Kathryn a la grippe encore, et elle est trop fatiguée pour une longue voyage. S'il vous plaît lui dites 'à bientôt' et 'merci beaucoup' pour nous.

(If a Mr Hussein telephones for Miss Kathryn or Mr Larry, please tell him that we have changed our plans. Kathryn still has a cold, and is too tired for a long journey. Please say goodbye and thanks very much from us.)

Prudent or paranoid? Sometimes the hardest thing about travel is to know the difference.

Winter in America

We took a *grand taxi* on to Taroudant, a town of blood-red ramparts on the Souss River, between the High Atlas and the Anti Atlas. After exotic Essaouira, Taroudant was something of a let-down, a dusty, nondescript town sprawling within its fortifications. We found a hotel in the main square, past which a queue of buses and lorries endlessly rolled. The hotel was virtually empty, and but for a lush central courtyard with a magnificent purple bougainvillea, would have been depressing.

The townspeople had the eccentricity of desert fringe dwellers, with a fetish for shoes, haircuts and false teeth. There were hairdressing salons all over town and the men – only the males actually showed their hair of course – kept their heads fastidiously coiffed. Almost as numerous were the dental surgeries with sets of false teeth displayed out front in glass cases. Did these people eat more sugar than other Moroccans, or just have thinner tooth enamel? The old woman who cleaned our hotel room showed full stainless steel uppers and lowers whenever she smiled. And everywhere there were shoe shops, the wares ugly-chunky for the women, beige or bone vinyl and phallically pointed for the men.

The bus we boarded for Ouarzazarte ('Wah-zah-zart') had new bodywork but antediluvian shock absorbers, and delivered six or so hours of excruciating jolts. We started out cruising through flatlands of red dust and miles of orange groves, but after an hour or so climbed an arid plateau with soaring red bluffs of bare scoured stone, their flanks cut away into jagged gorges. Here and there the first wildflowers of spring blossomed up through the cracks in the dry earth. Red mud villages were huddled into the hillsides, walled houses enclosed the oasis of a lone orange tree. We passed flocks of sheep and goats on these harsh uplands, white, brown, piebald, grazing on mean tufts and framed by the white-capped shelf of the distant High Atlas, the herders retreating from the cold into the depths of their *djellabahs*.

Rest-stops were few, and at one point I had to ask the driver to pull over. He did so in a little town, and pointed to what looked like a café. I ran inside, and found the place dark and disused. It was just a shell, no tables or chairs, the floor stripped right back to the earth. The only indication it had once been a café was a cracked Coca-Cola sign on one wall. An old man was inside, sitting on the floor as if he lived there. I asked for a toilet. With a nod he indicated a room running off the main one. I opened the door, stepped in, and found the man shutting it behind me. It was utterly dark within – the darkness of caves, pits or mines. When I felt for a light switch something alive and hairy moved under my hand. I had no idea where the bowl, hole in the ground or whatever, was. All I knew was that I was desperate to pee, that a man outside had shut me in here, and that the bus had just sounded its impatient horn.

I sniffed. There was an organic smell emanating from a far corner. I took a step, and my boot mired in something soft; mud, I earnestly hoped. The bus horn sounded again. In the end I did what I had to do where I stood. Then, horror of horrors, I could not find the door. But a moment later hard light flooded in when the old man, mouth wide in a big grin, opened the door and looked inside. I saw then that I had urinated into what appeared to be a well-stocked larder. 'Oops, sorry,' I said. He laughed gleefully, and I realised the larder probably belonged to a relative – one with whom he was no doubt on less than good terms just then.

Ouarzazarte was an extremely strange place, a modern city thrown up in concrete out in the high desert, with an international airport, five-star hotels, even a Club Med. The Moroccans have invested a ransom in infrastructure here, expecting Europeans to flock in by the Jumbo load to play golf on the courses newly planted in the desert.

Golf. I will never understand the lengths to which people will go to play that signature sport of environmental vandalism. Golfers will have rainforests razed, reefs pounded into coral landfill, endangered species extinguished, all in order to putt balls around manicured greens in baggy caps and funny shoes. They will fly halfway round the world to lose balls in exotic water traps. They will even come to a weird, windblown, dusty place like this one, a place as charmless as Ouarzazarte, all in the pursuit of this meanest of games.

It being Ramadan, the Europeans had stayed at home. Their travel agents had no doubt been a bit more candid than our London bucket shop man. 'Rumudun? No problem guv,' the pimply bloke in the tie behind the comically cluttered desk had said. (His coffee cup was stamped with 'My other cup is a Wedgewood'.) 'No, it's great. More intristing during Rumudun, innit?'

The five-star hotels were all big musty boxes, half-lit and skeleton staffed. We shared a beer – at least one can get a drink in these tourist sandtraps – in a red velvet lounge like the vestibule of a credit card brothel. We paid the routinely exorbitant bill and headed for the front doors, only to encounter a maze of doors marked 'No Exit'.

'Ah,' said Kathryn, 'I see we really have reached Hell's waiting room. If this is Monday, this must be Ouarzazarte.'

We stayed the night in a little place near the bus station. The next morning a freezing wind blew up from the Sahara. Tumbleweeds clattered down the deserted main street as we hunted for breakfast. We finally found a café which bore some of the characteristics of being open, in that the doors were unlocked and there was a depressed-looking young man in an approximation of a white apron sitting at a table – but his head rested on it, and he snored. The place was unlit, shadowy. In the dim recesses I could make out the shapes of several men in *djellabahs* sprawled asleep across tables.

The waiter awoke, shambled behind the counter and turned on the radio, which played *Winter in America*. The only edible items in the whole place were two stale croissants in a dirty glass case. Kathryn didn't want any so I ended up eating both – hard, dry as the desert, wind-blown sand grinding between my molars. We stirred our syrupy lukewarm coffees and watched the tumbleweeds roll down the empty street. When we got up to leave the waiter was already asleep again, his head nudging an ashtray spilling butts left over from the night before.

Sweet Tea and Vexation

We rented a car for the trip down the Draa Valley to the Sahara. The cheapest available was the Renault 4 – a tough little tinplate box with one of those eccentric gearshifts you push or pull from the dashboard. We drove through a bare and chilly, inhospitable terrain of rust-red peaks. For miles there was little sign of human habitation beyond the ruin of a hilltop mosque, a silent moonscape running away on all sides.

It was on a stretch of road high in these hard ranges that we encountered a Citroën up on a jack, and two or three Moroccan men standing around it. One of them flagged us down, and, in French almost as rudimentary as my own, explained that he needed to get help from the car's owner, who ran a café in the town of Agdz further down the road we were taking. He dictated a message which I transcribed as best I could, and we promised to deliver it.

About half an hour later we descended into Agdz. We located the café with relative ease, and I waited in the car while Kathryn dropped the message inside. She was gone for some time.

'They're so grateful for us delivering the message, they're insisting we come in for mint tea,' she said through the open window.

'I don't know. It's getting on a little. If we want to get to Zagora by dark we should really keep going, rather than stopping off in a café now.'

'Actually, it's not a café,' she said. 'It's a carpet shop. But they're very nice. They're desperate to show us their gratitude.'

'And their carpets presumably.'

'What?'

'Oh, this is all probably just a scam.'

'You're saying those guys hang around all day in the sun and the cold up there in those awful hills telling people their car has broken down, just to get them into a carpet shop?'

'Probably.'

'Come on now,' she said. 'Don't be like that.'

We were conducted into a building adjoining the café, and then through a succession of narrow corridors, until we reached a room resembling Ali Baba's cave. It was lined with fine carpets and fabrics, and abounded in what seemed to our eyes fabulous *objets d'art* – jewels, intricate rings, gold bracelets, lacquered wooden chests with damascene inlay, pots of silver, of amber, finely worked brass teapots. The walls were hung with a fearful array of weapons – pistols, blunderbusses, scimitars, daggers.

Our hosts invited us to sit on the deeply carpeted floor, repeating how grateful they were for our assistance with the car, and poured mint tea *à la Maroc* – the pot held high, dribbling the tea down into the cup, then the cup emptied back into the pot and the procedure repeated two or three times to ensure tea of a good strength. As we sipped, our two hosts, both dark-eyed, bearded men in full Tuareg indigo robes pattern-stitched with gold thread, watched us with silently smiling approval. Inevitably, our eyes wandered over their cave, its carpets and weaponry, all its assorted treasures. If our gaze happened to linger a moment on a particular prize, the elder man would click his fingers, and his junior would collect it and respectfully place it before us for closer inspection. Also inevitably, after a few minutes of handling these beautifully crafted objects, the words came automatically to the tip of the tongue, and were finally uttered: 'Sir, how much is this?'

'Oh madam,' the elder man smiled, shaking his head, 'it is not for sale. You are our friends. We are not here to sell to you.'

More tea was poured, everything conducted with ceremony, at a measured pace. 'What about your friends out there by the side of the road?' I asked.

'No problem,' the elder said, with a dismissive wave. 'Help is being sent out to them.' I nodded, and finished my tea. Yet more was poured before I could say no. Another silence, as if we were all waiting for something.

Kathryn admired a small amber jewellery case, and again enquired after a price. This time, after some protestation, a price, rather a high one, was quoted. She put the object down then, still regarding it with warm admiration but saying sadly she could never afford such beautiful things.

The elder man smiled benignly. 'If you want it, then you shall have it, dear lady.'

And so began a good hour of negotiation. At the same time, the younger man, seeing me notice the especially intricate pattern in the *killim* upon which I sat, began a carpet show, tossing down rug after rug with terrific pomp and seriousness. The dramatic structure of these routines is always the same. First there is the showing itself, each rug tossed down with a flourish, sometimes accompanied by a little sigh from the dealer at the loveliness of the piece; then, a simple enquiry as to one's favourites. To the protestation that one does not want to buy, that one is only look-ing, there is merely a repetition: 'Yes, please, and what are your favourite pieces?' Finally, one nominates some favourites, and then, by a process of elimination, chooses a favourite. Then you are asked to name a price. You may refuse, in which case the dealer nominates a price. If you make any counter-offer to this inflated opening price, you are already bargaining. A deal of some form is then hard to avoid. You have as good as bought another carpet.

When we finally returned to the car in the declining afternoon, Kathryn had the amber case and two long, indigo-dyed Tuareg scarves – and I had a new carpet. A big one. I was full of sweet tea and vexation.

'What an utter scam! That bullshit out on the road!'

'You didn't have to buy the carpet. No one forced me to buy these things,' Kathryn said patiently. 'And anyway, they're lovely.'

'It's more subtle than that. They're just very good, that's all. They know every trick of how to get money out of you.'

Perhaps it was all the sugar and the hapless sitting and the chat, or perhaps it was the late afternoon sun, which was still strong. Perhaps it was just us and our predicament, the interpersonal predicament we rarely mentioned, as if it could be filed away until our month here was up.

'I mean, it's late. We're driving on narrow roads we've never driven on before. It's stupid! And why is it *me* who always ends up buying carpets?'

'I don't know,' she said, peering into the fading light. 'You've just got a weakness for them. Come on, it's a nice carpet. And I love my amber thingamy.'

It was our sixth carpet so far. *Sixth*. Was I taking leave of my senses? I couldn't afford it and I didn't have the floor-space at home anyway. And 'home'? Kathryn had recently bought her own flat and was moving into it on her return to Sydney. Was not this, truly, the end?

'Come on, just drive,' she said.

'Well if we have an accident, it's your bloody fault.'

The late afternoon spread a heavy golden sheen over the stony desert as we encountered the first *palmeries* – watered settlements with a few palm trees and a scattering of wildflowers. Then, after more winding roads and barren ranges, the road linked up with the River Draa, flowing down from the High Atlas into the Sahara. The vista widened to a gloriously fertile valley, thick with date palms and green with waving fields of young wheat. The Draa ran on determinedly, a hard slate-blue, with an almost unbroken human habitation following its banks, mud-walled villages from which children sprinted out, or waved at our car with wicker baskets of dates for sale.

'Divine,' Kathryn said, breathing in the balmy air. 'Who knows, we might just enjoy ourselves yet.'

The Cowpat in

the Sahara

Zagora is best known for its old sign, '*Tombouctou 52 jours*'.

'Funny, that's probably when I'll get there.'

'What?' said Kathryn.

'Fifty-two days. I want to try to get to Timbuktu after the show opens in London.'

'Oh,' she said.

We stayed in a hotel called La Fibule ('The Pin'). It was Moroccan Santa Fe. Our mud and straw room was painted china blue, with big white clouds in the crevices. The restaurant was good, the bar unhurried. But as is so often the case with a nice hotel, we had a terrible night's sleep. Dogs, in the block next door, down the dusty road and way over on the far bank of the Draa, barked all night. It is just possible that the dog is man's best friend, but it is absolutely certain that it is sleep's worst enemy. The infuriating thing about dogs is that they never seem to get hoarse, barking out the same dumb things to each other, over and over.

Dog 1: This is my place.
Dog 2: So what?
Dog 1: I am big.
Dog 2: Oh yeah?
Dog 1: And strong.
Dog 2: I am stronger.
Dog 1: Who says?
Dog 2: Mahmoud's son. I nearly took his leg off today.
Dog 1: That sissy? My pup could take a leg off him.
Dog 2: Your pup eh? That pussy cat.
Dog 1: Hey, you just watch your language!

Dog 2: Look, we could argue like this all night and keep everyone awake.

Dog 1: So?

Dog 2: My master will beat me.

Dog 1: Your master never hears. No master ever hears.

Dog 2: Oh, I can't be bothered with you.

Dog 1: Why not?

Dog 2: You're stupid.

Dog 1: Look who's barking.

Dog 2: I'm bored. I'm going to sleep.

Dog 1: No you're not.

Dog 2: Yes I am.

Dog 1: I'm going to bark like this all night.

Dog 2: Why?

Dog 1: I want to bark like this all night.

Dog 2: Why??

Dog 1: Because I am a dog. I am big. And strong. And this here is my place. Okay?

The next day we started the final leg down to the Sahara. We crossed a rocky plain which became ever more inhospitable, our little white Renault alone on the thin black band of roadway running downwards. We breasted two low ranges of red blistered stone, not a leaf to be seen. It was hot now, the last of winter left behind far to the north. Then, in a swirl of sand across the road, we arrived at the Sahara. It was almost strange that something so large – a desert into which all of Australia could fit – could have a definable 'start'. Yet here it was, the first low range of sandhills. They were a far cry from the grand *ergs* – the massive sandhills of the wide desert – and yellow–pink rather than that hard, fatal white, but it was the Sahara alright and we were driving into it, and the moment possessed a palpable magic.

We got out and walked up into the first hills. We shared a feeling of unbounded liberty, so much sky, horizon, such a multitude of directions. We walked on, up and down the hills. The sand was clean and powdery, misting in the breeze. We found wind-sculpted pebbles, emerald-green, yellow, rust-brown, smooth as the bottom of the sea. Then the afternoon sun became too hot, so we found our way back to the car and drove on looking for a place to spend the night.

Just before the tar ran out at a desolate outpost called M'Hamid, we saw a hand-lettered sign, 'Kasbar Tuareg'. We drove down a bumpy track through a cool *palmerie*, to a compound of mud buildings dominated by a crumbling turreted kasbah. The patron was an old man. He had two rooms to rent. One was quite large, but already taken. The other was small with no bed or mattress, so we would have to sleep on carpets on the mud floor, but the kasbah was a peaceful place nestled in palms, and we decided to stay. We took a sunset stroll through waving fields of sprouting wheat, bright lime-green like new rice in Bali.

We were greeted on our return by two Dutchmen dressed in 'full Tuareg' robes and turbans. Marc and brother Jean were fleshy, fey and forty, tripping about Morocco accumulating carpets, jewellery and bric-à-brac. They were accompanied by Fis, a supple young Moroccan. Marc was a beautician, Jean a jeweller. Both spoke English with a lazy, affected tongue. They were staying in the big room. They had spent the day buying several enormous, hideously ugly Berber carpets, which they now spread out on the floor and arrayed themselves upon.

'Aren't they just so beautiful? And we could not have got them without him,' Marc said, with a nod towards Fis, who sat quiet and self-conscious in a corner. 'He was a genius with the bargaining, took no shit from them, you know.' He looked at the shy Moroccan, blue eyes lingering. 'But then, there are many things we could not do without him.'

He carelessly tossed over a packet of cigarettes and a plastic bag containing papers and a block of hashish, and Fis obediently started rolling joints.

'You really must stay here for dinner,' said Jean. He was a few years younger than his brother, not quite so corpulent yet.

'Besides, we've already arranged it with dear old Mr Mohammed, the patron. We just love company.'

Though we were tired from travel, they insisted, and in the end we stayed. They had a tape machine, and it was soon playing a mix of thumping disco and insipid New Age music while dinner got later and later. Kathryn and I escaped from the smoke to lie on our backs in the soft night and look up at the Milky Way, vibrant in the desert sky. Then the food finally came, and we were called back in to eat an oily couscous and gritty *tajine*.

We took our leave soon after eating, but I awoke before dawn on the cold mud floor, feeling at first queasy, then just sick. I spent the day with diarrhoea, and left behind a tan, cowpat-like deposit on the edge of the Sahara as we drove back out towards Zagora.

The staff at La Fibule were not the least surprised at my illness, given our indiscretion of eating anywhere in the region but at their restaurant. Their diarrhoea treatment was a full tablespoon of cumin powder, mine, Immodium capsules. After two less than memorable days, one or both cures finally worked.

Spain, Sicily, Senegal

A blur of days followed, travelling north up the desert side of the High Atlas, stopping off at the gorges that cut a path down from the mountains with clear, icy streams. Birches grew by the edge of streams fragrant with spring blossom – almond, apple, plum. Then another long stretch of stony desert came, with recurring images in the windscreen – laden women bent over like quadrupeds; men sitting in rows behind earthen walls to cheat the desert winds, patiently awaiting the 6.30 p.m. siren; a nomad, staff in hand against a barren horizon.

We stayed a night in a dusty barracks town called Errachidia before turning up the Ziz Valley, and entering the snows of the

Middle Atlas. As we climbed through the snow-line, the world transformed dramatically. Hillsides wet with melted snow sprouted spring grasses. Up on the plateau we traversed a snowy moor reminiscent of the Scottish Highlands. We descended through dense forests of pine, passing through a wealthy ski village of Swiss-style chalets, down into a balmy afternoon and rocky hills like Greece, with farmlets of grazing goats, towards our next destination, Fès.

'Have you been thinking about her very much?' Kathryn asked as we sat alone in the gloomy dining room of the Grand Hotel. Chairs were stacked up in corners, tabletops were dusty, the staff difficult to interest. Paper curled and paint peeled. It felt like Brighton out of season. Curtains heavy with dust were drawn over the big windows, which otherwise would at least have admitted the lights and clatter of the city.

'Well, have you?' she repeated, when I failed to reply.

'Sometimes, yes.'

'Do you miss her?'

'Do you miss Manolis?'

She sighed. 'That was different.'

'Was it?'

'Oh, what are we going to do?' she said. 'And don't just say "I don't know".'

The waiter, a thin, stiffened man, terminally depressed in his later middle years, his once-white jacket a palate of old stains, approached with funereal gait and informed us that both of the dishes we had ordered were 'off' tonight.

'*Parce que la Ramadan?*' I submitted.

'*Oui,*' he agreed with a deep, tragic nod.

This meant there was only one item 'on' tonight. 'Then I'll have the chicken *tajine,*' Kathryn said.

'*Deux, s'il vous plaît,*' I said.

'*D'accord.*' His parting footsteps were strangely loud across the parquet floor. Melancholia lingered when the echo died away.

I poured us another glass of Moroccan rosé. It was quite a good wine, and very drinkable. I wondered if there might be a second bottle out in the kitchen refrigerator. Kathryn raised her glass. I raised mine to hers, and we clinked.

'To what?' she asked, then smiled. 'And don't say "I don't know".'

'To the waiter,' I said.

'The waiter,' she replied. 'May he grin.'

As we drank down our wine, a large woman in sackcloth black crept in with a bucket and started to mop the floor.

'She seems so sad,' Kathryn said. Then she looked at me. 'We just don't know what's going to happen, do we?' She offered her glass, and I poured more rosé. 'No, we don't,' she said, answering her own question.

The following day we took a taxi to Fès-el-Bali, the oldest of the three conjoined cities which together comprise Fès. Founded in 809 AD by Idris II on the Oued Fez, this truly remarkable city has one of the last major medieval centres, or medinas, in the world, with a population of 200,000 within its walls. We were determined to explore its maze of alleys by ourselves, without having to submit to a guide.

But on being dropped off at the Blue Gate, we were immediately confronted by a jostle of touts. One of them, young, leather-jacketed, with the body language of a standover man and the oil slick of a coke dealer, muscled up and attached himself to us like a bushfly to a back. To our patiently repeated, 'No thank you, we just want to explore by ourselves,' he parroted that we must have a guide, that it was illegal for us not to have one (it wasn't), that we would not understand what we were seeing, that we would get lost, that the city was dangerous and we would need protection. After several minutes of trying to ignore him hustling along beside us down the narrow alleys of the old town, I stopped and confronted him.

'Please, go away.'

'What?? What you say to me??' he said, his eyes widening.

'I said just go away. Leave us alone!'

'Hey! This is my country!' he screamed. 'I cannot go away! You tell me to go away I smash you fucking head in!' He seethed, standing feet apart, face white, clenching and unclenching his fists. He turned to Kathryn. 'And you, you think you're so free, you fucking women! You're a slave! A fucking slave! If you not a woman I smash *your* fucking head in too!'

At this point the other would-be touts – there was still a jostle of them following us – went into what is probably a routine as old as Fès-el-Bali. Holding back their psychotic colleague, each of these young men pleaded with us to hire them because they were educated, they were reasonable, they were good. They were not like *him*. One young man whispered that if we did not hire one of them, 'the crazy one' would follow us all day. He pointed to a side alley and beckoned us to follow. In the heat and chaos of our welcome we hesitated, then went with him. The others pursued at first, shouting and cajoling, but slowly dropped back. Finally, the psychotic one did so too, though still eyeing us menacingly.

We found ourselves in the heart of that massive, decaying city where human beings have hustled, cuckolded, killed and prayed for all thousand and one nights, a *medina* of eternal fascination. The alleys were just wide enough for a loaded donkey to pass, and flanked either side by the tall, crumbling walls of houses butted hip to shoulder. Through the milling crowds, men pushed carts piled high with ripe red tomatoes, artichokes, enormous bunches of mint. Young boys on stools beat age-old patterns into brass plates. Old men wandered through clutching live chickens by the feet. Hole-in-the-wall shops sold brassware, rugs, medicines, honeycakes, cassette machines. At the crossroads of two major alleys human currents intermingled, and we were buffeted this way and that in the eddies. Unseen hands grabbed. A face pushed close and screamed something in

Arabic. A toothless crone extended her hand for a coin. A frightened horse bucked. Its master screamed and pelted it with stones.

Our guide, Moulay, conducted us to the entrance of a mosque which we could not enter, being non-Muslims, and began his facts and figures spiel, the number of artisans that worked on it, the number of tiles used, who paid for it all, how many can worship there at once.

'Are you a student?' I asked Moulay, to break the rush of barely decipherable words.

'Yes,' he said. 'At university.'

'What are you studying?' Kathryn asked.

'*Excusez-moi?*'

'What are you studying? *Quel sujet?*'

'Arabic Studies. I have half of it memorised now.'

'Pardon?' she said.

'I have half of it memorised now,' he said. 'The Koran.'

He produced his battered copy, and with his fingernail showed us the very point to which he had memorised.

After the mosque, Moulay conducted us through a carpet shop and a brass artisans workshop, the prices absurdly inflated by our status as tourists. When we showed no inclination to buy, he whisked us off to the next stop on the route, the tanneries.

We passed down an alley where the smell of human excrement hung in the air. We turned off through a doorway in a crumbling wall, and a colossal space opened out before us within the cramped confines of this ancient city. The eyes were grateful at first for some sky, then they recoiled. Blood ran in rivulets down the gutters at our feet, oozed into chocolate mud. In a dark, stinking room severed cow horns were piled to the ceiling. Skins hung in the sun, alive with flies. At one end of the courtyard a massive water wheel turned, Fellini-esque, a medieval vision of hell. The stench was staggering, overwhelming. We climbed steps for an overview of the honeycomb of vats filled with yellow urine, dyes and water for the various stages of curing and dyeing the leather, young men up to their waists in it. The work was appalling, filthy, yet we learned that these jobs were fiercely held onto, passed down feudally from father to son.

Emerging back into the main alleyway, we encountered two men fighting. One of them had the other down in the mud, punching and kicking with incredible ferocity, screaming what we could only take to be obscenities at his victim. '*La Ramadan,*' Moulay said, shaking his head and grinning.

A few minutes later we told him we'd had enough for one day. We paid him and made for a gate, where, fighting off yet more touts, we managed to find a taxi.

'Why must they behave just like the racial stereotype?' Kathryn said on the drive back to the hotel. 'They're so rude, and so violent. I'd really like to get out of here. It's *inhuman*.'

'But where to?'

'There must be an airport. We could fly to Spain. Sicily. Senegal. Anywhere it's warm and they're not trying to kill each other.'

The taxi pulled up in front of the Grand Hotel, and we braced ourselves for the usual argument about the non-metered fare, but the young driver leaned over the seat and grinned. 'You find Ramadan difficult?'

We looked at each other. 'Well, it's just . . .'

'It is alright. I understand. Tell me, have you read that book, *The Satanic Verses*?'

We looked at each other again. 'Well, we . . .'

'You see, I would like to read that book. I am a student of English literature. I made friends with a tourist, and asked her to post it to me. But my brother who works at the post office says it could never reach me. The censorship, you see.'

'They open the mail?' Kathryn said.

'Of course. We have not rights like you do.'

We paid and got out, and watched the cab coast off into traffic.

'It must be so awful not to be able to read the books you want,' Kathryn said as we lay in bed that night.

'If he actually was a student, that is. Or a taxi driver.'

'What do you mean?'

'He could have been anyone, trying to get us to say something incriminating. Who knows, in a place like this?'

Kathryn looked at me, shocked, but half-agreeing now with my patent paranoia. 'The world isn't *that* crazy, is it?' She thought again. 'I wonder if it's warm in Sicily yet.'

The Best *Tajine* in Morocco

It turned out that Sicily would be a very expensive flight indeed, and Royal Air Maroc adjudicated that our bucket shop tickets were not changeable. We could not even take an earlier flight back to London. So we were stuck in Morocco for the rest of Ramadan. We dropped off the car in Fès and took a train to Rabat.

'I'm sure it'll be pleasant there,' I said. 'It's the capital, it's by the sea. They say there are no touts.'

This matter of touts was now of extreme importance to us. It wasn't just the relentless harassment to which one was exposed in tourist magnets like Fès-el-Bali – it was the same nearly everywhere in Morocco. Saul back in London had been right about that. The level of harassment was far worse than anything I had ever encountered. We were too jaded by it even to go on to Marrakesh or Tangier because they were reputed hotbeds of touts. All we wanted was to be left in peace.

There were other depressing aspects of life here too. The people were subjected (or had submitted) to an unrelenting authoritarianism. The lack of democracy was disturbing. People seemed frightened even to mention politics. In Fès we met a man who did want to speak, but looked up and down the street and lowered his voice to a whisper before he did so.

'There is no freedom in this country. No personal freedom. No political freedom. No freedom of the press. We are trapped here. Worse still, we have let it happen. And that is the most tragic thing of all.'

In Rabat we stayed at the Hotel Terminus, a concrete three-star near the railway station in the heart of the Ville Nouvelle. It was pleasant enough, and considering its location on a busy street, relatively quiet. We strolled the beach, shopped at the markets and read in the Andalusian Gardens just below the old kasbah out on the headland. These shady, formal gardens, enclosed from the road outside by high stone battlements, afforded a commanding view down over the river where it ran into the Atlantic surf. Spring grasses scattered with vibrant red geraniums danced in wind-blown waves on the ruins below.

Each night just before 6.30, we stepped out of our hotel onto the palm-lined boulevard, the normally busy Avenue Mohammed the Fifth. Now it was deserted, and apart from the *muezzin*'s amplified call, silent. All across Morocco people were crossing their thresholds. Harira was being poured steaming into bowls, tea brewed, cigarettes tapped in impatient fingers. In the cafés, waiters were bustling about, taking orders. In the most out of the way shoe shop or olive stand, a man sat on a little stool, a bowl before him, awaiting the cannon or siren. At this moment the boulevard exuded a wonderfully soothing calm. There was a stretch of greenery out in the middle with a fountain and park benches, and we sat out there savouring the quiet. The only sound was the trilling of swifts as they swept past on their exultant rounds. The peace persisted for fifteen minutes or so, until the first of the cars and motorcycles made their return.

We dined at the hotel on artichokes from the market, fine herb omelettes, Moroccan rosé, crème caramel. The other guests were an old Japanese man, and two young Englishwomen. The man, white-haired and frail, was from Osaka. He was eighty-six years old. He'd flown here via Moscow with Aeroflot, and was travelling the country alone. He spoke no Arabic or French, and only a little English. Obviously nothing was going to stop him seeing Morocco. The Englishwomen were cousins, backpacking. They had 'been warned' about Moroccan men, but hadn't had any problems so far.

'I think it's all a racist exaggeration. You get far more trouble in England if you ask me,' the elder one declared. 'I'm Helen by the way.'

'And I'm Constance,' said the younger woman.

'You're Australians, aren't you?' asked Helen.

'Yes. Though we're actually on our way back to London.'

'On holiday?'

'Sort of,' Kathryn said.

Tension was building on the streets. With the end of Ramadan imminent, people were excited and happy, but also nervy. We had been told that Ramadan did tend to reach a big climax – that a month of disturbed living, eating and sleeping had a cumulative effect, that there were ever more fights on the streets, more people were wounded and died. But Rabat still felt safe enough.

We happened across a fish restaurant on Mohammed the Fifth and decided to try it. We were greeted by a personable young waiter who suggested we sit upstairs where it was quieter. It turned out to be very quiet – we were the only diners up there, with a balcony table overlooking the street. The waiter chatted with us a few moments, telling us about his university studies, and suggesting some local landmarks we might like to see.

We ordered fish *tajines*. They were some time coming, and when they finally did, Kathryn enquired after the toilet. The waiter said he would show her the way, and conducted her out a side door. She had been gone quite some time when the waiter re-emerged from the side door and went straight downstairs. Kathryn sat down a few moments later, an odd look on her face.

'Where was it, right down in the basement?' I asked.

'Not exactly. It's actually just here, behind that door.'

'You were a very long time then. Is everything alright?'

She looked towards the stairwell, and lowered her voice. 'Don't get too angry. But there's been a little incident.'

'What incident?'

'Don't over-react. Just stay calm.'

'What's happened? Are you alright?'

'Yes, I'm alright.'

'What is it then?'

'Well, when that waiter directed me to the toilet, I went into the cubicle, and locked the door. When I came back out into the washroom, he was still there in the dark, with the door locked.'

'What?'

'Look, he's alright really. He's just young and repressed.'

'What happened then? Tell me.'

'Well, he took my hand, and put it onto his chest. His heart was beating very hard. Thumping in his chest. And he had an intense look on his face. He just kept staring at me.'

'Why didn't you call out? Weren't you scared?'

'Not until he tried to kiss me.'

I was astounded. 'But this was all just a few feet away! From where I was sitting in front of this bloody *tajine*!!'

'Don't shout. It's alright,' she said, with another look towards the stairwell.

'It's not alright!!'

'Please!' she hissed.

'Well, what happened then?'

'I said, "*Excusez-moi monsieur, j'ai peur. Ouvrez la porte s'il vous plaît.*" ' ('Excuse me, I'm frightened. Open the door please.')

'And?'

'He didn't do anything at first, so I repeated it, and he thought about it a moment . . . and then he finally did open it, thank god.'

'Hang on, you're trying to tell me this guy expected you to have sex with him in the toilets, while I was sitting here? Or rape you?'

'He wasn't intending to rape me. No, one scream and you

would have heard. He just thought I'd fuck him then and there. In the toilet. While you sat out here and my dinner was going cold.' She smiled then, lifted the lid on her fish and lemon *tajine*, and calmly started eating. 'It's alright. He's a sweet boy. He wasn't going to do me any harm. He must just think that Western women will do that. Fuck a stranger in a toilet, just like that.'

I got up, but she put her hand hard onto mine and gripped it. 'Stay here. Please.'

'He can't do something like that! Lock himself in a room with you and . . .'

'Look, it was nothing. No harm done. You'll cause a lot more harm if you go down there and make a fuss. I don't want to go through accusing him in front of his boss. Besides, who are these people going to believe? What's a woman here, particularly a Western one? It'd just get more ugly still.'

I remained on my feet, but she slowly drew me back down onto my seat. 'Come on,' she said. 'Eat, and let's just get out of here.'

'But . . . he could have raped you. I can't believe how calmly you're taking it.'

'What use is there taking it any other way? Let's just go, and not come back,' she said. Then added, 'Which is a pity really.'

'Why?'

'Because this is the best *tajine* I've tasted in all Morocco.'

We both felt too agitated to go back to the hotel straight away, so we went for a walk along the teeming boulevard, and dropped into one of the student cafés for a *chocolat chaud*. The radical chic of Rabat convened in these hangs. Girls wore skirts, even stockings and heels. Their boyfriends smoked French cigarettes and drank long blacks, wore skivvies and intense expressions. After what we had seen in other parts of the country, it was all astonishingly normal.

It was past midnight when we got back to our room. In the instant I extinguished the lamp on the bedside table, I saw

Kathryn's copy of *The Whirligig* by Morris Cox, her amber case from Agdz and sunglasses, three oranges, and a half-empty bottle of Sidi Ali mineral water.

The darkness of the room settled on us, then gradually thinned out with the ambient streetlight, to a ghostly grey.

'Would you like some water, darling?' I asked.

'No, thank you,' Kathryn said, kissed my arm and slept.

Isn't Travel Wonderful?

We had almost finished breakfast the next morning when the two Englishwomen came in. Both were grim-faced, and short with the waiters. Constance trembled, and Helen held her hand. 'She got robbed yesterday, poor thing,' Helen said.

'No . . . what happened?' Kathryn asked.

'It was awful, just awful,' said Constance. She showed us an ugly mark on her arm which was just beginning to come out as a massive bruise. 'I went out alone yesterday to the outskirts of town, to see this archaeological site that's meant to be out there. Of course I can't find it, and there's no one close by to ask. It's very desolate where I was, just fields with rubbish in them. Anyway, I was waiting for a bus back when a boy rides by on a motorcycle. He sees me standing there, turns round and comes back. I thought he was going to offer me a lift, when he grabs my arm, really hard, and just starts squeezing it.

'He was so strong, there was nothing I could do. He just keeps squeezing harder and harder, his eyes are wide and mad and he shouts at me to give him all my things. So he gets my camera, my walkman, watch, money . . . all the time I'm screaming in pain of course and shouting to people in the distance who can see it happening but just keep walking and don't do anything. It was so horrible, I can hardly bear to think about it now. I've never been robbed before you see. Oh, he was a bastard, a mean bastard. And crazy.' Constance sobbed, and Helen put an arm around her. 'People don't tell you about this place do they? What a shit-hole it is!'

'I think it's made a lot worse by Ramadan,' I said.

'Maybe,' Helen said. 'Or maybe they're just like this all the time. Jesus, who'd be a woman here, hey? Kept locked up all the time. Bearers of children, hewers of wood and drawers of water, that's what they are here. And hidden away in sacks behind walls.'

Constance looked up angrily. 'And what about all these educated Muslim women they have on the telly at home all the time? The ones who say we just don't understand them and their culture and they're not really suppressed and they don't mind wearing that sack and veil. Why doesn't any stupid interviewer ever ask them why the fucking *men* don't have to cover their hair and wear a sack too? How come the *men* can get around in jeans and lounge about in cafés and ogle tourists and rob people and cause trouble! Why do the women let them get away with it?'

Her tirade ended with another bout of sobbing just as the old Japanese man came in.

'Why she cry?' he asked.

'She was robbed yesterday,' I said.

'I rob too.'

'What??'

'In market. Boy knock me, money gone.'

'Christ,' Kathryn said. The two Englishwomen were listening too. Constance had stopped crying.

'There's some very bad people here,' Helen said.

'Oh, bad people everywhere,' the Japanese man shrugged. 'Pass coffee please.'

It was our final evening in Morocco. We walked through the *medina* towards the beach to watch the sun set into the Atlantic.

'I can't wait to get out of here,' Kathryn said. 'It's ridiculous,

I mean, it's so beautiful . . . the medieval turrets of the castle, the little fishing skiffs darting by in the river . . . it's lovely, but . . .'

We saw a crowd up ahead on a rubbish-strewn stretch of wasteland. An ad hoc game of soccer was being played on a pitch chalked out in the dirt, and a couple of hundred people had gathered to watch. Kathryn said she'd like to watch for a minute or two, but just then the final whistle blew. My watch said 6.25, time for everyone to rush home and eat. It was also, so we had been told, probably the last night of Ramadan. Probably, because no one seemed to know for sure. They wouldn't know until they saw the moon that night.

As the rival teams milled about shaking hands, two opposing players starting jostling each other. Seconds later it was a fist-fight. A wave of anger surged through the players and spectators, and everyone pushed forward to see. Suddenly more people were fighting. The tumult spread in an instantaneous venting of fury throughout the crowd, which in a twinkling had become a mob. Men screamed abuse, others grabbed rocks from the ground and threw them, seemingly at no one in particular. We retired to the river, where gangs of boys chased past us and brawled on the water's edge.

The *muezzin*'s call came then, and tempers cooled. The fighting factions dissipated into angry knots. Some men walked away with cuts, others nursing bruises. A tall player grinned, proudly holding a small trophy aloft. That was what this fight had been all about – that and a month of fasting, thirst and lost sleep.

We reached the seafront. It was a balmy spring evening. Surf pounded the empty beach. A heavy sea-haze drifted over the deserted streets of Rabat. The first stars were just appearing in the pale, blue–grey sky. The lighthouse out on the point came on, silvering the pink horizon. We sat on the sand and looked out to sea.

'Morocco really is beautiful,' Kathryn said. 'It was probably just us.'

'Yes,' I said, 'it probably was.'

The next day we took the train to Casablanca Airport. On the way, a young student informed us that Ramadan was indeed over. It felt bizarre to sit in the airport café and see Moroccans drinking coffee, Moroccans eating croissants, chatting happily in daylight hours.

'Funny, isn't it?' I said. 'When we bought our tickets in London, Casablanca seemed such a romantic destination. Now it's just a sprawling industrial city.'

'See the things you learn?' Kathryn said. 'Isn't travel wonderful?'

Our flight was delayed, so we sat in the café looking out at the green fields and yellow flowers beyond the tarmac, sharing a bottle of rosé.

'I think that sleepy-looking airliner over there is ours,' she said, pointing to a lone 737 out on the edge of the apron.

'I wish they'd hurry and wake it up,' I said.

Casablanca Toujours

Susan, the woman I had been seeing in Sydney, had sent several letters which I received on our return to London. When I read them now, they were written by someone I barely knew, much less had spent six passionate weeks with. There was also a declining graph of excitement in them. The first ones sent were intimate and amusing; the latter ones little more than news updates.

Icy rain beat on the telephone booth in Highgate. I could hear the crickets down the line from her summer garden in Sydney.

'Thanks for the postcard from Morocco,' she said. 'I always wanted a photograph of a camel.'

'Susan, I'm sorry, I meant to write more . . . I wanted to.'

'Then why didn't you?'

'It was difficult. I was with . . .'

'I know who you were with. You told me in the camel card.'

'But you knew we were going to Morocco together. I told you before I left.'

'But I didn't need to hear it again,' she said. 'Look, I have to go.'

'Susan . . .'

'Goodbye.' She hung up.

Back at the apartment, I told Kathryn what had happened.

'Are you alright?'

'I feel a bit odd.'

'Well, that's a shame,' she said. 'Now you mightn't have either of us. But then, that's always the risk, isn't it?'

London theatres remind me of cinemas I went to as a child – tatty, seen better days, hangdog as a Fleet Street hack. The ushers' uniforms look as though they've been sewn from old velour stage curtains, there are sweet-sellers at intermission, and the seats are soft and you sink in too deep. The bar reeks of smoke and drinks spilt by patrons long passed on.

The preparations for the show went smoothly enough, although there had been some problems with the sound: radio-miking tap dancers must be a sound mixer's worst nightmare. The Queen's Theatre stage was not ideally large for *Hot Shoe Shuffle*, and it was raked too: we wondered whether some of the dancers' daredevil slides might end up in the front row. But one by one the hitches were overcome. There were a few changes to the script, though not as major a rewrite as we had anticipated. Then the previews came. Everyone was very nervous for the first one, but it went off well. The audience comprised telephone salespeople who organise big group bookings. I sat next to a plump woman with nicotine-stained breath, who of course did not know I was involved with the show.

'What do you think?' I asked when the cheering subsided after the final encore.

'Oh, it'll be a hit, no doubt about it,' she said. Then she thought for a moment before adding more soberly, 'Well, ought to be anyway.'

Every audience gave the performers a standing ovation, yet each preview felt completely different, as previews do. One night we would go back to the apartment with a bottle of champagne, the next with a Bulgarian red.

Before we knew it, the cast were taking their bows at the last preview before opening night.

'Terrific final preview,' a young usher said to his elder.

'Aye, and you know what that means for opening night don't you?' the other said grimly.

'But isn't that just an old stage superstition?'

'Oh, aye,' said the old usher. 'That it is, boy. A very old one.'

The following day I joined a smattering of soup-stained business drunks, Italian hippies and soccer louts shuffling in the pre-dawn chill of Piccadilly Circus, waiting for the tube station to open. The first train took forever to get out to Heathrow. By the time it did her flight had already been processed through Immigration and Customs. She sat waiting for me in the Arrivals hall.

'Sorry I'm late,' I panted. 'Have you been waiting long?'

'Only a few minutes,' she said. 'Now give me a kiss.'

It was only the second time my mother had been out of Australia, the first being a ten-day holiday I took with her and my father in Bali a few years before. But this trip was something else entirely.

'I can't believe I'm going to see my own son's musical open in the West End tonight!' she enthused as we took the escalator back down for the return train. 'It's the night of nights!'

We got out at Green Park and took a taxi for the last mile or so to the apartment in Saint James. 'Look, Mum,' I said, 'Buckingham Palace.'

She peered through the rear windscreen. 'That grey one? Is that it? Not very big is it? I thought it would be bigger.' She looked a moment longer, than settled back in the seat. 'But the taxi's very nice.'

We rode on a few moments, the cab chugging up Buckingham Gate. 'So have you heard from that Susan girl?'

'It's over,' I said, looking straight ahead. 'And Morocco was dreadful. How's Dad?'

'He's a lot better. How's Kathryn?'

'She's well. Pull up here please, driver.'

We came to a halt in front of the tower block where cast and crew were staying, and I helped my mother from the taxi. 'Can you still see Buckingham Palace from our rooms up there?' she asked. I nodded. 'Just wait till I tell your father,' she chuckled.

My mother had flown non-stop from Adelaide to London, and caught up on sleep in her room all day while we read, had lunch, and tried to relax before opening night. It was a windy spring day, the tulips buffeted in Saint James Park.

We woke my mother at five. We were ready to go by six-thirty, but hung about, watching TV, taking it easy. At 7.15, we went downstairs and hailed a taxi. Traffic was heavy from Trafalgar Square onwards, and the West End impossibly choked. We had to walk the last stretch, but it was still only 7.45 when we neared the theatre. We saw a big sandwich-board sign outside which read, 'Tonight at 7'.

'That's odd,' I said. 'Must be a mistake.'

But the foyer was almost completely empty.

'Most of them must have already gone in,' Kathryn said. 'If you wait in the foyer for Dirk, I'll get the tickets from the box office.'

Kathryn encountered an old friend from Perth, who was having a night off from performing in the Gershwin show, *Crazy For You*, around the corner.

'Isn't your show going just so well!' the friend enthused.

'What?' Kathryn said.

At the same moment, an usher was confirming it for me too, 'Went in bang on seven, guv'nor.'

'But our schedule said eight,' I said, horrified. 'No one told us it was changed.'

'Everyone was so busy,' Kathryn said, returning. 'They must have forgotten to tell us.'

'Have you just arrived?' came a worried voice from across the foyer.

It was the producer.

'Why, yes . . .' I said.

'But . . . but there are five seats for you. Right in the middle, down the front. There's a *hole* in the middle of the theatre! On opening night!'

'We're sorry,' I said. 'We thought the show went up at eight.'

'But you're the writers! You can't be late!'

'We just . . .'

'It's always seven on opening night,' she said with rising pitch. 'Seven.'

'Our schedule said eight.'

'It's seven,' she affirmed. 'Seven on the West End on opening night. Seven.'

'Sorry,' I repeated. 'It is our first opening here.'

She gave us a look which said 'and probably your last', and went.

Just then Dirk and his guest, Bonnie, a neighbour of around my mother's years, appeared.

'Sorry,' Dirk said, slightly out of breath. 'There was a delay on the tube. We thought for a while we were going to be late.'

We slipped into our seats as intermission ended, and disapproving throats were cleared all around us. The show went brilliantly, and ended with three standing ovations. The final Tap Truck routine, in which the dancers perform astounding tap steps on seven small boxes, left the audience speechless. The bows were exultant, triumph and relief shining on the faces of the young cast. The theatre buzzed as the audience bustled out. Flashbulbs popped at stars in the foyer. TV cameras got instant responses from audience members. First-nighters in their formals spilled out excitedly onto Shaftesbury Avenue.

The five of us walked through the crowded streets to the Café Royal in Regent Street for the party. I had been looking forward to it – but now regarded it with some degree of trepidation. What else could go wrong?

Situated at 68 Regent Street, the Café Royal was opened in 1870 by Daniel Nicholas Thevenon, a Parisian wine merchant. During the closing decades of the nineteenth century and the early twentieth century, the French-style Café became famous for the literary and artistic crowd it attracted to its bistro, its Domino Room, Billiard Room and private rooms upstairs. The roll-call includes Wilde, Shaw, Somerset Maugham, J. B. Priestley and T. S. Eliot. It was painted and sketched by Beardsley, and appeared in D. H. Lawrence's *Women in Love* as the 'Café Pompadour'. Whistler is reputed to have signed his bills with a butterfly mark. The Prince of Wales and Duke of York were regulars. A notice was issued to waiters that the pair 'Lunch frequently. Always plain food. No fuss. Call Head Waiter at once and notify Manager.' The Café Royal was so greatly loved by its literary and bohemian habituées that when it closed for renovations during the mid-1920s, T. W. H. Crossland wrote, 'They might as well have told us that the British Empire is to be pulled down and redecorated.'

I found the modern Café Royal typically London – formerly charming, a bit pompous, somewhat unwashed. We were shown into a grand hall where a swing band played much too loudly and conversation was near impossible. My mother and Bonnie found it particularly hard to communicate, coming as they did from a generation not routinely subjected to auditory assault in the name of entertainment. Because of the racket issuing from the band, the party guests tended to congregate at the far end of the hall, which quickly became a flushed, sweaty crowd. Drinks came around in liberal quantities, but not so the food. This was largely confined to vols-au-vent with a scrap of chicken swimming in mayonnaise, or a shrimp in what looked like clotted cream. With the show going up at seven, and most of the audience presumably having missed out on dinner, by the time the paparazzi started snapping most faces were as pink as a Pom on Bondi Beach.

I was introduced to a very grand American couple. 'You're the rider?' shrieked the woman in black and gold silk, hung with what looked like Christmas tinsel strung with seed pearls.

'Co-wrote it, yes. Did you enjoy it?'

'Jesus fucking Christ, did we what!' boomed the man. 'How do you spell Tony!'

The noise level rose by uncomfortable degrees. Everyone in the room was shouting. The band played on, even louder. I spotted Kathryn in a group with Bob Geldof. 'So, did you or didn't you like *Ulysses*?' someone was shouting at him. Sir Bob replied with a pained sigh: Kathryn had spilt her drink all over his trousers.

In the meantime, Bonnie and my mother were attempting to find something in common between Bonnie's lifetime in puppetry and my mother's lifetime in the suburbs of Adelaide, over 200 decibels of *In the Mood*. Dirk had wandered off somewhere and didn't look like coming back.

'God, I feel horrible,' I said. 'Awful.'

'Me too,' Kathryn said.

A waiter came around and asked if we wanted coffees. The notion of caffeine was soberingly attractive, yet equally so too was a final descent into the chill Dantean depths of alcohol. There seemed only one thing for it.

'I'd like a Café Royale please,' I said.

The waiter looked at me curiously.

'I think it's coffee with brandy in it,' I said. 'And even if it isn't I'd like it anyway. A nice big decent slug of brandy please. More like brandy with coffee in it, actually. That's what I'd like.'

'Me too,' Kathryn repeated.

He gave us another curious look, and wandered off.

The cast arrived to enthused applause, and posed for a battery of photographers. Later we danced to the band, or tried to, but didn't have the heart for it. In the end we found we were quite

65

miserably drunk. So that had been our London opening, our night of West End glitz.

Back at the apartment, we took turns at the toilet bowl. Out it came, all of it: the vols-au-vent, the scene with the producer in the foyer, Morocco down to the last grain of couscous, and us.

A week later I said goodbye to Kathryn at Heathrow. It was six in the morning. We'd just had a mad drive to get there, down country lanes and motorways under repair, from Henley-on-Thames where we had stayed the night before.

Kathryn's bag disappeared down the conveyor belt, and she turned to me holding her boarding pass for the flight back to Sydney. She looked as entrancing as when I had met her here on her arrival from Paris so long ago, in the mustard overcoat, the pert dark hair, the deep red lips.

'So, you're on your way back then, to your new flat.'

'And you're off back to Africa.'

'I'll miss you.'

'I'll miss you too.'

'Funny how things work out isn't it,' I said, utterly uselessly.

Kathryn smiled. 'Still, no matter what happens – we'll always have Casablanca.'

We kissed one last time. She went through the barrier, turned and waved, and was gone in that final, final way peculiar to air terminals. She was already being processed through the machinery of international air travel.

I looked down at my hands. The skin looked aged. 'When will you learn, you fucking old fool,' I told myself.

Bloody
Mary's

PRESUMABLY, human beings started travelling to trade. Travel was still the root *travail* then – work. People would journey hard and perilously across land or sea, turn up on someone else's plot or island clutching gifts and trade goods, share a cup of *kava* or two, exchange the odd legendary dance drama, and with any luck not end up roasted on a spit. Back in pre history, you respected your hosts.

Nowadays travel usually equates with tourism. We fly to the tropical Third World country of our holiday choice, and are conveyed by vanette to a 'resort', a well-guarded enclosure on a beach or mountain-top. Upon arrival we are 'processed', and 'familiarised' with the workings of our new world. As it turns out, it's much like our old one. We have our street and our number, only now it's a corridor and a door number, or a pathway and a hut number. We have the same facilities, hot and cold water, TV and video, booze in the fridge. The only thing that is different is the view. And the cost of it. Needless to say, this place is sucking several villages worth of water out of the local supply, and the lion's share of power from the regional grid for our hair dryers, shavers and vibrators, but who's counting? We've come here to rest, read, swim, fish, eat, drink, and, if the stars are shining propitiously, indulge in a holiday fling. The most common thing people say of a holiday like this is, 'I just want to veg out for a week or so, do nothing and think nothing.' This would be understandable, were it not for the fact that we spend most of our lives at home doing exactly that.

Once ensconced in one of these citadels, certain iron laws of human behaviour become apparent. Fat people are usually friendly. They have to be. So too are old people, unless they're squabbling among themselves. Pretty people are not as a rule friendly: it's not in their contract. They will only be so when they need something – help with a pesky lizard or spider, a stubborn lid or a money transfer that hasn't 'come through'. The best place to meet people is on one of those excursions to the mountains or the reef that hotels are always running. With good luck, you find a new friend, confidante, lover. With bad luck you spend a lot of time in glass-bottomed boats enduring stilted conversation with retirees from Miami and honeymooners from Osaka.

The most bizarre thing about being in one of these citadels of tourism is the cultural 'items' imported for us. Each night, there they are, the choirs of singers in 'traditional native costume', the dancers, the snake charmers, the carvers, tie-dyers and basket-weavers, all temporarily admitted from the grubby world outside the front gates, into this gleaming hotel lobby where for an hour or so they give us a teensy sample of their culture. Trinkets are sold. Sarongs are bought and worn. Salarymen start wearing shell necklaces and blowing conches. Then the 'performers' are paid off and dismissed, and that does it for the local colour. It's back to the gin slings by the pool.

But this soupçon of local colour is *de rigeur*. Otherwise, on return what is one to say to friends, family and co-workers? 'I went somewhere . . . dunno exactly. There were these huts and coral reefs. I got pissed a lot and almost scored a root.' No, it's, 'Oh, Tahiti is *marvellous*. The traditional dancing is fantastic. Look at my intricately carved Tiki.' Or, 'I went to Bali. Stayed up near Ubud of course, out in the rice paddies. Aren't the gamelan orchestras wonderful? I brought back a tape. It's here somewhere . . .'

Resort hotels are of course extremely ugly. What is it about them? The gold embossing on the soap box, the tacky little bottles of French champagne in the mini-bar? The too-heavy, paisley-print bed coverlet and the ghastly upscale bordello furnishings? To me, the five-star resort is an extension of the inside of a jet airliner, the perfumed domain of Chanel, Hermes scarves and Rolex watches. The very excess which is its putative beauty, is its definitive ugliness.

But with the ever-increasing blandification of global culture, the great flattening of human diversity being wrought by mass transit and communications, travel is an increasingly banal, ersatz experience. Travel agents already provide videos of the resort of your choice. There's the pool, there's the bar, the reef, the dancers from the village. It's almost as if you've had the trip before you've left. It's not such a step from there to experiencing one's first African safari, Indian market, Japanese temple, through a virtual reality headset. And no doubt that will come to pass too, soon enough.

A key component in the mechanism of mass tourism is the glossy travel magazine, which pre-masticates destinations for readers. In the often futile pursuit of trying to make a living, I had convinced such a magazine that I was a credentialled, reliable writer of travel material, and had somehow been sent on assignment for a week in French Polynesia.

Where objectivity is the stated ideal for most journalism, with destination travel writing it is *adjectivity*. 'Bora Bora is the most seductive of tropical islands. Gothic spires of black volcanic basalt thrust up out of the Pacific, peaks festooned with jungle green . . . a coral lagoon shading from turquoise deeps to tranquil aquamarine shallows, coconut palms overswaying beaches of finest sandy white . . .'

I felt I was getting the hang of it. But what I should have added was don't even bother locating Bora Bora on the map unless you're rich. You not only have to be rich, but a certain kind of rich, preferably French, with a penchant for white shorts with fascistically pressed pleats, polo shirts with silly, quasi-regal monograms, and a bottom that will fit into an egg cup.

Polynesia's fool's gold glitter goes back as far as Defoe and Diderot, to Melville, Robert Louis Stevenson, Somerset Maugham and James A. Michener. Michener was stationed on Bora Bora with the US forces during the Second World War. His *Tales of the South Pacific* was adapted into the Broadway musical, *South Pacific*. 'Here am I, your special island,' Bloody Mary sings, 'come to me, come to me.' And, flashing gold Amex, they do.

The French Polynesian travel rep back in Australia had insisted I must get to Bloody Mary's restaurant on Bora Bora, no matter what. One of the greats, he said. Thus I now found myself, fetched from my hotel by the Bloody Mary's minibus, zipping down the bitumen road that runs the ring round the island, the night perfect, cool and still, seated beside Carlotta, the good woman of Caracas. Carlotta was sixty, tall and gaunt, masculine as a drag queen. Her horsy face was runnelled with sun and Scotch. Her wedding ring had grown into her knotted finger-joint like wire into a tree trunk. She had just come from Morocco where she had lounged around on carpets in some very big striped tents with King Hassan at the thoroughbred sales. She wore a silk shirt in hibiscus print, beige slacks with a little gold belt around them, gold shoes and gold watch. Everyone on Bora Bora has a gold watch.

Carlotta warmed to her favourite theme in idle conversation – global chaos. Apparently she enjoyed confronting strangers with their apathy. 'The real issue is over-population,' she declared to all in general and no one in particular. 'In Colombia they're down from six to 2.6 children per couple. But here, the French subsidise them to have families. Six to eight kids. Everybody's pregnant! They'll run out of land soon.'

Beyond the Very Wealthy like Carlotta, the only other major sub-genus of visitor to Bora Bora is the American Honeymooner. Our companions aboard the minibus that night were a

Honeymooning couple from New York, and a Second Honeymooning couple from Montana. We had all nodded greetings as we boarded, but as Carlotta warmed to tonight's impromptu lecture, the Americans seemed to gain a profound interest in the bird shit spattered on the windows. Carlotta's husband was there with us too, almost. He sat up front, beside the driver. A squashed, wordless man, he was in the process of osmotically merging himself into the upholstery of his seat.

'And water,' Carlotta strode on, as if anyone might be foolhardy enough to cross her. 'The real issue is water. The politicians don't tell you about water, do they? Where's the water coming from for all these extra people? The sky?? And plagues. Cholera. Typhus. AIDS. Do you know in some Central African villages there's no adults left? My country Venezuela is so corrupt. So corrupt! They don't take millions. It's billions. They never clear away the garbage. They expect us to live in filth. That's the real issue.'

With a collective sigh we pulled up outside Bloody Mary's and escaped onto the white coral grit driveway, which became the floor of the restaurant. There was a painted board displayed outside, with the names of famous diners who had been through the place. Raquel Welch, Dudley Moore, the Carpenters (is it bad taste to put that out in front of a restaurant?), Nelson Rockefeller, Dorothy Lamour, Tony ('Tie a Yellow Ribbon') Orlando, Rowan Atkinson, Cadillac Jack (whoever he is), Roman Polanski, Ron Wood. I wondered who invented the phrase 'Jet Set'? Marshall McLuhan? 'Where the jet routes meet, that's where you'll find Peter Stuyvesant – the International Passport to Smoking Pleasure.'

We were greeted by easy-listening Rick, with the tan body language of a gay windsurfer. He showed us to the counter where the night's offerings were laid out on cubes of ice – big pink–grey slabs of yellowfin tuna, lumps of snapper and chunks of mahi mahi, mullet fillets, black lobster hand-caught out on the reef, as well as crab from Australia and tiger prawns from Thailand. I ordered the mahi mahi grilled with lime, the Americans went for the lobster. Carlotta ordered steak. Very rare.

Over a Bud or two at the bar the Americans introduced them-selves as Americans will, and I ended up sitting at their table. The red-faced, balding man opposite me was Randy. He was a genetic counsellor. 'I take samples of the amniotic fluid and advise on possible defects. It's a bitch of a job but someone's got to do it.' Randy's tartan shorts were tight, and cellulite bulged up yellow above the pink of his knees. His diminutive bride Ramona – navy top, white mini-skirt, loafers, hand clutching his tightly – described herself as a para-legal. 'We do all the work, the attor-neys make all the money,' she squeaked. They were from New York, 'Queens born and bred.'

The other Americans were Jeff and Jenny from Bute, Montana. They ran a burrito place called 'Sierra Madre'. They handed me their business card – Humphrey Bogart curled around a cigarette. Jenny was another tiny woman, of rodent-like timidity. Jeff was a solid slab of white goods. He liked Montana but didn't like the bears a whole lot. They were pesky when you put out your trash.

I sought out their impressions of Bora Bora. 'Oh, fan*tas*tic,' Randy enthused. French Polynesia? 'In*cred*ible,' Ramona con-curred. I asked what they thought of the French being here. 'It's good for the natives, isn't it?' Jenny surmised. And the nuclear testing? 'Yeah? We didn't hear about that,' Jeff shrugged.

Randy and Ramona were early thirties, liberal, east coast. Jeff and Jenny were forties, northwest, tending redneck. Yet the two couples got along fine. Jeff complained about taxes and insurance, Ramona the para-legal had some answers. Randy cautioned on birth defects, Jenny detailed her sister's breech delivery. Although the four had only met on the minibus, they were already planning a joint snorkelling trip the next day.

I heard Carlotta's voice from an adjoining table. Glancing across, I saw her propounding a Papist conspiracy to a French couple, the woman very young, back honey-smooth, linen dress very short and very white, legs bare, gold lacquered toenails to match her gold watch, her white-flannelled husband heavy-souled as the older Mastroianni, hair going going gone, neck sag, gut flopped out with a lifelong load of *boeuf* and *crêpes*, poking at his lobster drowned in mayo.

Meanwhile Randy was complaining about how hard it is to get a park mid-town, and Jeff was proposing a distinctively American Solution to Carlotta's global problems. 'I'd just like to get an AK-47 and blow them all away! Boom! Boom! Kamboom!' I didn't pick up if he was talking about Iraqis, blacks or Communists.

'So how'd you two meet?' Jenny asked Ramona in a voice just above a whisper, down the female end of the table. Randy saved his new wife the trouble of answering. 'It was at this Renaissance festival – you know the kind of thing, all these mummers and jugglers. She [he always referred to Ramona as 'she' or 'her', never by name] was this, like, *beer wench*. I was a Shakespearian fencer. I must have been okay at it too, because I made enough money each summer to put myself through college [he also had that unfortunate knack of drawing even the most incidental conversation back to himself] and she gave me free beers. And it all just happened from there.'

'Oh, now, isn't that just the most *romantic* story?' Jenny patted the hand of her man. Beside him she was almost pathetically minute. Where Jeff's legs were tree-trunks, hers were twigs. In fact, there was an overfed quality to both the men, only Randy was bagel, Jeff was burger. Randy was bicycle, Jeff was pick-up. Randy was Seinfeld, Jeff was Roseanne. I tried to imagine the trunks and twigs having sex. Such massive men could so easily crush these magazine-dieted, mail-order-made-over post-post-feminist women. The disparity in physicality – grain-fed macho versus culturally-acquired fragility – was disturbing close up.

Over my shoulder Carlotta was telling the honey-backed Frenchwoman about King Hassan and his horses. They all agreed the fall in the birth-rate in Colombia was a very good thing. Mastroianni shoved away his lobster and sulked.

'Another beer?' Jeff asked me quickly as our Tahitian waitress tried to flit past unnoticed. She was shapely, tall and resentful. Why, she was wondering, was she still here, waiting on these bloated, stupid tourists? Where had she gone wrong? How come she hadn't got into one of those libido lagoon movies the Americans are forever making here? All her friends had. Now they partied in the Hollywood Hills while she waitressed in Bloody Mary's. Life just isn't fair.

I ordered a Hinano beer and she went off in a sombre shuffle of thong. The table drifted into American domestic policy. 'No one will ever get a health care bill through in America. We're all protected,' Randy said. 'I've got health cover through my job. Everyone's just taking care of themselves.'

'I suppose that's really our problem, as Americans,' Jenny mused, thoughtfully. 'The only thing we do as a community is shoot each other.'

'That's right!' the others agreed, and burst into laughter.

I finished my fish. It had been okay, not special, vastly over-priced. 'You know they say this is one of the great restaurants of the world,' I said, knowing full well the Gouger Fish Café in Adelaide was better, fish just as fresh but far less fussed, and a fraction of the price. But then Adelaide is not a French base, and bases are expensive.

'This place . . . naw,' Jeff muttered, chomping down the last of his lobster and wiping his mouth of mayo. 'If you wanna eat in one of the great places, hey, come up and try a "Sierra Madre" chicken burrito. Just watch out for the bears.'

'Aw, Jeff,' said Jenny, with a little 'leave off cleanin' that shot-gun and come to bed honey' sigh. Randy caught Ramona's eye across the table. Beneath it, his bared foot went down on hers in the coral grit. Paradise tonight, baby? Come to me, come to me.

Back in my room, reclining upon the paisley quilt and familiaris-ing myself with the mini-bar, I wondered what I could write for the magazine back in Sydney. I thought of writing about Carlotta and Marcello and his honey-backed wife in white, about Jeff and Jenny and Randy and Ramona, about easy-listening Rick and Cadillac Jack (whoever he is) and the waitress who never quite got to boogey in the Hollywood Hills. But I knew better – the travel magazine wouldn't want a story like that.

After perusing the mini-bar price list (I was, tragically, paying for my own drinks) it wasn't long before I scratched out a paragraph of appropriate adjectivity about the fame and allure of Bloody Mary's. I popped open a twelve dollar can of beer, and bent my back to the task. Another cog in the industrial wheel of tourism dutifully turned in the island night.

The

Sea Breeze

I was brushing my teeth when a pale, freckle-faced woman knocked on my compartment door. I recognised her, having seen her in a restaurant back in Mysore some nights before. Then she had been radiant in a lacy see-through blouse, her long red curls down, yieldingly soft and enigmatic, a high hippie queen and her court a cabal of chillum-smoking-velvet-vested-bare-chested Frenchmen in their later middle years. But now she looked fragile, her eyes puffy and pink. Her curls were worried, squashed down beneath a black beret.

'Hi. Do you have any Vitamin C tablets to spare? My sponge bag got ripped off with my passport back in Goa.' Her voice was soft and submissive, the sentence endings upturned. The accent was immediately Antipodean.

'I do actually,' I said. 'Please, come in.'

With a tired sigh, she entered and sat down on the vinyl bench-seat. She introduced herself as Caetlin. Up close I saw a forty-ish face beneath the beret and curls, a pretty face, but losing out quickly to the South Indian sun.

'I also have some good sun blockout.'

'Do you?' She looked about distractedly. 'I've actually got some but I haven't had the mental space to use it. It's all been taken up avoiding a man.'

'Anyone in particular?'

'Oh, this Italian guy,' she said. 'You're Australian too aren't you?' I nodded. 'I met him in Goa.' She coughed harshly, her chest heaving. 'Sorry, my cold. And now I can't get rid of him.'

'You've been travelling together?'

'Travelling, smoking, fucking, driving each other crazy. I mean, he's really wonderful, Alfredo. But he's just too much, you know? Never sleeps. Never. Hyperactive. Manic depressive. Fucked up basically. Maybe *he* stole my Vitamin Cs.'

'Why would he do that?'

'They were with my dope and passport.'

'He stole them too?'

'Oh, I don't care. I only want him to stay away from me. Mind you, I wouldn't mind my passport back. Doesn't the bureaucracy here suck?'

We were getting close to Cochin now, and the train was travelling very quickly, as trains seem wont to do as the pull of the destination gets stronger. It was foggy and rainy outside, a blur of shabby grey–green. Schoolboys with black slicked-down hair waited impatiently on bicycles at barred rail crossings.

'But he'll come after me,' Caetlin went on. 'I know he will, bastard.' She glanced around quickly, as if posing for an unseen eye. 'You from Sydney?'

I nodded. 'And you?'

'Uh-huh.' She yawned. 'Nice of you to offer me the vitamins.'

'They must be here somewhere,' I replied to the prompt. I pulled my medical kit from my bag and opened it.

'I haven't been myself, haven't been taking care of myself. PMT, break-up, ripped off, period, flu,' she snuffled. 'I've just come from Poona. The Rajneesh place, you know. It's like a fucking concentration camp that place. They tell you what colour clothes to wear, when to eat, how to wipe your bum, everything. They censor the bloody mail. You have to have an AIDS test when you get there. When I first arrived I had to piss in the Non AIDS-Tested toilet. The place is run by these Germans. For Italians and Japanese really. Like a war reunion or something. There's no Australians there. They couldn't hack it. I had to wear a pair of maroon bathers or they wouldn't let me swim in the pool. I spent so much fucking money and I don't even know why I was there. No, yes I do. I was there to get a salad. You can eat the salad there, tomatoes and lettuce, washed in filtered water and made up by people with these plastic gloves on. That's what Rajneesh is good for, the only safe salad in all of India. But you know what? I still got sick there anyway. Vomiting. Shitting. It's where I met Alfredo.'

'Didn't you say you met him in Goa?'

'That was the second time I met him. First time it was in Poona. Then in Goa. I see him all the time. He's everywhere. Probably on this train.'

I laughed, but she lowered her voice.

'No, I mean it. He's near. I know he is. I can feel his presence. The countryside is lousy with him.'

I handed her the vitamin bottle, and she spilled out a handful of tablets and pocketed them.

'My real problem is I broke up with this guy just before I left home,' she said. 'We'd been having a really good relationship, just really nice. I was taking him through the whole process. Full initiation. Kundalini energy, Tantric sex, the lot. And then he goes up to Cairns and just fucks this fucking Brazilian woman there. Totally blows it.'

'How long were you seeing each other?'

'Weeks, months,' she shrugged. 'We were just so compatible. That's the really, like, galling thing about it. I was so pissed off that he fucked it up. So now I'm just cruising, just enjoying being in India. Slowing right down.'

The train also seemed to be slowing, entering a big town of some sort. 'I think we might be coming into Cochin.'

'Ernakalum,' Caetlin said. 'Not Cochin. They're twin towns. The station's in Ernakalum.' She drew a quick breath. 'Did I tell you I saw The Mother last week?'

'I thought she was dead.'

'No, no, that's the *Pondicherry* Mother. The French one. This is the *Indian* Mother. You really should meet her. She lives right here, in Cochin. You'd like her. There isn't anything she can't give you. She told me my new show's going to be a success. She says to me, The Mother, just complete it and it'll be a big success. All I have to do is just keep painting. Her ashram, it's vibrating with this awesome God Consciousness. Before I got to talk with her I was sitting outside her little, like, hut. And I was thinking she doesn't love me any more because of this guy back home, you know the one who fucked things up with the Mexican bitch in Cairns . . .'

'Didn't you say she was Brazilian?' I heard myself quibble again.

'. . . and I was thinking how he'd, you know, filled me up with all this darkness? But, The Mother, she *knows* everything that's going on in my head . . . and she *knew* I was still carrying it all around inside me, all this fucked up darkness, and she told me my problem was lack of awareness, right? Over the initiation I did with the guy? That I shouldn't have done that? That I shouldn't have gone through with it because it was wrong for me to do that initiation, because I'm not a guru? Which is fair enough – I'm not. I'm an artist. But because of all this I was thinking she didn't love me any more, right? So I was deeply depressed. Then, you know what? She called me right back in, she just smiled at me, and gave me a *lot* of attention. You see, she knew what I was going through. And I asked her if I should go with her on this, like, pilgrimage she goes on up to Calicut? And she said yes I should go with her if I want to. So that's why I'm here. And I should be really happy but I'm actually really fucking tense because I don't want to run into that cunt Alfredo again. And now I have this cold. And I really appreciate you giving me your Vitamin Cs by the way . . .'

She stopped. 'Oh shit, there, you see, I've done it again.'

'What?'

'Spent ten straight minutes just talking about me all the time. What about you?'

'What about me?'

'What are you doing in India?'

'Just travelling.'

'Alone?'

'Yes.'

'By choice?'

'Somewhat.'

She nodded. 'Uh-huh.'

With a sudden harsh braking we were pulling into Ernakalum Station, and with a gasp that she had to rush back to her compartment and collect her bags, Caetlin was gone as quickly as she had come.

I was intrigued to see Kerala, touted as it was as an ideal coconut state, a happy and bizarre collision of Hinduism, Islam, Christianity and Marxism. As the taxi rolled out over a series of bridges across natural and man-made islands towards Fort Cochin, an Indian Venice of sorts revealed itself. The hammer and sickle was all about, on signs, banners and bunting, stencilled on roads, the walls of houses, but just as common too were temples, mosques and churches. The driver continually honked, just avoiding a column of oncoming trucks garlanded with flowers and emblazoned with signs declaring allegiance to some movie star, to the Virgin Mary or Joseph Stalin.

Cochin Harbour was deep and handsomely wide, scattered with green islands. The tropical waters shaded down to cobalt-blue, and as the taxi pulled up on the foreshore out at the old Fort I saw a tall white ocean liner, a single tug in its train, making stately progress down the narrows of the main channel towards the green enclosing folds of the harbour.

I took a room in an alley near the Church of Saint Francis, and made a sortie to see da Gama's tomb before returning to sleep an hour or two that became three. Thus it was mid-afternoon before I found my way to the Sea Breeze, a restaurant on a headland with views up and down the shipping channel where scrubby ferries plied and high-prowed fishing smacks traipsed. As I entered, I could not help but notice Caetlin, in a long and billowing scarlet silk shirt, alone at a table writing with fierce attack into an antique leather-backed journal. She happened to glance up, and saw me.

'Oh, look, sorry, do you mind if we don't sit together right now? I can't really talk. I've just got to get these ideas down for my next solo exhibition, and you know what it's like when people interrupt and want to talk? I'm sure you understand. You do, don't you?' She looked about. 'Oh, fucking Alfredo's going to find me here, I just know he will. Bastard.'

I managed to extricate myself and sat at a table on the other side of the room. A waiter came and I ordered a *thali* – the South Indian staple of assorted vegetarian dishes and *dhal* served in little pots on a platter with rice and *chapatti*. Next to me a group of Germans joked across a table cluttered with empty Kingfisher beer bottles, while directly opposite me an obese Englishman, a fiftysomething cetacean in sandals, toyed with a bright-eyed Indian boy who had somehow strayed into his clutch.

The Englishman was loud in mid-complaint to the waiting staff, that he had not received the four eggs he had ordered for his breakfast, one entire meal back. He threatened to deduct these lost eggs 'orf' his lunch bill if they were not immediately 'supplied'. This little sideshow went on for some time, the words 'four eggs', 'deduct' and 'ets jest the prenciple of the metter' loudly repeated by him at regular intervals and overheard by the other patrons, none of whom tried to conceal their amusement. The Englishman finally got his way, received a compensatory deduction from his bill of a few rupees, and promptly ordered a celebratory tumbler of milk for himself and an ice cream for the boy. As he toddled off later, arm draped proprietorially about the child, I wondered whether the kitchen staff hadn't spat into his milk.

My *thali* arrived. I ate slowly, sipped a cold Kingfisher. The lunch crowd thinned until there were only a few other patrons left. One was a pink–blonde German woman who sat alone and lonely, forlornly drunk. Well on her way to sixty and obviously once quite beautiful, she was now very much a wilting bloom, if not actually dropping the petals. She had bailed up one of the waiters, an attentive, sparrow-like old man, and held him in her captive orbit while she recounted the woes of the world.

'I am not a happy person. I am wealthy, yes. But not happy.'

Her worn grey eyes looked up at him, demanded a response.

'I am sorry to hear that madam.'

'I will never be happy, not in this lifetime.' She drained her glass. 'Four or five lifetimes, then maybe I am happy.'

She watched a dirty little freighter chug down the channel while she forcibly retained the old man's attention. 'You do believe in reincarnation don't you?'

'Pardon madam?'

'Pasht lives.'

'Yes madam.'

Her lips twisted in a smile, and a claw clutched his arm. 'You don't want me to die, and be re-born as a dried-out camel in the desert do you?'

'No madam.'

'Then get me another drink. I'm thirsty.'

He turned to go, and the woman chanced to make eye contact with me. I watched her a half-moment. To be fifty-seven years old, drunk and alone at 3.30 p.m. in a tourist café, I thought, age holds such appalling potential.

She looked about blearily and spoke up loudly, not to me but to Caetlin in her blazing red silk on the far side of the café, still scratching frenziedly into her journal.

'And what is a young woman like you doing alone here in India, eh? What is wrong with all the men these days?' Her sideways glance alluded to me. Caetlin looked up, forced a smile, returned to her page. The German woman went on. 'I tell you. I tell you what's wrong with them. What has always been wrong with them. They are more interested in each other than us, and that is the truth.'

Her fresh drink arrived on the waiter's tray. She grabbed it, stood and turned sharply to me. 'And what do you think of that, young man? Do you think they are more interested in each other nowadays, the men?' She laughed harshly before I could speak, and raised her glass with a flourish. 'So here's to you men!' As she downed her drink, I saw a big tear glisten down her powdered cheek. Then a low howl erupted from her, and she doubled over in pain.

'Madam has had enough now I think,' the old waiter said, extending his arm round her quivering frame.

She did not protest as he helped her up. Caetlin glanced over and watched for a half-instant as the old man shepherded her out the door.

'Sad,' I said.

'Uh-huh,' she agreed. 'Such low consciousness.'

As I rose to leave, I glimpsed a male face she was sketching in violent, staccato thrusts into her journal.

'Oh, and thanks again for the Vitamin Cs,' she said, not looking up.

'I hope they did the trick.'

She nodded.

'So what did you think about what she said . . . about how men aren't really interested in women any more?'

'They're not, if you're like her.'

'You don't feel any pity for her?'

She looked up. 'Why should I?'

'But . . . isn't that what all this searching is meant to lead you to? Some kind of compassion?'

She shrugged. 'Look, I'm really sorry, but I've just gotta keep working here. You understand don't you?'

The waiter came back in. 'The lady is alright now,' he said. 'She is sleeping.'

'You know her?' I asked.

'Oh yes, sir. She comes in every day. She stays nearby. It is a pity she must drink so much.'

'I'd like another coffee,' Caetlin said. And with a final worried scan around the room, went back to sketching her lost but ubiquitous Alfredo, his lean shadowed face like a gunslinger in a Wanted poster.

A moon a sliver short of full crowned the sky as I strolled the deserted alleys of the old fort town that night. I passed down twisting lanes between houses, two or three storeyed, sandy coloured for the most part, dogs asleep out front, goats and cats scouting the gutters. From the upper window of a hippie dosshouse came the closing chords of *The Dark Side of the Moon*. A candle flickered up there. In a dormitory sack somebody, perhaps it was Caetlin, would be reading *The Celestine Prophecy*. A lazy cyclist passing a fraction too close by me whispered, 'Opium?'

The Pale Café of
the Unexplained

MY favourite café is the Mali, in Crown Street, Sydney. I have been going there regularly for more than a decade. When it first opened, they only had three tables and six chairs. When they got new ones I bought the original chairs, white wrought iron with green seats, for my kitchen. I still have them.

The story, or legend, of the Mali goes like this: a young man called Xerxes started it up after a trip to West Africa – thus the name. It is said he reached Timbuktu. Xerxes was lithe, dark, very serious. He always wore white, baggy pants and a slightly ragged shirt with long sleeves. There was a red bandanna knotted at his neck and a leather belt around his waist, from which his various chisels, pliers and screwdrivers hung. He was always engrossed in some very important task of renovation. Yet the miraculous and wonderful thing was that despite all his constant work, the café never seemed to change. For years it was in a state of coming into being. Walls were painted, painted over, then painted again. Sand sat in drifts in corners. Some patrons believed the café itself was an art installation.

The walls inside ended up a lime and lemon wash; outside, a very pale green, giving the place a feeling at once desert and marine, like sands at the bottom of the sea. The sinks and basins were hand-moulded, and encrusted with seashells. The counter upon which the San Marco cappuccino machine sits like a throne was hand-made too. The curtains are rough white muslin with cockle shells sewn in.

Over the years came the decorations – a line of pastel starfish above the entrance to greet the arriving patron, a curving strip of pineboard over the counter swum along by hand-cut wooden turtles. Weird *felucca*-like craft sail high over the tables, and there are also hand-painted wooden animals scattered about, giraffes and gazelles, and plaster of Paris tiles painted in watercolours of African *kraals*, rhino in savanna, a lion in wait for prey. At one stage these were offered for sale. I bought two (I believe trading was a bit thin otherwise).

The café is tiny – ten people and it's crowded. There is a scattering of seating on the pavement outside, big sandstone blocks and milk crates for the most part, where the overspill can sit in the sun watching the bumper-to-bumper traffic of Crown Street shunt by. Although usually relaxed, the place has its own intensity: a hollow-cheeked desperado scratching out a haiku in spilt sugar, an art student gloomily deconstructing a pastry. The coffee itself is rich, with a creamy texture, never bitter. It is hard to imagine better. And the menu, though minimal, is unique. Lunch is a lemon juice sweetened with rosewater, Spanish coffee, and a Turkish bread sandwich of salad, olives, chillies and haloumi cheese. But the truly magnetic attraction of the Mali comes not from its menu, but its mystery. The unexplained. Battered sepia postcards of the Pyramids appear on the walls one day – the next they are all gone. Then a sign in tiny hand-printed letters appears: 'No Photographs In The Café Please.'

A few years ago I was asked to write a magazine article on my favourite café. Needless to say, it was the Mali. There was a problem, however, as I was unsure the management would find the publicity desirable. It seemed unlikely they would even allow photographs to be taken. Thus I was in the absurd position of writing a piece which could gain the café business, yet I had to do it surreptitiously. And if it worked, and too many people came in, I might even ruin my favourite café through the very act of writing about it. In the end, no one knew the story was being written, and the photographs were taken from out in the street. I didn't return for months, and when I finally did I ordered a very circumspect caffè latte.

An elegant Frenchwoman named Sylvie took over when the Xerxes clan moved interstate. She ran the place a little differently. French fashion magazines appeared on shelves, and soon the café was frequented by a new crowd, size eight models with navel rings, boys with nascent dreadlocks and the faraway eyes of the young Brando. I didn't feel I quite fitted in so well any more. Was the original spirit of the place dissipating? Now it was all so, well, 'cool'. Or had the café grown younger, myself older? Was I merely experiencing slippage from the demographic?

A winter's day, chilly but sunny. Inside, people were huddled near the single kerosene heater traditionally put out in the middle of the café, the only recognition of the cold months. Boys in pre-loved duffel coats and beads, girls jacketed in recycled fluffy bath-mats. I was just finishing my sandwich when there was a sudden commotion: a pigeon had strayed into the café. The girls looked up from their *marie claire* magazines, the boys from their angst and cigarettes.

Startled to find itself indoors, the bird flew hard for the street beyond – only now there was an invisible barrier blocking its escape, and with an awful thud it smashed its head against the glass. All of us, eight in number, stared as the big grey pigeon picked itself up, fluttered randomly around the café, just over-head, panicking. We all knew it would do it again, and surely enough it did, flying straight and hard at the barrier, smashing itself brutally against it, so that it slid down half-stunned onto the magazine counter, wings flapping helplessly.

No one moved. The bird would keep doing it until it rendered itself unconscious or smashed its brains out. Someone had to do something, but everyone seemed unwilling, or incapable. Besides, it was just a pigeon, the lumpenproles of city birds, 'rats with wings'. They don't command a fraction of the respect of native urban birds, cockatoos or currawongs. Yet up close one could clearly see the ter-ror frozen in its eyes, and sense the intelligence behind them.

Again the bird flew at the glass, again the horrible thud of head on glass, the scrape of beak, the panicked flutter. But then I found myself on my feet, stretching towards it. I had never handled a bird in my life: patting cats and dogs is about as far as my contacts go with fauna. But my hands joined around the bird's body. It was surprisingly soft. It did not resist. If this were to be its moment of death, it felt ready. It relaxed, and I lifted it and carried it to the open doorway. The winter sun on Crown Street beckoned. I raised the bird and released it. It hesitated a half-second, then flapped off.

Just a simple street pigeon, but I felt for that moment as if I had released a wallaby from a rabbit trap. When I turned back, the others in the café, those of the frozen cool, discreetly applauded, even smiled. It was a strange feeling, a sense of belonging renewed in that pale café of the unexplained.

The

Blue Man

I sat at one of the jumble of plastic tables of Le Café L'Homme Bleu, out in front of the hotel. I was alternately writing in my diary and watching the black and white TV mounted on a Seven Up crate in the corner. It was past mid-afternoon, but the day was very hot, and as the sun swallowed up one segment of shade I kept moving tables to another. The TV programme appeared to be a fundamentalist franchise of 'The Price is Right', in which contestants were quizzed on their knowledge of Islamic holy sites. Though I did not understand Arabic, the thing which made it such compelling viewing was a studio audience of women screaming and shouting like a game show audience anywhere, but all of them in full veil.

I was interrupted by a male voice. *'Excusez-moi, monsieur.'*

As I had to look up into the full glare of the afternoon sun, it took me a few moments to appreciate fully the bizarre appearance of the man who stood above me. He was dressed in what must once have been a long military-style jacket, but was now a mess of mottled threads, a shagpile collage of blue hair. The garment was fastened at the waist with a crude steel fibule. This was just as well as the young man – I could see now that he was indeed still young – wore no trousers beneath the coat, in fact no other clothing at all beyond a pair of sandal-like shoes cut from old truck tyres and fastened to his feet with frayed lengths of rope. His deeply tanned face had the serenity of the desert itself, and from it sprang a profusion of curly blond beard. His hair, which was also blond and curly, had entrapped specimens from the landscape through which he had passed – twigs, seeds, fragments of dried blossom. His eyes were African sky blue, the whites as white as the albumen of a freshly poached egg.

'*Oui?*' I said.

'*Excusez-moi,*' he repeated, as I blinked up into the sun. '*Je cherche Tombouctou.*'

Fastening onto his meaning, I broke into English, half to myself. 'You're looking for the way to Timbuktu?'

'Oh, you speak English,' he said with obvious relief.

'Yes.'

'Thank god,' he smiled. 'Haven't spoken it in months so it seems.'

I gestured to the chair opposite mine, and with a long sigh like a tyre deflating, he collapsed into it.

'You're going to Timbuktu,' I confirmed, when he had settled.

'Yes. Well, it's on my way at any rate.'

'Bus? Bush taxi?'

'Foot.'

'Walking?' I said, with barely disguised incredulity. 'You're walking there?'

'Yes. You can do a good deal of walking in Africa. It's a big place.'

The slim shade was already moving on from us, and all the tables were subjected to the full weight of the afternoon sun. The hard blue air was motionless, the heat stifling. His gaze strayed past me to a rusted '*Buvez Coca-Cola*' sign at my shoulder.

'Thirsty?'

'I am somewhat, yes.' Then without warning he swayed forward in the chair, wilting before my eyes. I just managed to catch him by the arm. It was sinewy as rope.

'Are you alright?'

'Yes, yes, don't worry about me,' he said, but his head settled down onto the table and stayed there. Enlisting the help of a boy who waited at the tables, we took him up the dusty terrazzo-tiled steps to my room on the first floor above the café, overlooking the street. We settled him onto the bed, and I got him to drink some bottled water. He drank seriously, like a camel at a well.

'Not too much all at once,' I suggested.

But he drank on, as if he knew what he was doing, and would know exactly when to stop. When he finally did so, he carefully capped the bottle and set it down on the bed beside him. 'Thank you.'

'Feeling better?'

'Much.'

The boy took his leave, retreating with measured, backward steps until he slipped out through the doorway, and eased the door shut behind him.

Eyes accustoming themselves to the room's shadowy interior, the man took in his new surroundings by degree, the blue luminescence of his gaze alighting here and there.

'You're sure you're alright now.'

'I am, thank you.'

'You're English,' I said.

'Yes. From London.'

In his ragged blue coat and truck tyre sandals, he looked like a post-apocalyptic harlequin or a saltbush preacher. Only the eyes seemed at odds with this raffish impression. They were remote. The word 'purified' came to my mind. I watched him as he looked out my window onto the street below. A cloud of burnt orange dust hung out there, punctured by the rush of the occasional bush taxi.

'Is there anything else I can do to help you?'

'Not really.' He returned his gaze to me. 'You've already done enough. I don't usually allow people to do so much for me.'

'Why not?'

'Because then I'll come to expect it. And one simply cannot do that. Not here. Not anywhere for that matter.'

'Where have you come from?'

'Down south.'

'South Africa?'

'Harare. Zimbabwe. I was robbed there. Thieves broke into my hotel room.'

'What did they take?'

'Everything but the clothes I was in.' Then he smiled. 'No, not these ones. I picked up these on the way.'

'The police didn't catch the thieves?'

'I didn't report it actually.'

'Why not?'

'Didn't seem much use, to tell you the truth.'

'Surely you phoned home though.'

'No.'

'I take it you're not married.'

'Yes. We have three children'

'But . . .'

'Oh, Helen would have tried to talk me out of it.'

'Out of what?'

'Well, you see . . . I wanted to go far away, very far away. Before the robbery, this was. That was the plan. I'd told Helen I simply had to have a few weeks' break from everything. Right away, by myself. Find myself, you know the kind of thing. But in my heart I actually wanted to go even further than that. I wanted to go so far I'd forget my address, my bank balance, my bloody phone number . . . Just utterly fed up with everything I suppose. But when I got to Africa, to Harare, I found myself in a hotel just like any hotel. It was Africa, but it was anywhere and nowhere too. It felt hopeless. I didn't know what I was doing. I felt strange, like I was trapped there in that hotel, that room.

'I saw the sights, met a few people. But it was no good. I knew I had to go further, deeper, if the experience was to mean anything. But I didn't know quite what to do. Felt I was probably going mad or something. Probably was. Then the robbery happened . . . and curiously enough it fixed everything. Freed me to do what I'd wanted to do all along, because suddenly I had nothing. No credit card, money, passport. Not even a photograph.'

'And . . . after the robbery . . . you just started walking?'

'Yes.'

'Where? Where were you going?'

'North.'

'Just north? That's it?'

'More direction than most people have. Oh, I know it sounds peculiar, but I just walked north, through all of Africa. And I found it was . . . land. That's all. Land. That itself was a revelation. It wasn't some terrible place, like you see on TV. I found myself walking through land, land like it had always been, long before anyone called it "Africa". How can I explain it properly . . .? A benign terrain stretched away before my feet, like a carpet. Grassland and jungle, mountains and desert. People living in straw huts, with *kraals* and dogs and pigs and cattle, with families and cooking fires, and stories. And outside, the forest and the savanna, all the elephants and giraffes, wildebeest and warthogs, lions and hyenas, hippo and flamingos . . . magical beyond words . . . beyond anything you can even dream when you take the tube to a job, when you sleep every night in some barred-up cellblock you call home and your feet don't ever even touch the earth because there's leather covering your feet and tar covering the earth.'

'But without any money, how have you fed yourself?'

'I've gotten by.' He patted his taut stomach. 'Though it has been somewhat slimming.'

'How did you cross borders, without a passport?'

'Walked. Or waded. Or swam.'

'Borders didn't mean anything?'

'Most times I didn't even know which country I was in anyway, unless I came to a town. Borders became irrelevant.'

'Like they are to a Tuareg,' I suggested.

'Yes,' he said, the tanned face suddenly animated. 'A blue man.' He got up and sauntered around the room, tyre-track shoes slapping softly against the floor tiles. 'You're Australian aren't you? My brother lives out there. In Perth. He's an engineer.'

'It's a nice place, Perth.'

'So he says.'

'Would you like some coffee?'

'Yes, thank you.' His tone was suddenly dreamy as he conjured up the genie of coffee. 'With milk.'

I went out onto the landing where I called downstairs for '*deux*

95

cafés au lait, s'il vous plaît'. On return I was taken aback at how shadowy the room had become. Evening comes on quickly here, but its rapidity still surprised me. He had returned to my bed, stretched himself out, rough hands with fingers knitted together resting on his chest. His beaten sandals were neatly paired at the foot of the bed, as if he were retiring for the night. In the dark gold light his bared feet looked like crude but trusty implements, fashioned from clay.

'Sorry, I'm a bit tired.'

'That's alright, make yourself comfortable. Did you come far today?'

'Not so far. A few hours or so.'

I resumed my place in the chair. 'They'll bring the coffee up in a minute.'

He turned to me, eyes bluer than ever in the gloom, the whites glaring out. 'Do you know what I was thinking about, all those months walking? You may think I'm truly mad – if you don't already that is.'

'No, tell me.'

'I was thinking about the Mystery of the Holy Spirit.'

'Oh,' I said, unable to conceal a tone of disappointment.

'No, no, I'm not a religious nutter. I am not.' He looked hard into my eyes. 'I am not a lunatic. I am like you. Look at me. Please.'

It was more a command than a request, and I was unused to being ordered about. But finally I levelled my eyes with his. We looked at each other a moment or two, then he smiled enigmatically. 'Yes. The Holy Spirit. Shall I tell you about it?'

'Alright. If you wish.'

He paused a moment, cleared his throat formally, and finally began speaking in a soft, confiding voice. 'God the Father, God the Son, and God the Holy Spirit . . . to tell you the truth, I was always rather amused by that as a boy.'

'By what?'

'The Holy Spirit. Always imagined a ghost in a white sheet. Could never quite picture a face. Could you?'

'I didn't have much of a religious education.'

'But you must have seen representations, pictures of the deity.'

'Jesus, you mean.'

'Jesus. And Jehovah. God the Son and God the Father. I recall Jesus always had milk calf eyes, clear olive skin, and a nicely trimmed blond beard. His father was seated up on a cloud, with a long white beard and a stern look on his face, usually giving Moses curry about the Ten Commandments.'

'I remember Hell the most,' I said. 'A schoolfriend's family once took me to hear this famous visiting preacher. He was fierce, all fire and brimstone. And for months after I used to lie awake in my bed at night seeing demons with pitchforks and sinners boiling in vats of oil.'

He chuckled. 'But you *must* remember God with the long white beard, and Jesus with the clipped blond one. But the Holy Ghost never had a face, did he? The Paraclete, that's what the Catechism called him. I used to get mixed up because the Paraclete was sometimes depicted as a bird, and when I was a child I thought he was called the *Parakeet*. I was often confused in class. Often caned too.'

'Weren't we all?'

'The Holy Spirit,' he mused further. 'A faceless god. Yet, he impregnated Mary, if I'm not wrong. Imagine that, a god bonking a virgin. A human virgin too. And why was she still a virgin anyway? Couldn't Joseph get an erection? Were the hours too long in the carpentry business? Too many tables and chairs on order? Too many cabinets and shelves . . .'

There was a low tapping on the door, and a small, slightly stooped man with a serious expression entered. It was Amadou, who ran the hotel's errands and delivered food and drink to the rooms. He entered furtively, with a sidelong glance towards the figure lying on the bed, and deposited an aluminium tray bearing two mugs of muddy-looking coffee onto the rickety bedside table.

'*Merci*,' I said, and paid him.

Amadou nodded and slipped away. Neither of us spoke as my guest watched him disappear out the door and close it behind him.

'Hotels are full of people whose lives haven't quite worked out, aren't they?' he said gently. 'The tragic old man who delivers the room service. The teenage girl who wipes down the tables. The haughty bugger at the desk. And the guests, clutching ever so tightly onto all their pathetic baggage – if that isn't a metaphor I don't know what is.'

He sat up, and I passed him one of the mugs. The steaming surface of the coffee trembled lightly in his grasp. I saw his beard stray into it, before being drawn back with a reflexive movement of his hand. I took the other mug and sipped. It was the usual, Nescafé with condensed milk.

'What was I talking about again?' he asked.

'The Holy Spirit.'

'Was I?' His eyes were clouding over now, into a half-lidded sky.

'Yes. And about Joseph and the hours he worked and him not being able to get an erection perhaps.'

He smiled and took another sip, his hands clearly shaking. 'Oh, I really must apologise. You don't want to hear about all that crazy stuff.'

'Actually it was just getting interesting . . .'

'No, I know you don't want to hear it. And rightly so. Why would you?'

'Please, continue,' I said.

'No,' he repeated firmly. 'I've just been alone too long, that's all. Too much silence and too much to think about.'

I was so surprised at his change of tack that I was unprepared for the next one.

'So what are you looking for here?' he asked.

'Me?'

'Yes, you,' he grinned.

'Well, I don't know precisely.'

'What brought you then?'

'I suppose I'd just reached the end.'

'Of what?'

'Everything. Nothing seemed to have meaning any more. So I

got on a plane and went to Paris. I spent some time there, very pleasant, but that ended up pretty meaningless too.'

'So you boarded another plane and came here.'

'Yes. Strange, isn't it?'

'Not entirely, no. And where to after here?'

'I don't know.'

'That's the problem, isn't it. One is already at the end of the earth. There's nowhere else to go.'

'I suppose not.'

'You don't have relatives back in Australia? Children? Wife?'

'I was married once. That was enough.'

'Girlfriend?'

'I did meet someone I liked, just before I left.'

'What was she like?'

'Nice. Very nice. But then my departure date came, and I left.'

'Have you heard from her?'

'We exchanged a few letters when I was in Paris. She's an odd girl actually.'

'In what way?'

'For one thing, she froze some of my sperm.'

'What?'

'Yes. The last time we made love, just before I left, she took the condom, knotted the end and put it in her freezer. Just in case I didn't come back, she said.'

'Extraordinary. But do you think she'd actually do something with it?'

'I don't know. Could she?'

'I must admit cryogenics is a bit outside my field. But these days, who knows?' He mused a moment longer. 'Bloody extraordinary.'

It was now dark in my room. For some reason, it seemed perfectly natural to be conversing about my sperm in a lover's freezer back in Australia, with an English ragamuffin who had just walked across most of Africa. Perhaps it was the heat. I realised I knew very little about him – we had not even exchanged names. I was tempted to do so, yet felt perhaps we had gone past that point.

'You haven't told me what you do for a living,' I said.

'Haven't I? Industrial chemist, with a big pharmaceutical firm. Backroom boffin basically. Very tedious.'

Something caught my eye just then, and I got up and walked over to the window. In the poisonous yellow light of the street, a gang of boys had gathered around an old Citroën like ants round a dying roach. They already had its engine out, and signalled to each other with little grunts and quick movements of their hands about the next phase of the gutting.

'And where to now?' I asked him.

'North.'

'You're really going to walk across the Sahara? How will you find your way?'

'Oh, there's plenty of tracks through the desert. *Pistes*. Loads of people out there too. Tuaregs. There's water . . .'

'Food?'

'One finds it.'

'And when you cross the desert?' I had thought better of saying 'if'.

'Morocco. Spain. France. London. Crouch End.'

'And Helen?'

'If she still wants me.'

'How long have you been gone?'

'A year, perhaps longer. Seasons do get very confused when you walk from hemisphere to hemisphere.'

He fell quiet then, and I thought he might have drifted off to sleep. But when I looked at him closely I saw his eyes were alert once more, and fixed on me.

'Now, would you like to hear about the Holy Spirit?'

'If you want to talk about it, yes, I would.'

'I'm not mad you know.'

'I know that.'

'And you may find it of use later, in your life. But you must want to hear it. That's why I stopped before. Unless you really want to hear it, I'm wasting my breath.'

'No, please, speak.'

'Are you certain?'

'Yes, please. I want to hear.'

'Very well then,' he said softly, resting his head back onto the pillow and closing his eyes. 'When you arrive in some places, no matter how dusty and awful they are, there it is, the Holy Spirit. Floating through everything, before your eyes, like a veil of the finest desert dust, a sweet film over all, through all, like pollen. A miasma of divinity. Then you reach somewhere else, it doesn't matter what it's like, where it is . . . the hills may be green, streams clear and cool and flowing hard, the people happy and friendly . . . but it is lacking. The place lacks the Holy Spirit. Well, my friend, let me tell you that Africa is awash with it, bathed in the Holy Spirit. It's like no other place you could ever see. I know this because I have been blessed, blessed with my little ramble through this place. I've seen the Holy Spirit. Drunk it in the rivers, breathed it down from the stars. I have stared down into the dust and seen it there, the lovely face of the faceless. That is what you seek, too, in all your travels and tribulations. I knew it from the moment we met. That is what you seek in love as well. You wish to give a face to what must be faceless. But you see, the Spirit . . . love . . . cannot be so very . . . *defined.*'

His voice trailed off. I finished my coffee and put my mug back onto the aluminium tray, causing the metal to clatter. Peering into the darkness, I saw his eyes open, startled, and look about as if he had just awakened from a long sleep. Then they closed again.

'Do you want to get back home?'

He did not respond, but I saw a smile spread across his cracked lips, disappearing away into his beard.

'To your wife, family?'

He nodded, still smiling. 'And my bed. Yes. I would like my bed again now.'

'Well, you won't get there. You're tired. Thin. Sick too, most likely. After what you've been through, you can't cross the Sahara now. No one can. Not on foot, alone.'

'People walk across Africa,' he said. 'Lots of them.'

'But they have support teams, camera teams usually.'

He chuckled. 'If only the company I work for, the big chemical concern, knew about the Holy Spirit,' he said. 'Silly buggers, they'd be forever trying to bottle it.'

'Listen,' I said insistently, 'you can't do this.'

He did not respond, and I saw this time he was indeed asleep, chest rising and falling in an even rhythm, the empty mug toppled from his grasp.

I slept in the next room. When I awoke next morning, he had gone, as had the return coupon of my airline ticket to Paris which I had left on the bedside table with a short note imploring him to take it. There was the briefest of acknowledgements: 'Thanks. I must admit my feet were getting a little tired.'

So now he was to be me. And I him. I had only a couple of thousand or so French francs left – not enough for another ticket out of here. All I could hope for in return for this act of momentary folly was that I too would see the face of the faceless, the Holy Spirit in the ribbing of the desert sand, and, like him, arrive at something like a destination.

I awoke at a party. A woman in a little black dress was saying something about an art show, while a bearded man in jeans levered the cork from a bottle of champagne. There was the smell of hashish in the crowded room, which boomed with loud, generic rock. I felt slightly faint, made my way to a window and stuck my head out into the cool night. There was a tangle of creeper in the garden below. The horn of a distant ship sounded through the mist that hung over the dark waters.

'Had enough?' came a female voice from beside me. It was the woman in the black dress, clutching a velvet wrap. I nodded. She smiled and took my hand. Hers felt warm, comfortable. But somehow she must have sensed reticence, or confusion in me. 'What is it darling?' she asked, with a look of concern.

'Oh, nothing.'

She swept an auburn wisp aside and snuggled into me as we left the party with kisses and farewells, and made our way down into the street. It was quiet there, the air pleasingly cool and still.

'Tell me,' I said, 'have I just . . . been somewhere?'

'There and back,' she said gaily. 'Come on, the babysitter will be wanting overtime.' She skipped off down the pavement. 'Oh, do come along now darling. You don't want to be blue all your life, do you?'

Far away, a clock struck. I wondered if perhaps it was not Big Ben.

the Pearl .of the Orient

Mr

Stevie Wonder

D IRK and I strolled across Hampstead Heath the day before I left London. It was Easter Saturday, early April, early spring, but the day was cold and turbulent, the sky frantic. Rain whipped our cheeks and low stormclouds whorled about us like suds round a plughole. Halfway across the Heath an arctic gale gusted up, flinging a hail which encrusted the back of my denim jacket with a gravel of freezing glass. Dirk barely noticed, talking on head down about how the galleries weren't interested in his work, how the London art scene was tied up tight and he didn't know where he was going anyway, how tired he was of being called a JAFA – 'Just Another Fucking Australian' – how he sometimes really wanted to piss off out of England to somewhere pleasant, Spain perhaps. He was also tempted to go home to Australia. That night we toasted the arrival of spring with Bulgarian red, and then we toasted Kathryn and Sally, women in general, then the continent of Africa.

I had a poor night's sleep, awakened repeatedly by sirens up and down Kentish Town Road. I gave up trying to sleep at 6.30, ate a bowl of muesli, did a final check of my bag, ticket, passport, money, and left with a decisive closure of the front door. I walked the half-mile down through a very cold, clear Easter Sunday morning to Kentish Town tube, past the shambling row of kebab joints, the travel agency doubling as a child minder, the 'turf accountant' (England still can be so quaint in an Arthur Daley kind of way) and estate agents offering the same rows of sad-eyed terraces. A gritty, grimy, down-at-heel, mean-spirited, over-touristed, pompous, polluted and penny-pinched old town London is, but you can't help but like it.

At Gatwick I took off the moth-eaten sweater I had worn beneath my denim jacket, and left it in a rubbish bin. Now I was travelling light, Africa light. I felt buoyed up, as if the sun were already on my shoulders. I had for months pictured myself in the back of trucks bumping through the desert, or half-asleep on a dusty afternoon in some remote outpost. I intended to write a novel in West Africa. I had heard about a place in Ouagadougou ('Wuh-guh-doo-goo'), the capital of Burkina Faso. The place was called the Hotel Le Pavilion Vert. Small rooms with ceiling fans around a garden courtyard, I had been told. Very pretty, very quiet. A good place to work. I pictured myself there, each day at an old table, writing in my stout, red-covered notebook from Ryman the Stationer. I saw the bottle of mineral water at my elbow, the beads of perspiration on my brow, the dusty tiles at my bare feet. I saw the palm trees in the courtyard, and the head on the first beer as the sun slipped below the horizon and the desert sky washed blue to pink. After roughing out the great African novel in Ouagadougou, the idea was to push north to Mali and out to Timbuktu, towards which I had strained my eyes from Zagora, in Morocco, those fifty-two or so *jours* previously.

It all seemed perfectly possible from looking at a map of Africa. I knew it might be difficult here and there, I might even get a bit ill on the way, but it should be no problem to an experienced traveller like myself. I had even already started on the great African novel. Some of it existed in draft form, as a short story. I had written it in London in Dirk's basement, on a borrowed portable typewriter. The piece was based on an anecdote Dirk had related to me, about a young man who had been robbed in Southern Africa, and who had decided to walk back home to England, across the entire continent of Africa. Of course, a few people *have* walked across Africa, but this fellow had done it without support – without money in fact.

A version of that story was to be the basis of my novel. I had devoted a couple of days to drafting it out. I set the story in a wayside hotel in a dusty West African town, as a meeting between two equally lost men. As I wrote, I wondered if it would be obvious to the reader that the writer had not been to West Africa – and whether it would be possible to write an entire African novel in that musty basement in Highgate. After all, a deal of the exotic lexicon has been written with little more than a good atlas and imagination.

There was someone who looked very like Jerry Rawlings, the Ghanaian leader, in the departure lounge at Gatwick Airport. He wore a long white African robe. His Afro ringlets and funky sunglasses were very Mod Squad. I asked the blue-suited African man behind me in the check-in queue if the man was indeed Jerry Rawlings. He glanced up from his *Daily Telegraph*, and looked the man over.

'No,' he said, 'but I do believe he is Mr Stevie Wonder, the American singer.'

I read my short story over on the flight down to Accra. I didn't think much of it, but decided it was a start at least. I put it away, ate my airline food, drank the miniature bottle of claret that came with it, daydreamed, dozed. As we flew ever south, my thoughts parachuted down through thirty thousand feet of cloudless sky, to the floor of the yellow Sahel. Down there in Mali were the places I had come to see: the Niger River, the great sand mosque at Djenne, the market port of Mopti, the Dogon Country, Timbuktu. In a few days I would start out from my base in Accra, north to Ouagadougou, then later on to Mali. Soon, lulled half-asleep by the food and the cheap, warming claret, my thoughts drifted further, off towards the rim of the world.

As a rule, people did not travel when I was a child. They went away. We used to go away for two weeks each January, to a spot never too distant, always by the sea. We rented a shack or holiday flat. One time it was rooms behind a country bakery – my memory is the smell of warm currant buns. We would fish and swim by day, play cards through the hot, sticky nights. I remember the sheen of perspiration on my father's sunburnt back as he fetched another beer from the ice box, cigarette clenched between his teeth as his lips parted in a laugh, sitting down to deal another hand.

Of course, some people did travel – interstate, even overseas. My bachelor uncle, a policeman, somehow managed it. He sailed off to America and Japan, more than once. People were a little suspicious of this, wondering why anyone would ever want to go to Japan. My father wondered why anyone would ever want to be a policeman.

The first time I 'travelled' anywhere it was with my aunt, to Brisbane. I was five years old, and the transcontinental journey from Adelaide was an adventure. The states still had different gauge tracks then, and we made endless sleepy stops in the middle of the night to change trains.

We passed through Sydney first. The air was so clear you could still see the Blue Mountains from the city streets. I bought a plywood boomerang at a souvenir shop inside one of the pylons of the Sydney Harbour Bridge, and took it back to Adelaide like an icon foraged from a far off land. In Brisbane, my aunt took us on a day trip in a canvas-topped riverboat, and it felt like we were sailing into an African jungle. Next we travelled down to a new place called Surfer's Paradise, and stayed at the Motel Rio. It had a kidney-shaped swimming pool, and I had never seen anything like it. All around the motel were sandhills, violet blue under moonlight. Not far off, marked out in the sand, was the ground plan for the Broadbeach Hotel, later to become a Gold Coast landmark.

The last thing I recall of the trip was the hotel we stayed at in Melbourne on the way back. It was opposite the Spencer Street Railway Station, a gaunt building, grey stone in big chunks, forbidding as a hospital. When I got back my parents made a fuss over me, and I was very proud of my adventures. It was as if I had achieved something. And, I considered now, dozing in my acetate airline seat flying down to Ghana, there is that satisfying feeling of achievement with any completed journey – just as there must be a feeling of defeat, of being cheated even, with one not completed.

Dusk was closing in on Accra as the airliner banked around and began descending into Kotoka Airport. Out the window I saw an orange plain studded with young green growth, not unlike the South Australian outback after rain. Yet there was a dusty, unkempt quality to it too, a wan melancholia.

I had no real idea of what to expect of Ghana. I was arriving with a bare mental sketch of its recent history. I knew something of the charismatic people's hero Kwame Nkrumah who had steered Ghana to independence from Britain in 1957 – the first colonised country in black Africa to gain it – and of the young flight lieutenant, Jerry Rawlings, who seized power from a corrupt and moribund military regime in 1979. Rawlings is a remarkable character – three months after staging the 1979 coup and at the peak of popular power, he voluntarily stepped down and held elections. Two years later he staged a second coup, and has been in power ever since. For an avowed and outspoken leftist and critic of the West, he had nonetheless engineered a free-market style revival of an economy devastated by decades of misrule. These days he remains a canny and resourceful national leader, but a dictator nonetheless.

I had one local contact. I had recently become acquainted with a young Ghanaian back in Sydney, and she had given me her parents' telephone number in Accra. I had rung Tom from London, and now he met me at the airport, a short, jolly man of seventy. He was successful businessman with a Peugeot and driver and a comfortable bungalow.

The Penta Hotel which he had booked for me was more expensive than I'd hoped for – around US$50 a night – and the windowless room was stuffy and depressing. It seemed the management believed you wouldn't notice the broken furniture if they gave you a colour TV and bar fridge. The air conditioner rattled like a steam train, but with the baking heat still pushing in from outside I realised I would probably have to keep it switched on all night. I had packed ear plugs: human beings cannot be trusted with stereos, car-horns, dogs, relationships or machinery.

As I lowered my bag to the floor, Tom slapped me on the back and announced I was invited to a big party that night. He handed me a long blue African shirt embroidered with gold. 'There, now you are a true Ghanaian.'

He checked that the mini-bar was properly stacked with beer – 'I know how you Aussies love to drink' – and left saying his driver would be back in an hour to pick me up.

Alone, I sat down on the bed and perused my cell. A man wandered past the partition wall outside, whistling. I heard the corridor toilet flush. Off in a kitchen, a pan clattered. Someone shouted at a crying child. I turned on the TV set. It was a local broadcast, a trio of men glumly discussing the defeat that day of the Ghanaian soccer team at the hands of rivals Côte d'Ivoire at the African championships in Tunisia. It felt like a national crisis. The coach stared out mournfully from the gyprock set like a convict on the scaffold and conceded, 'I have no excuse.' The presenter, heavy-browed in this difficult moment, nodded. An advertisement for Club Beer came on, followed by one for Panther Condoms, and then another beer advertisement, this time for a brand called ABC. It looked like the same bunch of partying actors were in the beer and the condom ads, having the same goood time. Then we were back to the sports post-mortem, to the stern-faced presenter and the coach on the gibbet. I turned it off and took a shower. Dressing for the party, I wondered whether Rawlings might be there, with his presidential guest, Mr Stevie Wonder.

Hard White Light

A perfect party night settled over the tropical dictatorship. The occasion was the seventieth birthday of a trucking magnate, and everyone was going to be there. We pulled up outside a modern whitewashed house behind a high wall in Accra's embassy belt. As I followed Tom, his wife Evelyn and daughter Roberta through the gates, I saw about two hundred people milling about up ahead. Everyone was hugging and laughing as they greeted old friends. The costumes were vibrant, the women in brilliant flowing prints, bright greens and golds and bold reds, the men in togas of *kente*, a cloth densely woven in narrow, complex strips of dazzling colour. I was warmly greeted by everyone. A glass of champagne found its way into my hand. We were conducted to our table as a band played breezy hi-life, guitar lines rippling up into the starry night. We were placed with some of Tom's old friends, and I was sat near two of the other few white faces at the gathering, a European Ambassador and his wife.

The evening got underway with testimonials from the magnate's old friends. The speeches were erudite, warm, most of them very witty. Everyone seemed to quote Shakespeare or the Bible, 'three score years and ten'. The freshly septuagenarian guest of honour sat at the top table, surrounded by his family.

When the speeches were over and dinner was served, I found myself talking to the Ambassador. He was a big man, well into his fifties. His hair was white, but he still had all of it. His eyebrows thrust up like hard weeds in the desert. His wife was twenty years younger, fine boned, cool in white linen, with slender arms and a dancer's legs. He kept his eye on her as he told me about all the Russian tanks he'd seen left behind by the Libyans after their defeat in the desert in Chad, and how he knew the Soviet Union had always been destined to fall. Capitalism, he said by way of extension, is more natural to the human beast than socialism. 'A problem of evolution,' the Ambassador mused. His gaze slipped

113

back to his young wife. 'She is a painter,' he confided. 'I met her here in Africa. Ten years now we have been together.'

The food was superb. Aromatic plantains, sweet potato, cassava, a robust spinach and fish dish, chicken wings glazed with something piquant and earthy. More drinks came. People were up on their feet now, dancing in a slow, measured rhythm. I let my head loll back and looked up at the stars. So here I was, back in Africa, my third time, and it was perfect and I was having a wonderful time except for the fact that I was suddenly a little drunk and very tired. How long ago was it that I had climbed out of bed into that chilly room in Highgate?

I danced with the Ambassador's wife. She was pleasant and polite, if remote. She painted still-lifes, she said. As we danced, I saw Evelyn, Tom's wife, watching me, and when I sat down she asked me to dance. Out on the floor, she spoke to me in a firm, almost disciplinary tone.

'Dance *seriously*,' she said. 'You must follow the beat. Follow the beat, that's all you have to do.'

I tried following the beat.

'Oh, now really, sir,' she said, 'you must learn to dance like a Ghanaian if you are here. That is what we all do, dance.'

Looking around, I marvelled at the sight. Here was the hoi polloi of Accra, socialist greybeards who had been with Nkrumah, young guns who had cut their teeth with Rawlings, and plenty of the brash new capitalists, yet everyone was dancing to the band, and dancing well. I tried to compare it to a Labor Party 'do', and it didn't. My dancing wouldn't have been out of place there.

Back in my room that night, I practised steps in front of the mirror. Easy – one, two. One, two. A simple shuffle of the feet. I looked in the mirror, watching myself 'dancing seriously'. Oddly, the sight of myself made me wonder where Kathryn was, what she was doing, right now. I felt a barb in my intestine. What, I asked myself, am I doing here? Chatwin's title never seemed more apt. Sitting on the bed in that dingy room, I experienced it again, the malaise of the solo traveller. There is so much romance, allure, which attaches itself to 'I Travel Alone'. It's one of the last authentic adventures in this world, yet so often it is like this, finding yourself shipwrecked in a nasty, airless room.

Kathryn had gone back to Australia three days before I left for Africa. Gone back to move out of our house, into a flat, a flat which did not even have a telephone yet. And when she got her telephone connected, I would not have the number, because I was travelling through West Africa, the land that Telecom forgot. I would not see her for months, perhaps not even hear her voice. After seven years, it all seemed so abrupt. And who would she meet while I was away? Someone who would no doubt treat her better than I had. Who would value her beauty, charm, her intelligence, sensitivity. What Am I Doing Here? I wondered again.

In the hard white light of day, the Penta Hotel was fully revealed as a sixties concrete box, gone at the seams, as charmless as it was airless. The corridors were dark and the traffic down them was African carpetbaggers, shifty European gold dealers, and call girls. You got the feeling from the guys at the front desk that if a guest were murdered in their room, their only concern would be the wear and tear on the linen.

It being Easter Monday, everything was closed. I had slept in. It's odd how things like public holidays, festivals and strikes affect the traveller. Even when you know they're coming they still leave you beached. Hungry, I ventured out into the early afternoon. Usually I enjoy the heat, but my first encounter with the equatorial West African sun was memorable. It was the kind of radiance that bakes mud into pots and burns skin into tumours. It thudded down in heavy waves, and I felt the impact hard on the shoulders, like a lag the lash.

I wandered down a red dirt alley nearby, looking for anything open. I passed shacks, modest bungalows and big houses behind high walls. Scraggy banana palms were everywhere, and horny thistles. Then, in the shadows of walls, in rubbish-strewn ditches, I saw men, first one, then a second and a third, sitting in the dust. They were thin men, skeletal, their heads mere skulls stretched with black skin, the eyes and teeth disconcertingly large. Their faces were fixed, eyes far off. They gave no indication of seeing, merely stared. I knew of course that AIDS was rife in West Africa, but I was shocked at coming face-to-face with it so quickly, and to see its victims abandoned to the street, to the sun, wind and flies.

I found a stall selling fruit. It was run by a large middle-aged woman, and there were two or three of her women friends hanging around, swishing flies from the papayas. They made some remark about me in their language, and broke out into giggles. I smiled the obliging smile of the tourist, and made my purchases. Back in my room I ate a late lunch of papaya, banana and mango, cut into slivers with my knife, a spread-out plastic bag my place-mat.

After eating, I hailed a taxi and went looking for a better hotel. The driver was young and cool and strangely suspicious.

'Which hotel do you want to see?'

'Any place better than the Penta – but not too expensive, please.'

He barely nodded. The taxi was small and matt black, like a very old Toyota but impossible to identify positively beyond a collage of crushed panels held together with rust and desperation. My seat felt glued with chewing gum.

The young driver must have seen me looking. 'You don't like my taxi?'

I shifted uncomfortably to evade a steel spring poking up into my groin. 'No, it's not that. It's just . . .'

He cut me off. 'Here on business?'

'I'm just travelling.'

'You have friends in Ghana?'

'Yes.'

'White friends?' His tone verged on accusatory. He turned to look at me.

'No,' I said. 'Black.'

He relaxed, almost smiled. 'Okay, let's go. I show you some hotels.'

But none of the places turned out right. The better ones were generically dull and far too expensive, the cheaper ones bombed out, near-deserted, listlessly malarial. I didn't like the look of anything.

'Take me back to the Penta please,' I said.

He smiled knowingly. 'Of course.'

As he drove, I began to take in the city in more detail. It was a typically British colonial layout, built from the core of a Victorian post office, cathedral and park down by the main beach. Running along the blue line of the Gulf of Guinea were the more recent additions, the concrete administration blocks dating from the reign of the various military dictatorships which had followed the overthrow of Nkrumah. We passed Black Star Square, a colossal expanse of paved parade ground backed by the sea, Nkrumah's answer to Moscow's Red Square. Then we followed the British ring-road and roundabout system out into the suburbs, past rows of houses and public buildings. Some parts were miserably shabby, but I got the feeling that although Accra had seen some bad times not too long ago, things were improving.

I asked the taxi driver what he thought of Rawlings. He looked at me for a long moment, sizing me up with a cynical eye.

'Good,' he said.

Back at the hotel, I hunted through the rumpled rooms of people just checked out until I found one with a window, a working air conditioner and a firm mattress. I went downstairs and told the desk staff I wanted it.

'Take it,' said a tall, impossibly bored one whom I took to be the manager. He yawned at me. 'I'll send a girl up.'

A few minutes later I moved in. The fridge chugged, the air conditioner chugged, but it was clean. Out the louvred window I could see a row of timber shacks below, the yards strewn with wrecked cars. Hens pecked in the red earth. A naked child ran after a ball, an enormous black dog barked. I got my ear plugs out and put them on the bedside table.

A Part of Life

That evening I dressed and went downstairs into the panelled bar that adjoined the dining room, and ordered a beer. I was about halfway through it when an African woman in a sunflower yellow dress and sandals slipped onto the stool beside me. It was still quite early, and we were alone there with the barman.

'Hello,' she said gaily, 'I'm Celeste.'

I introduced myself.

'Well, hello to you then,' she said. As we shook she dug her finger into my palm.

She was in her late twenties, full figured, ever smiling but with a slightly tired look. I wondered if she was friendly, forward, or a prostitute. As she sipped the beer the barman set down in front of her, she conversed with a knowing ease one usually reserves for old friends.

'My job is driving me crazy you know, just crazy. Who would be a hairdresser, eh?' She kept smiling. I noticed how her leg quivered like a jumpy adolescent's. 'Anyway, now I've finished work, and I want some fun.'

Not knowing quite what to say, I actually replied: 'Nice night for it.'

She continued smiling, prattling, sizing me up with a pair of wide, dark eyes. 'I'm single. Divorced. I was married to a British guy.'

'Do you have any children?'

'One daughter. Eight years old,' she said. 'Very expensive.'

'I'm sure, what with education, and . . .'

I took another mouthful of beer, and noticed she had already emptied hers. She sat over it expectantly.

'Would you like another drink?' I asked.

'Two more beers,' she told the barman, before I could say my current one was enough for me for the time being.

'So, what are you doing tonight?' she asked. 'What are your plans?' She swivelled in her chair and faced me. Her breasts were

118

thrust forward in the yellow dress, and the frayed hem rode up, exposing gleaming black legs.

'I'm probably having dinner with some Ghanaian friends of mine. Parents of a friend back in Sydney.'

'Oh, that's too bad.'

'Why?'

'I thought we might be able to spend some time together.'

'That's what we're doing, isn't it?' I said.

'No. We're drinking together. It's not the same thing.' She put her hand onto my thigh. I could feel the sharpness of her thumbnail through my trouser leg. 'We can have a good time together.' Her voice dropped a half-octave, and her flighty chat was replaced by a sales purr. 'Take me up to your room. Just a little while, before you go out.'

Out the corner of my eye I could see the barman watching but not watching. He had seen it all a thousand times before, but was still intrigued enough to half-watch and half-listen while he polished glasses and whistled along to the muzak.

'I'm sorry, Celeste.'

'But why not? Don't you like me?'

'It's not that. It's . . . I have to see my friends,' I lied. 'And besides,' I lied again, 'I'm married.'

'Married?'

'Yes.'

'Well,' she said, looking about us with comic exaggeration, 'I don't see her here now.'

'She's back in Australia.'

The hand worked on my thigh, massaging its way upwards. 'Yes, and it's a long way, Australia. And you're here. Come on, it's a part of life.'

'But I couldn't do that. I couldn't lie to her.'

'Oh, I understand that,' she said. 'That's good.' She produced a mischievous tweak of her lips, and raised her eyes towards the bedroom upstairs.

I drank down my beer. 'Actually, I have to go in a minute,' I said. 'My friends . . .'

Her hand fastened urgently onto mine, and this time there was no play in it. 'Just five minutes,' she said. 'In your room. It's a part of life.'

I stepped off my bar stool, breaking her grasp. 'I'm sorry Celeste.'

'Just five minutes. For my child.'

'I'm sorry Celeste,' I repeated. I paid for the drinks and walked out.

Back upstairs I wondered whether she was a prostitute or just a hard-up girl looking for some extra cash. I also wondered what all the thin men out on the street meant to her, if she felt she could worry about it, or whether that too was just another 'part of life'.

Returning from dinner later that night, I passed by the bar where four people were drinking. Two of them were loud, hearty Germans, gold dealers. The younger of the two had his arm around a pretty Ghanaian girl, modelishly slender in a black silk slip. The other German had his hand halfway up Celeste's dress, and her arm was curled around his neck in a drunken headlock. As I walked by, they all burst out laughing at something very funny.

In London I had only been able to obtain my visa for Ghana itself. This meant I still had to get visas for Côte d'Ivoire, Burkina Faso and Mali. But when I visited the Embassy of Côte d'Ivoire the next morning, I was told there would be 'quite some delay' in granting me a visa. Whether this was because of my Australian passport, the colour of my shirt or a go-slow in the office, I could not discover, despite my protests. In the end I decided to skip Côte d'Ivoire for the time being and fly direct to Ouagadougou in Burkina Faso on my way to Mali.

I went downtown to the offices of Ghana Airways and Air Afrique, only to discover there were no direct flights between Ghana and Burkina Faso. I could fly via Côte d'Ivoire – for which I would need that visa – or I would have to take the bus. I discovered there was one bus a week, on Saturdays, a straight twenty-four hour trip.

The bus station was out on the ring road – called Ring Road – that runs around the centre of Accra. It was jammed with traffic, a fog of fumes rising through a hot blue sky. At the station I was directed to a seemingly disused building on a bare square of wasteland muddy with diesel and motor oil. A tiny sign indicated the hole in the wall which sold tickets for the international service north. For some reason, a bench seat had been set at right angles to the one-foot-square ticket cubicle, and you had to manoeuvre yourself over the obstacle to reach the cubicle.

'Hello, is anyone in there?' I called, straining forward. The day was the hottest yet, and sweat stung my eyes as they tried to make out any sign of life within the darkened hole before me. There was a mesh of wire between myself and whoever was inside, the experience of speaking into it rather Confessional.

There was no reply at first. Then, finally, a girlish giggle. 'Yes?'

'Do you have any seats left on Saturday's bus?'

Another pause. Another giggle. 'Yes.'

I enquired after the price, pulled out a stack of greasy 200 *cedi* banknotes, and pushed the correct money into the black void. As my eyes adjusted to the darkness of the little room behind the mesh, I saw my payment had been received by a young woman with short curly hair, and chin-beard.

'My name is Ophelia,' she said.

'Hello, Ophelia.'

'Tell me, what is your marital status?'

'Do you need to know that for the ticket?'

'No,' she laughed. 'I just want to know.'

'I'm single,' I said.

Ophelia giggled again. I saw that unlike the beards I had occasionally seen before on women, hers was luxuriantly thick and carefully trimmed. I waited a few moments, expecting a ticket to emerge from the darkness, but none came. I cleared my throat, drummed my fingers, still it didn't come.

'May I have my ticket please, Ophelia?' I asked at last.

There was no reply – then a high, sweet laugh. 'You come back and see me tomorrow.'

'I can't have it now?'

'No.'

'I'd like my ticket please. I've paid you for it.'

'We are doing numbers for the bus now,' Ophelia said. 'Come back to me tomorrow and I shall see about your ticket.'

I realised I could either demand my money back, try to find someone to complain to – both difficult and probably counter-productive responses – or just come back.

'Alright then, I'll see you tomorrow.'

'I shall look forward to that,' Ophelia said with a final chuckle, and from the darkness emerged a crumpled slip of paper scrawled with pen. Deciphering, I realised it was my receipt.

There was a message at the hotel from Tom. He was coming around to take me to the Ghana Club. I went upstairs, had a cold shower and dressed just in time to go downstairs and meet him.

The Ghana Club is the old British colonial club of Accra, only now the members' faces are black rather than white. I was apprehensive it might be stuffy and awkward, a leather lounge of port and cigars, but it turned out to be a breezy, timber clubhouse on stilts by the sea. It appeared to have remained a male preserve, but there was an easy informality in the way the judges, politicians, bishops and businessmen drifted up to the bar or clustered about tables over pints of Club Beer. Tom was sanguine and gregarious as ever, introducing me to everyone, calling over old friends, men who had been shoulder to shoulder with Nkrumah, most now grizzled and grey.

Tom quickly downed his first beer and ordered another while introducing me to Sammy, a softly spoken, grey-whiskered man. He was lean, almost silent. It turned out he was Tom's family doctor. They quietly chewed the fat, Sammy responding to each item of Tom's gossip with a sardonic half-smile. Nothing about the world, it seemed, could ever surprise him now.

Then a man wandered in who looked different from the others. He was dark-suited, but rumpled as if he had picked his jacket up off the floor on his way out the door. His hair had not consented to the comb, and although he was probably in his late sixties, his eye retained a mocking gleam. 'That is Harold,' Tom confided. 'An actor.'

Harold had been the finest Ghanaian actor of his time, Tom told me. He had done the first productions in Ghana of plays by Shakespeare, Chekhov and Ibsen, as well as plays written by Nkrumah himself. Tom was still extolling his praises when Harold joined us at the bar. He affected a politely bemused expression as Tom went on, but accepted a beer. We were already on our third pint, and by now my bar stool was threatening to disengage and drift up off the floor. But Tom was ordering more, urging Harold to introduce me to some local thespians, take me to see the new National Theatre. Harold smiled obligingly, then was called over to another table.

'He is out of favour now,' Tom confided. 'He is financially hard up, but uncompromising. Very sad, you know. He even acted on the stage in London. Now I think he rents a little room somewhere.'

We finished our drinks, and unsteadily made our way down the wooden steps and back outside. The early evening air was clean off the sea. 'I thank the Big Man upstairs for our lives here, you know,' Tom said, patting his stomach with satisfaction.

'You mean, god?'

'Of course. He is the most terrific chap, and so easy to speak with.'

'I didn't realise you were religious.'

'Oh, yes, we all are here. Presbyterian.' He studied me a moment. 'What is your faith?'

'Well I . . . don't really have one.'

'No?' he said. 'That must make life rather difficult for you.'

'Yes, I suppose it does.'

He laughed at this and slapped me on the back. 'By the way, I took the liberty of mentioning you to my son, and he wants to meet you. He makes films. Perhaps you can give him some help with his writing.'

'Well, I'd be happy to try,' I said, as we got back into the car and the driver started the engine. 'What sort of films does he make?'

'Devotional,' Tom said. 'He is into . . . what do you call it? Televangelism.' He called forward to the driver. 'Penta Hotel, then home.'

Back at the hotel I decided another beer wouldn't hurt now, and went down to the bar. Within ten minutes I was being propositioned again – this time by Clara, a sleek girl in a short dress. When I said I didn't want to take her up to my room, she was amazed. I realised this was what all the Europeans who passed through the hotel did while they were here – took on a 'girl-friend' for the duration of their visit, who would deliver sexual services in return for meals, drinks, a 'good time', and some spending money. That was the situation of every other white male guest here, I realised. All of a sudden the Penta felt like the Rose Hotel in Bangkok. And how long would it be until a night came when I'd had just a little too much beer, the girl was that much more enticing, and I would reach that point of asking myself, 'Hell, why not?', answer myself with, 'A lot of reasons, including HIV,' and reply to myself, 'Well, you've got the best condoms money can buy – and as for the other reasons . . .'

I went back up to my room, stretched out on the bed and stared up at the ceiling. The damp warmth of the tropical night streamed in through the open window, but I couldn't stand the racket of the air conditioner. I had drunk quite a lot of beer, much more than I was used to. I felt bloated, my head ached.

I awoke thirsty in the small hours and couldn't get back to sleep. Was it not inevitable that something new, hot, tumultuous would sweep aside the foundations Kathryn and I had laid down in those seven years? We loved each other, yes. But we no longer experienced the intoxication of love. Nothing strange about that – it happens to everyone. We had both tried the limited alternative, the fling, the 'affair' – that ugly word. But these sorts of things only take on a passionate reality when control is released. And when control is released, the centre has a habit of not holding, and things of falling apart.

As day broke, my third dawn in Accra, I felt that the thread which had invisibly bound us these years, and which now stretched all the way between here and Sydney, would snap. If I stayed here these two months I had planned, it would. But I loved Kathryn, I knew. So what was I doing here then? What was more important in life than love? What did it matter that I had spent a few thousand dollars getting ready, getting here, that I'd planned to write a book here? I looped the loop again.

Finally, as the first hard shards of sun came through my window, I slept. When I awoke a few hours later, I turned on the radio and heard a news bulletin on state-run radio. There was word of a plane crash, unconfirmed reports that the presidents of both Rwanda and Burundi had been killed. Shot down, it was believed. The radio spoke of madness unleashed in Rwanda, an orgy of killing, people hacked to death with machetes on the streets, in their houses, as they stood in their front yards.

I got out of bed and looked out the louvred window. Dust hung lazily in the alley below. My limbs felt tired and my head ached. I wished I hadn't had so much to drink, thanked my stars I hadn't had more, hadn't ended up with a Clara or a Celeste. Did I really have so little self-control as to be untrustworthy even to myself? As I took my shower, more reports started coming through of the mass murder unleashed on the far side of Zaire.

Italian Heels

After breakfast I went out and collected my ticket from Ophelia at the bus station, and got my visa for Burkina Faso. Later in the day I visited the Ambassador. His residence was a white mansion, a tall clipper on a field of green. He greeted me warmly and led me inside across the parquetry of the living room. He showed me his wife's still-lifes of birds and flowers on the walls. I could tell just how much he loved her by the fact that he genuinely admired them.

We sat outside at a table with a view of the swimming pool set in palm gardens. A white-jacketed African waiter served us wine, cognac, biscuits and nuts. The tenor of our talk was something of a re-run of the first time, but with a few fresh elements. The European Community, the reunification of Germany, the Japanese economic miracle and its problems, and, lastly, Australian wines. He was just as urbane as on the night of the party, a cultured man. I was struck, oddly, by the notion of him as a figure out of Conrad: the 'Before' figure, before Africa works its arcane bewitchments upon the white knights of European progress.

He went inside, and came out with a crude-looking bamboo arrow with a barbed metal point. 'When it gets in, it can't get out,' he said, passing it for me to inspect more closely. 'They dip them in snake poison. Half an hour and you are dead. Even from just a scratch. It's quite efficient.'

'Where is it from?'

'The north of the country. There are some ethnic troubles up there. You may see some evidence of it on your bus journey.'

We talked of the news from Rwanda. 'It can happen anywhere,' he shrugged. 'Look at Bosnia. Nowhere is safe.'

A large bird had been circling the gardens for some minutes. When it touched down by the pool I saw it was a vulture. 'They are a very shy bird,' the Ambassador said. 'They come in to drink from the pool, but they won't do it while we sit here. When we go inside, the bird will drink.'

The waiter poured us both another cognac, and I saw a card had been placed on the table before me. It was an official card, bearing the Ambassador's imprimatur. 'There is no Australian representation where you are going,' he said. 'Please, take my card and use it at any of our missions, if you need it.'

I picked it up and looked at it. 'Thank you,' I said.

'You never know when you might need it in Africa.'

We finished our drinks and watched the vulture watching us, awaiting its turn to drink from the cool blue. As I was about to take my leave, the Ambassador's wife turned up from a luncheon appointment, crisp and tall in Italian heels.

'Oh, hello.' She saw the arrow on the table. 'Has my husband been amusing you?'

'He has, yes.'

I saw the Ambassador's eyes seek her out as she held her pose in the doorway. When she turned and went back inside, his gaze followed. I felt sorry for him: the powerlessness love can bring.

'Are you married?' he asked.

'No.'

'Why not?'

'To tell you the truth, I don't believe in it. For me, that is.'

'Oh, yes,' he said, 'we were all like that once.'

As he walked me indoors, I saw the vulture dip its beak into the pool. I said farewell, and was going up the gravel driveway when the Ambassador came after me, holding out his card which I had forgotten to pick up from the table. 'Please,' he said, handing it to me. 'Here you never know, eh?'

English Tie

The following day I took a taxi with Harold, the actor, out to the university to visit the national drama school. Even though it was another oppressively hot day, Harold was in the same crumpled dark suit, frayed white shirt and tie. He spoke with a smile both world-weary and shy about his glory days on the stage, how people had flocked to see his Shakespeares and Chekhovs, how they had been staged on so little money, but were triumphs. A lifetime of struggle had ebbed the strength from his eyes, but he still had wit, even when relating how bad things were now. I asked if he was 'out of favour' with the people or with the regime, but he was disinclined to answer. Perhaps it was too painful. Or perhaps it meant both.

The drama school was a cloister of demountable buildings around a dusty quadrangle on the edge of the university. Besides a group of bare-chested students rehearsing a modern dance piece, there didn't appear to be much going on. Harold led me down shaded walkways, knocking on the doors of old friends who, it seemed, hadn't seen him in years. These were invariably men, also in their later sixties, who sat at untidy desks hemmed in by shelves of yellowing play scripts. Harold introduced me, and we sat and chatted. More than one of his old friends told him that, funnily enough they had just been thinking about him lately, and asked whether he might be interested in a part that might be coming up. It was the 'might be maybe, let's do lunch and cancel it now' universal language of the theatre. Harold, who of course had heard this all so many times before, smiled sagely. I wondered just how long it was since he had worked, how it must be eating him out, remembered how Tom had said he was living in a little rented room somewhere, like all the other little rented rooms the world over where the used up people of the theatre eke out their days on tea and marmalade, on vicarious gossip and scrapbooks of brittled reviews.

Next Harold got the taxi driver to stop off at the National Theatre, a new 'complex' built for Ghana by the Chinese. It was massive, impressive, but felt jerry-built. I wondered how many doors would have handles in five years. But it was here, on the stage of a village folkloric piece being rehearsed, that Harold received a genuinely warm welcome, from a group of young actresses who ran up and clustered gleefully around the old man, who threw their arms around him, kissed him and called him 'uncle'.

As we drove back to the hotel and I worked out the fare with the driver, a request Tom had made of me on the telephone that morning came back to me. It was a difficult request, yet one I knew I must honour. All the way back to the Penta I put it off, but then finally spoke up.

'Tell me Harold, how are you fixed for cash?'

He looked up, his expression a mixture of surprise and embarrassed bemusement.

'It's just, I wondered if you might need a little.'

He still said nothing.

'Would you mind if I gave you some? I'm travelling on a bit of a tight budget, but . . .'

He looked at me a moment, then out the window. 'Oh, well . . .' he said, his voice trailing off. Then, quickly, he added, 'Alright then.'

I handed over a small wad of notes and he pocketed it without looking. The taxi rattled onwards. Harold stared down into his lap, at the frayed white shirt and his old English striped tie, perhaps the last remnant of his days on the London stage. 'Thank you,' he said.

Meat

Drinking alone at a table in the bar that night, I was joined by the two Germans and three Ghanaian women. One of them was the modelish woman I had seen with the Germans a few nights before, but I hadn't seen the other two. It turned out they were her sisters. As we sat over a round or two of beers, one of them began flirting with me, running her toenail up and down my leg under the table. I was becoming used to this by now, and chatted on and smiled.

A Ghanaian man in his fifties, slight, with heavy spectacles, walked in and sat down at our table. The Germans seemed to know him. I thought he was a doctor, but he introduced himself as a businessman. His name was Terence. He sat next to me, and we talked a few moments before he asked my nationality. When I said 'Australian', his face fell and he looked away. He didn't speak for a few moments, and when he did so he apologised, saying that his wife and two young children had died in Australia.

'In Queensland, in a plane crash,' he said. 'In the sixties.'

He said the memory still hurt, whenever he heard the word 'Australia'. I gave my condolences, and he shook his head and said it was his problem – so much time had passed since he had waited for that plane that never touched down on a dirt strip in the Queensland scrub.

Terence ordered more beers and we drank. The Germans drank on too, into the mid-evening, when they got up and summoned the three sisters to follow. The girls suggested I accompany them, but Terence whispered in my ear not to have anything to do with them. As one of the Germans passed by me, he bent into my ear and suggested that I shouldn't have anything to do with Terence. When I told him I intended to stay and have another drink, the German shrugged, curled his arm around the slender waist of his girl, and led the way out.

Terence said he knew a jazz bar nearby, and we went. We passed down a darkened, deserted alley. As we walked, he pointed out a Chinese restaurant, the Pearl of the Orient. One of the best in town, he said. When we arrived at the bar, I found myself in a long, low-ceilinged room, almost empty, blue-lit with dingy corners. A Nina Simone tape played softly.

We sat at the deserted bar. 'It's still early for this place,' Terence said pre-emptively. He called over the proprietress, a large, jolly woman called Margaret, and she lined up beers. 'Drink up,' she said. 'I'll run a slate for you.'

Terence and I downed our first beers, and I looked around. Here and there people loitered at tables in ones and twos. There was a TV above the bar, showing a news broadcast. I saw Stevie Wonder beside another man in matching white African robes and long, curly hair. A young man beside me at the bar spoke up.

'Bastard. This used to be a good country,' he said quietly. 'But that bastard Rawlings . . . he's a killer. We never used to have killing here, you know. But he has soaked the land in the people's blood. And do you know why?' he asked vehemently. 'He is half-Scottish. There is no people more violent in this world than the Scots. Look at them, soccer hooligans, the tartan army . . . Well, Rawlings is half-Scottish, half-African. If he was all African, he would never have killed his own people.'

Feeling it wasn't quite the right time to mention Rwanda, I nodded. Terence spoke up at my other elbow. 'Come on. Let's play darts.'

A board was located and three sets of darts, and Terence, Margaret and I started up a game of 'Around the Clock', which I had not played since childhood. Margaret quickly showed herself to be an excellent exponent of the game. I was just beginning to get the hang of it again when the alcohol kicked in and I liberally perforated the woodwork.

Some time later, Terence had wandered off and I realised Margaret and I were playing by ourselves. She had an acerbic wit, and got no end of amusement out of my hopelessness with the darts. 'I thought Australians could drink beer.'

'We can. Just not as much as Ghanaians and still hit something as elusive as a dartboard.'

She laughed. Terence returned with a formal, middle-aged man whom he introduced to me as 'Lieutenant-Colonel' somebody. The bar by now was filling up, and the smoky air resounded to laughter over which I strained to hear.

'The Lieutenant-Colonel wishes to propose something to you,' Terence was saying.

'Oh?' I asked. 'What?'

'Pigs' trotters,' the Lieutenant-Colonel said.

'I see,' I said, as surprised as if they had suggested I run guns for them.

'Yes, you see,' the Lieutenant-Colonel went on, in clipped English, 'I do believe you have rather a lot of them down in Australia.'

'I must admit to not being utterly *au fait* with things in the pork regard,' I said, desperately trying to think of something more pertinent to say. Then a light bulb blinked on. 'Actually, our Prime Minister is in the pig business. He has an interest in a substantial piggery.'

'Excellent,' pronounced the Lieutenant-Colonel with a tweak of his grey moustache, obviously used to wheels being greased at the highest levels. 'Perhaps you could have a word with him for us.'

'Well, I suppose I could write to him, yes.'

'Very good,' Terence said enthusiastically. 'The moment I saw you I knew you could help us. You see, pigs' trotters are very popular eating here, whereas I would wager that in your own country they are thrown away as waste.'

'Or ground up for hamburgers or pet food,' I said. 'How many would you like?'

'One container load would be optimum to begin with,' the Lieutenant-Colonel said. 'Or as many trotters as you can get us for, say, 40,000 US dollars.'

'I'll see what I can do.'

'Very good then,' the Lieutenant-Colonel said, then stopped for a moment and looked at me. 'By the way, I'm sorry to have been so pushy about this . . . You're not Jewish are you?'

'No,' I said, 'although I am a vegetarian. Well, almost.'

'Vegetarian!' the Lieutenant-Colonel laughed with a British military bark. 'Vegetarian!! Oh, that's a good one, that's a very good one!'

We all laughed, and he gave me his business card, and asked me to get in touch as soon as I had the shipment organised back in Australia. I said I'd do what I could.

'Secure us the order, and we shall send the money. Five per cent is yours. Is that adequate?'

'Done,' I said.

We shook on the deal, and the Lieutenant-Colonel went away still chuckling, 'Vegetarian . . .'

'He really liked you,' Terence said, offering me another beer. 'It couldn't have worked out better.'

Terence and I parted like old friends, and I stepped out into the cool night for the short walk back to the hotel. There was a table outside, and a young man and woman talking in low tones. Strangely enough, I thought I recognised the man, who wore a stylish sports shirt and pants, and expensive shoes.

'I'm sorry, don't I know you?'

'I don't know,' he said, then flashed me a smile. 'Perhaps you do from the television.'

'Of course, you're the beer man!'

'So you have seen my commercials,' he said, still smiling.

'All the time. They're on virtually every five minutes. Talk about a hundred per cent exposure.'

'And do you know how much I get for each commercial? Just $200.'

'Is that all?'

'Yes,' he sighed.

'Well, you'll have to do something about that,' I said with the uninformed determination of the adequately inebriated. 'You'll have to get yourself a good agent.'

'But who, here?' he said. 'There is no one.' He stopped for a moment, and looked at me closely. 'You seem to know about the business. I don't suppose that you would consider . . .'

'Oh, I'm sorry – it's not really my line.'

'No? What are you in then?'

'Import–export,' I said. 'Meat.'

That Pretty Green

Country

When I happened across the Pearl of the Orient on my way back to the hotel, a sudden pang reminded me that I had not eaten. The hour was late, and the place dark out front, but a flicker of movement behind the plate glass suggested it might still be open. I went in.

It was shockingly cold inside, as if I had climbed into a refrigerator and shut the door on the balmy African night. A young man in uniform black and white greeted me with a smile and ushered me over to a small table in the window. I realised I was the lone diner, and hoped this was merely because it was late. I had eaten with significant care since my arrival. I had prepared most of my own meals, usually fruit, or bread and cheese and yoghurt from the local supermarket. But now, numerous beers into the night, I was too hungry to walk out on a mere suspicion. The waiter hovered. I ordered chicken and onions – whence the vegetarian now? – and steamed rice, trusting in the bland. As an afterthought I asked for a saucer of chilli sauce and another beer.

As I sipped the beer, I looked out at the alley. A vapour of dust lingered in the triangle of yellow light from a floodlight bolted to the restaurant's façade. The lack of any movement out there somehow made me feel more alone. I felt hollowed out, weak. Probably just hungry, I thought. Or drunk. A dog, a scrawny old mangy thing, stopped outside, propped up a hind leg and commenced a meditative licking of its testicles. A woman sauntered past, a rounded woman in a low-cut green floral dress. She progressed with a slow determined sway of her hips, like an ocean liner riding a swell. A male voice called sharply from behind her, but she threw back a high-pitched raucous laugh and kept on walking with the same navigatory sway.

My food arrived in a clump on an oblong plate. The white chunks of chicken looked like they had been dug out of the cadaver with an ice cream scoop. The onion slices were long and silvery half moons, glistening in a tepid bath of gelatinous goo. The rice was set down beside it in a hard-packed snowball, and the chilli sauce in a tiny blue china saucer. It smelt good enough, but I recalled a meal I had once eaten on a Thai island, at a vegetarian café, which had left me sick for a month. That had smelt good too.

Staring at the plate I had a momentary *Death in Venice* experience – Aschenbach staring at a glass of water which probably contains cholera, yet which he knows he will drink nonetheless. I got a dollop of chicken meat onto my fork and put it in my mouth. It tasted good. Salty, but good. What was I worrying about? This place had been recommended. It was no doubt one of the better places in Accra. Without any more hesitation I spooned rice onto my plate and began working my way down the pyramid of food. It was soft and slippery all the way.

It was well before dawn after another interminably hot, uncomfortable night when I awoke and regretted everything. Firstly, I regretted all the beer I had drunk. That most certainly. Then I regretted the Chinese food which sat in my stomach like a ticking time bomb. Next I regretted the human condition of sexual passion always fading, even when love does not. And lastly I regretted everything I was, a hopeless non-talent, shyster and bum.

I turned over, and tried to go back to sleep, but through the wall came the humps and groans of my German neighbour and one of the local girls. I marvelled at how impotent reason was against the sexual urge, how people can so easily ignore all the advice, the urgings, the implorings. A condom provides just a fraction of a millimetre of comfort against a wasting death, and even the best may break, or slip off. I thought of the thin men in the dust on the streets all around. Yet the Germans seemed not to see them. I thought about their wives and girlfriends back in Frankfurt or Dusseldorf, Hamburg or Berlin, and wondered how many of them would contract the disease. And there would be children too, born with it. That thought stopped me, and made me think of something else. I had never had any children. One slip on a beery night here, and I might never be able to – that would be that.

As the dawning day crept in through the louvres and I heard the whimpering of a child below, I stared up at the ceiling not

135

knowing what to do. This was my pure existential moment, the one of greatest freedom and most profound hopelessness. I was free. I was still young, had some money, no ties. I could go anywhere from this place. Anywhere. No one would stand in my way, even ask a question. No one would care. I was utterly unfettered. Yet, as I looked, each avenue seemed equally pointless, each option useless. What was the use, in the end, of even leaving the room? Where would it get me?

Technically speaking, it was an attack of the horrors, caused no doubt by the combination of alcohol-induced dehydration, MSG, anti-malarials – I later discovered a friend had his own episode of similar horrors in Nigeria, while dosed up with the same anti-malarial drug – and the unremitting heat.

I flicked on the TV. It was CNN from Rwanda. In towns and hamlets all across that pretty green country, people were being chopped into pieces with anything that would take an edge, a bloodbath of amazing ferocity. Neighbour pummelled neighbour into mash. Children with stumps of limbs screamed in filthy hospitals while their parents were washed down jungle rivers like lopped logs. In full colour satellite close-up, the faces of the murderers were expressionless, their voices muted, eyes dull. Dächau had mated with Bedlam.

Crocodile in a Stetson

Later that morning I managed to get through on the hotel telephone to Le Pavilion Vert guest house in Ouagadougou, and book a room. Down the line, the place sounded clean, friendly, pleasantly deserty. The man who booked me the room spoke no English but was considerate with my French. He assured me I would be most welcome in his guest house. Then Tom arrived, and we went to his house for a farewell lunch. Along the way I felt feverish, nauseous, or was I just hung over?

Tom's son Aubrey sat at a video editing desk in a back room of his father's bungalow. 'Stay and have a chat with Aubrey a few minutes,' Tom said, 'while I see how lunch is progressing.'

When I sat down, I realised Aubrey was watching a tape of an American televangelist, one of those choral-scored, primary-coloured sales pitches conducted from the virtual cathedrals of California and the South. I looked at video cassette boxes in racks, and saw they were all Born Again televangelists. As Aubrey played the tape, and the hideous white creature on the screen declaimed and reassured, wheedled and threatened, and the black back-up singers swayed and sang, and the caption came up on the screen reminding the viewer that all major credit cards were accepted, I felt the tiles beneath my feet turning to putty, into a quicksand into which I was descending, down into a cavern beneath the earth, a place of total and eternal darkness but for the blue flicker of a screen.

'What are you . . . doing with this material?' I asked shakily.

Aubrey didn't take his eyes off the screen. 'I re-edit for the Asian market. Singapore at the moment, but others too, soon. The market's exploding. We're taking the Word everywhere,' he said, turning and grinning a grin that pre-empted dissent. Perhaps I might have wondered whether this activity was licensed, or whether there was a global trade in pirated televangelism, but I could not because I was gripped by a cold sweat and a single notion: the televangelist out in Gumpville Alabama, the re-edit in a backroom in Accra, Ghana, and young Charlie Ho, five, dumped by his parents in front of the TV in a high-rise in some concrete estate in Singapore, getting the final product thrust down his throat along with his battery chicken and mash.

Aubrey made a final edit, turned to me and grinned again. 'Have a look,' he said, and before I could think of an excuse, any excuse – the chill in my limbs, the ache in my head – he ran the tape. I sank back into my seat, stranded in another of those moments from which there is no exit. A stetsoned crocodile with glittering blue sapphire eyes came on crooning at a microphone about the love of God. The music swelled and swept upwards, swirling round the cupola of the crystal cathedral. The elephantine woman in the front row passed out and was revived by attendants. Then the crocodile looked down the camera and pleaded for more money to be sent. The new building fund was falling behind. Freeze frame on the crocodile's tears.

'Well, what do you think?' Aubrey asked eagerly.

I could not speak. I felt ill. I wanted to run out the door, run and keep running.

Aubrey sensed my hesitation. His eyes turned to me again, seeking comment.

'Very interesting,' I said.

Lunch was served in the wood-panelled dining room. As we assembled around the table, Tom motioned to me to remain standing. He stretched out his arms, and I realised we were all to join hands. Tom, Evelyn and Aubrey bowed their heads, and I followed suit. Tom then spoke up clearly: 'Lord, we thank thee for these foods we are about to eat.'

The meal was typical Ghanaian – chicken, sweet potato, cassava, a spicy beef and spinach dish, the four of us sharing from bowls in the centre of the table. Evelyn poured tea into English cups and saucers and pressed us all to eat more. The meal ended with us rising in our places, linking hands and bowing heads again, and Tom speaking a farewell prayer for me:

'Lord, we ask you to give your protection to our friend from Australia, on the journey he is about to undertake.'

I said my farewells to Evelyn and Aubrey, and Tom drove me back to the hotel. As we said goodbye, I was touched at how kind he and his family had been to me, a complete stranger who barely qualified as a friend of their daughter back in Sydney. Yet it was a relief to be cut loose from them now, even though Tom was the closest connection I had here, in fact the closest person to me on the whole continent of Africa. If I had known him a little better I would have told him that for the past few hours I had felt dizzy and 'out of my body', that when I had stood up to pray at the table the world had spiralled about me. That perhaps I should see a doctor. But, then, I did not know him quite that well.

How Greene Was My Africa

That night I re-checked my preparations for the journey inland. I had received all the recommended inoculations for this trip: typhoid, cholera, hepatitis, yellow fever, meningitis, polio booster, and had stocked up amply on prescribed anti-malarials. My medical kit, packed in a clear plastic lunch box, comprised three hypodermic syringes in their virgin plastic wrappers so that I would never have to submit to a suspect one. The needles were packed with a doctor's note to police and border guards to the effect that I was not a junkie. The lunch box also contained antibiotics, anti-diarrhoea tablets (which I was now taking), tincture of iodine for wounds or sterilising water, sleeping pills, aspirin, disinfectant cream, sunblock, chap-stick and extra ear plugs. In addition to the medical kit, my canvas travel bag contained a broad-brimmed khaki hat, mosquito net, short wave pocket radio, walkman and tapes, paperbacks of *Buddenbrooks* by Thomas Mann and the African classic *God's Bits of Wood* by the Senegalese Sembebe Ousmane. There were five T-shirts, two pairs of shorts and a pair of jeans. There was a sewing kit saved from a swank hotel, a toiletries bag with the unopened packet of super-strength condoms from Boots, a reel of string, four pairs of socks and five handkerchiefs. In my money belt were 18,000 Ghanaian *cedis*, 15,000 Central African francs, thirty-five US dollars, 800 French francs, sixty pounds sterling and ten Australian dollars – around 500 US dollars worth of cash all up – as well as 16,000 French francs in traveller's cheques, my International Health Certificates and Visa card, Pilot Hi-Tecpoint pen, Swiss Army knife, the European ambassador's card, and a gold guardian angel good luck pin loaned by my mother. There was another 200 US dollars stuffed in a sock, a final fifty secreted in a seam of my travel bag: be creative I had been told – the road bandits are.

When I finished packing and checking, I took a long drink of water. It was a very hot night, the hottest and stillest yet. I showered to try to cool off. But it didn't help. After I dried myself, the perspiration poured off at an even faster rate. The diarrhoea worsened, and I felt feverish, increasingly disconnected. I felt in no way fit for a twenty-four hour drive in a bus through heat and desert. Yet, I reminded myself, this was what it was all about, hard travel. Remember the image of being bumped around in the back of a truck? Well here is the truck and here is the desert and here are you with your ticket, and notwithstanding the state of your bowels and your feverish for-god-knows-what-fucking-reason head, you have to be on that bus because there won't be another for a week – if you could get another ticket that is. But what about Kathryn, and the thread? I asked myself. You have no choice but to go on, I responded firmly. But surely love is worth more than the vicarious thrill of travel, I tried. You should have thought that through before now, I responded.

The mental chatter finally subsided, and I slept a little, but I was awake when the dawn came. I got up, ate a banana, packed my day pack with water and biscuits for the bus trip, shouldered my backpack and checked out of the Penta.

I felt nauseous on the taxi ride to the bus station, but at least the diarrhoea seemed to have settled down. The early morning was cloudy, dirty and polluted, and everything, the streets, the buildings, looked shabbier than ever as we whisked by. The traffic was thin on Ring Road, and it only took about ten minutes to arrive at the bus station.

I paid the taxi driver, and walked past the first line of buildings to the office on the big vacant paddock where I had got the ticket from Ophelia. Rounding a corner, I was amazed to see the previously empty yard now filled with hundreds of laughing, shouting passengers. Tribespeople in brightly coloured African robes, in Western jeans and loose-hanging white rags, milled around half a dozen buses which idled ominously in the heavy tropical air. At the same moment, a hard, brilliant sun burst through the low clouds and showered the scene with a blinding brilliance. So strong were the rays that one could feel them pierce the weave of a cotton shirt and embed themselves in the skin.

I hauled my bag through the throng, smiling apologies as I went, trying to identify the bus for Ouagadougou. When I finally located it, I could not approach within ten metres because the ground all around was carpeted not just with people, but with stupendous quantities of luggage. There were cheap suitcases and leather satchels, cloth-weave bags and string bags, food parcelled up into giant packages of paper and string, and row upon row of those large, rectangular plastic zip-up bags, each one filled to bursting point. Somehow all this luggage was going to be loaded onto that one bus, and then all these people would get on too. It did not seem possible.

I set my own bag down in what I thought might be the queue, and tried to get my bearings. But the heat was coming down in those slow, familiar waves now, each one beating a little harder against my head like a muffled sledgehammer. I saw the driver up on the top step of the bus, locked in one of those interminable arguments with a pair of passengers about tickets. The line did not move, and gave no hint that it would. Someone slammed the luggage compartment doors shut and locked them. They must be full, which meant these mountains of bags must somehow be getting loaded onto the bus proper.

The driver eventually finished his argument, and the line inched forward. Fifteen minutes later I was on the bottom step, then finally on the top step, handing over my ticket. The driver glanced at it, and motioned me to my seat. Getting there was easier said than done, as the bus was virtually completely full, in that all the interior air space was occupied by people and luggage. The central aisle was a mountain range stretching away from me, and I had to scale it, hauling my bag up and down over each luggage peak, towards the back and my numbered seat. When I finally reached it, there was nowhere to place my own bag, so I had to wedge it tightly under my own place, and sit with my legs crossed on top of it. My day pack I jammed between my elbow and the window. Fortunately the seat beside me was vacant, and I still felt I could breathe, but a few moments later a young woman climbed towards me over the mountain range of luggage, and took it. Once she was in place, other passengers and baggage handlers began packing in more and more luggage, literally bricking us into place.

That done, activity subsided. Everyone was in their seat now. Luggage was piled up to the roof in some places, so no one could move. The inside of the bus was airless, and the sun baked down on the roof inches above our heads. I saw perspiration running in a river down the back of the man in the seat in front of me. I had just enough room to turn in my seat, and see that there was no toilet on the bus. No matter, even if there had been, I would not have been able to get to it.

The bus was due to leave at eight, and right on time the driver started up the engine. But then I saw more people milling outside, down around the steps, and even bigger mounds of luggage arriving down there. So we all sat in the airless heat, unable even to move, and waited while the idling fumes from the exhaust crept up and insinuated themselves.

'*Vous allez à Ouaga?*' ('You're going to Ouaga?') the woman beside me said.

'*Oui.*'

She noticed my travel guidebook, and asked if she could have a look at it. I handed it to her.

'*La première fois à Ouaga?*' she said.

'*Oui,*' I said again. 'First time. And you? Do you live there? *Vous habitez là?*'

'*Bien sûr,*' she smiled.

She was open and attractive, and normally I would have thanked the heavens, the bus company, the bearded Ophelia for having sent me someone pleasant to sit with for the next twenty-four hours, but as the minutes ticked by, the heat intensified and the air disappeared from within the cabin, and my need for a toilet became more desperate, I admitted at last that for all my resolve, I might not be able to take this trip.

It was an appalling thought. Because if I did not stay on this bus, I would be marooned another whole week before the next one. Marooned in the Penta Hotel. With the Germans. And the hookers. And the beer.

The thread linking Kathryn and I was now at its extremity, stretched to its tautest, to breaking strain, between this dusty oily bus lot in Accra and a flat in a backstreet of Darlinghurst, in Sydney. If the bus moved off, I knew the thread would snap. Yet I was sitting here, had sat here in a swaddle of sweat for the past twenty minutes, the twenty minutes beyond the departure time, tempting fate. But now something moved in me with a finality, something literally in my bowels, and I knew I had to get up out of my seat, obey the call. I physically needed to get off it, and very quickly. Seconds passed, but my senses reported in that nothing had changed. I was still sitting in my seat, apparently patiently awaiting the departure of the bus. I had not moved. Indeed, so it seemed, I could not.

The back door of the bus sprang open behind me, and more people swarmed up the steps. On their heads they carried yet more luggage, which they proceeded to brick in behind us. So now I had to do something, or any movement would be truly impossible. If I were to get down off this bus without an appalling and embarrassing disaster, it had to be now.

I pulled hard on the strap of my bag wedged under my seat. It didn't budge. The woman looked at me quizzically. Perspiration coursed down my neck. My face was wet, gritty with dust. I pulled again, and this time the bag moved. I hoisted it up, then climbed up as well as I could onto the seat. Everyone turned to look at me, the sole white face on the bus, as if I were about to make an announcement.

'*Excusez-moi,*' I said to the woman.

'*Mais . . .*' she began, but I was already clambering over the high stacks of luggage set in place behind our seat, hoisting my bag and my day-pack, struggling onto the narrow stairs and pushing my way down towards the clear air.

I slipped on the steps and crashed down onto more luggage piled up for ferrying onto that already comically over-laden vehicle. Regaining my footing, I staggered away, followed by curious eyes. It must have seemed as if I had gone a little mad. Perhaps I had. I ran frantically looking for a toilet. There was nothing resembling one in that huddle of buildings surrounding the red dust quadrangle where the buses were pulled up. A man pointed to the main buildings, some fifty metres off – an impossible distance.

I ran in the other direction, behind the rusting hulk of an old bus, threw down my bags, my pathetic sacks of socks and T-shirts and medicines and biscuit packets, and pulled down my shorts. And there, in the rising dust and the appalling weight of sun, I released the foul contents of my bowel, spattered with globules of blood.

I was near fainting when I saw the rear door of the bus close, the glint of the silver body as it began to inch away. I felt too weak even to call out. The driver sounded the horn deafeningly, like the honk of a great rogue goose, and the bus picked up speed and charged down towards the gates and the main road. I collapsed onto the dust, sat there and watched it go, my bus. As I did, I was thinking about what Tom had said, about how inconvenient it must be to live a life without a faith, a belief in where we came from and where we are going and what it all means, and how that sentences one to a life of choices which are probably equally meaningless, so that one is forever a creature circling a blue pool, waiting to drink.

I remember a few things from the days that followed. Watching the cracks in the ceiling. Pacing my room like a prisoner in a cell. Showering again, then again, as if trying to wake myself from a bad dream. Running to the toilet, then back to the toilet. CNN was Rwanda, more hacked bodies, more opaque-eyed villagers relating blankly how they had slaughtered their neighbours. Being the weekend, these reports were bizarrely interspersed with Parisian fashion models on catwalks, high-tech car shows in Tokyo, big dollops of sport. I watched it all with a wide-eyed acceptance, that this was the world of which I was a citizen member, this was the infernal party to which I had been invited.

Then I remember a bright speck in the sky, and a French hippie at my shoulder pointing to it and saying, 'There, look, there it is, coming up from Lagos.' The speck grew and grew until it was a jumbo jet charging down a dark runway, and then it was a shrieking beast towards which we scurried, and into whose side we entered. At Gatwick I experienced a delicious rush of cold, but I did not awaken to full consciousness until the moment I was walking up from Kentish Town tube station towards Dirk's place, through a little alley, and I saw a profusion of white spring blossom against the blue of the early morning sky, and I realised that I had gotten myself to the airport and taken a flight out of Accra, and that now I was in London, on a cool and lovely morning.

Back in Sydney a few days later, still ill and very shaky, I managed to get her new number and dialled it.

'Hello,' I said, and waited.

'Where . . . where are you?'

'Home.'

Kathryn said nothing for a moment.

'Come over,' she said.

The

Custard Man

A vignette. Some years ago my then girlfriend and I were leaving London after a year working there, to return to Australia via Europe, Africa and Asia. Over the final breakfast in our flat in Muswell Hill, I extracted a promise from her. 'No matter what, please promise you won't pat any animals once we leave England. No dogs, no cats, monkeys, birds even.'

Mandy looked across the table, calm assurance in her pale green eyes. 'Of course I won't, darling.'

'Promise?'

'Promise. More tea?'

We set off from Victoria Station, took trains down through France to Barcelona, then on to Venice, Rome and Southern Italy. It was here, in a hilltop village, that we met a gang of boys whose exuberant hand gestures we filmed with our Super 8 camera. Afterwards they took us to a parents' *trullo* (a Southern Italian conical stone house built without the use of mortar) for coffee, and pogo-ed to punk music. A pair of mongrels chained in the back garden punctuated Clash and Damned tracks with raucous barks.

One of the boys challenged me to a game of table tennis. He had one of those floating, back-handed serves, and was in the process of bamboozling me when we were interrupted by a bellow from the dogs. Mandy rushed through the back door wide-eyed and panting, a hole ripped in the knee of her jeans. 'One of the dogs bit me!' she quavered. 'The little one!'

'Oh, oh no,' said Marco, the eldest of the boys, in his late teens. 'What were you doing to her?'

'Nothing. I was just patting the other one. And suddenly she came after me. She seems crazy.'

'She is only jealous of you patting her boyfriend.' His eyes emitted a twinkle. 'You know how women are.'

I parted the serrated edge of the denim and looked in. The white skin of her knee looked unbroken. Marco breathed a relieved sigh. 'You are lucky,' he said. 'It is only the jeans she has ripped.'

I looked Mandy hard in the eye.

'I know, I know, I know,' she said, raising her hands. 'Never again. Promise.'

After all the farewells from the boys, we found we were running late and only just made it to the station for the train to Brindisi, and the night ferry to Igoumenitsa on the far side of the Adriatic, in Greece. Among the last passengers to board the crowded vessel, we ended up trying to sleep in the dust on the floor, heads pillowed on a cotton bag stuffed with T-shirts.

A clear day dawned as the ferry docked at Igoumenitsa. We disembarked and found a sunny room in a guest house overlooking the Adriatic. I peeled off my dirty clothes, and, too exhausted to bathe, slipped under the sheets. Mandy did the same, her jeans being the last thing she removed. As she did so, a faint gasp escaped her lips, and I turned and saw what had caused the reaction. Just above her knee, previously hidden from sight, was a row of ugly red marks from the dog back in Italy.

'Jesus Christ . . .'

'Is it from the teeth, do you think?' Mandy asked fearfully.

I peered more closely. 'I don't think so. But even if it's only from the claws, some saliva might have got in.'

'But what are the odds of that?' Mandy protested.

'I don't know. But with rabies I know what kind of odds I'd deal with – zero.'

She stared at the row of scratch marks – their redness deepening almost as we looked – and slowly nodded.

The doctor's surgery to which we were directed seemed clean and proper, but the doctor himself had an arrogant leer which rarely left Mandy's bust. We had no Greek. He had no English.

'*La Rage,*' I tried, pointing to the red marks just above Mandy's exposed knee. '*La Rage. Du chien. La Rage. Chien. Cane.*'

He stared at me for a moment, then his hand dived into a drawer. Before either of us could say anything, he was squirting some unidentified yellow fluid from a syringe. It went high into the air – oddly, I found myself thinking, like a child's piss – and left a line of yellow dots along the dirty white ceiling. Then he plunged the needle into Mandy's arm.

'*Quest-ce que c'est!*' ('What's that?') I asked, still for some desperate reason persisting with a language this man had given no sign of comprehending. '*Que faites-vous!*' ('What are you doing?')

He shrugged and looked away.

'*Rabies,*' I tried again. 'She needs treatment for *rabies*. Is that what you've given her?'

With an uncomprehending smile he dropped the used syringe into an overflowing wastepaper basket at Mandy's feet, and stood there, quietly contemplating. What, I suddenly wondered, had he injected into her arm? The same thought must have flashed into Mandy's head just then too, as she looked across at me, lips parted slightly, her eyes widened with bewilderment.

A voice came from the doorway behind. It was the doctor's young nurse, who had arrived late for work and come in without us realising. 'Are those scratches from a dog?' she asked matter-of-fact, in English.

'Yes,' Mandy said.

'Whereabouts did it happen?'

'In Southern Italy,' I said. 'Is there much rabies in Southern Italy?'

'The place is bloody lousy with it.'

Surprised at the accent now revealing itself, and at her choice of idiom, we both looked at her. 'You're not Australian, are you?' I asked.

She indicated the school jumper she wore over her nurse's outfit. 'Randwick High,' she grinned. 'My olds have just moved back to Greece, and I decided to come for a while.' Then her tone changed as she turned to Mandy. 'And you've got to go to Athens, right away.'

'Why?' Mandy asked.

'Because Athens is the place in Greece where you can get proper treatment for rabies. It's the best part of a day to get there. And you only have two to three days from the moment of infection, to commence the treatment. Any longer than that, if you start to develop rabies – it's too late.'

My mind raced. 'Is it two days, or three?'

'Sorry, I'm not really sure.'

'It's very important.'

'I know.' She uttered a few words in Greek to the doctor. He shrugged in reply.

'But this is all so ridiculous,' Mandy said. 'The dog was probably harmless. It was a pet, chained up in a backyard. It's nothing more than a scratch most likely.'

The teenage girl regarded Mandy with nursely cool. 'Get down to the bus station.'

'Can't we fly?' I asked.

'With flight schedules and getting onto flights and getting to and from airports and all that, you'd be better advised to take the bus. It'll get there just as fast.'

We arrived in Athens early next morning, fuzzy after another sleepless night. We had only a few hours left to the forty-eight hour deadline, but there seemed no impediment to us making it. The city was quiet when the bus pulled in to the station, but soon traffic began to congest, the streets filling up quickly with people, cars and trucks. It looked as though the roads simply couldn't cope with any more traffic, yet it came, and with it a dishwater brown smog-cloud over the Acropolis.

'Surely this can't just be normal peak hour traffic?' I asked a young student as we got off the bus.

'No. Today is a national day.'

'What?'

'From World War Two. When we told the Germans we would fight to keep them out of our country.' He paused as the driver handed him his bag from the luggage compartment. 'What are you doing here in Athens? Holiday?'

'We're looking for the rabies clinic.'

He blinked. 'What?'

'A rabies clinic,' Mandy repeated. 'Do you happen to know where it is?'

'No,' he said. 'Sorry. All I can do is wish you good luck. And a pleasant stay . . . Oh, and there's a telephone.'

We went over to the phone he had pointed out and I called the Australian Embassy. I explained the situation to a young clerk on a posting from Melbourne. By four o'clock, I said, forty-eight hours would have passed since the incident in the Italian village. He found me the address of the clinic, out in the suburbs of Athens, and said he would ring and tell them to expect us. But he warned that this being a public holiday was bound to make things difficult. The streets would soon be blocked for the main parade, and everything would shut down at midday. The clinic itself might even be closed for the whole day. He told me to stay in touch.

We hailed a taxi and I gave the driver the address. We had only gone half a block when we ran head-on into a column of marching bands, men in traditional Greek costumes, all skirt and pom-pom and crowds pressing about them, everyone laughing, singing. Children ran shouting gaily past our stationary vehicle, and men stuck their heads in the windows offering food and drink. It was more like Mardi Gras than a military commemoration.

I looked at my watch. It was already past ten. We had less than two hours before the clinic closed for the day – if it was open at all, that is. (I had not mentioned this further complication to

Mandy.) Still more crowds surged by us, cheering. There was no chance the taxi would move now. We were a capsule of urgency trapped in a carnival. I realised that Mandy, until now a model of stoicism, was crying. 'We'll never get out of here,' she said. 'We'll never get there in time.'

I paid the driver. 'Come on,' I said, and we leapt out onto the street and ran with the crowds, pounding down the roadway in the white, intensifying heat of the day.

'Which way are we going?' Mandy pleaded.

'We've just got to get to the other side of all this!' I called back.

'The other side? But we can't! It just goes on for miles and miles! There's people everywhere!'

'Just keep going!' I said.

We ran through choked alleys. But they just connected with choked streets which connected with more choked streets. Everywhere there were soldiers, marching girls, donkeys, school-children, tanks. And through it all the awful thumping *oom-pa-pa* of marching bands. We had not even thought to get a map back at the bus station, so I feverishly tried to remember the layout of Athens from my one previous visit.

'We're not getting anywhere!' Mandy cried out. 'We're just going round and round in circles. We don't even know where we are!'

I smelt the aroma of herbed meat, saw a café open on the pavement. Two old men were playing backgammon outside, and I ran up to them panting, wild-eyed, and shoved in front of them the grubby, sweaty scrap of paper upon which I had scrawled the address of the clinic. They looked up at me, looked again at the address, conferred briefly in Greek, smiled politely and went on with their game. I appealed to passers-by. Several people stopped, but no one seemed to be able to decipher the script (or was it just my handwriting?) in which the note was written. More people stopped. Then more. A noisy, spontaneous crowd surged about me and my little scrap of paper, and I lost sight of Mandy.

'Mandy?' I cried out, frightened I had lost her. 'Mandy!!'

I managed to tunnel my way out of the crowd, and found her standing in the middle of the street, wilting in the full sun, weeping. 'It's just so stupid!' she wailed. 'Stupid!'

I held her, but my watch reminded me there was no time for this. It was nearly eleven. A police car materialised, slowly negotiating the throng, and I ran up and pleaded through the window for them to stop. The two policemen inside stared at me in amazement over their thick black moustaches, as if I were a madman or terrorist.

'We have to get to a clinic,' I declared. They continued mutely staring at me, and I knew I must have seemed like a raving lunatic. 'Hospital,' I shouted, and pointed to Mandy. 'Hospital, for my girlfriend!'

They looked at each other, but still did nothing.

'My girlfriend! Rabies! Hospital!'

They looked at Mandy, who still wept.

'Please, take us,' I said, and astonished myself by opening the back door and pushing Mandy in. The policeman in the passenger seat turned around and stared at me in blank surprise, but the driver seemed to intuit what we wanted, and somehow, magically, we found ourselves being conveyed through the crowds in our commandeered police car, siren wailing and lights flashing. Soon the crowds thinned, and we were out of central Athens. We sped down a highway and pulled up in front of an imposing building, obviously a hospital. The driver turned to us.

'Hospital,' he announced.

'Rabies clinic?' I asked.

He nodded. 'Go.'

We thanked them, and ran inside as the police car sped off. A moment later we discovered it was not the right hospital. I looked at my watch. It was 11.43. I begged a telephone and called the embassy again, and the clerk from Melbourne told me he had contacted the rabies clinic, that they were expecting us and would stay open a little longer if we were late.

We found a taxi, and this time, just after midday, we pulled up outside what looked like a modest suburban home. A short, white-coated doctor greeted us.

'Thank you for waiting,' Mandy said with profound gratitude.

'I would have waited all day and all night,' he said. 'Now, tell me about what happened.'

While he administered the first injection, into the stomach — she would need seven of these, each spaced two days apart – I looked out into the doctor's backyard, where a few sheep grazed. I thought perhaps they were there to keep down the grass, but later learned they were the source of the anti-rabies vaccine. A sheep would be injected with rabies, die, and the cells from its brain used in the vaccine the doctor was injecting into Mandy's stomach every second day.

We stayed at a cheap hotel in the middle of Athens those two weeks. Every second morning Mandy would return from her visit to the clinic with a self-conscious smile and the peace offering to me of a sweet custard pastry from a cubby house café on the street next to the hotel, its name translating roughly as 'The Custard Man'. I have always liked custard pastries, but the gentleman who made these was a true poet of confectionery, each morsel sweet as Mandy's contrition.

For the remainder of our trip through Africa and Asia, we wondered whether she really had needed those injections, whether the dog had actually been rabid. Six months later, back in Australia, Mandy received a postcard from Marco, the elder boy in Southern Italy. She read it to me across her parents' dining table where we had just finished a late breakfast. In the card, Marco joked: 'What is it about you? A few days after my dog bite you, she die.'

As Mandy showed it to me, I saw a shocked chill in those pale green eyes. She cleared her throat before I could speak. 'More tea?' she said.

Café 300

I had expected to love the food in Japan. I had always enjoyed it in Australia, but on arrival in Tokyo quickly discovered that while one meal a fortnight is fine, fish-mash, pickle and brine three times a day is definitely not to my taste. Although I still dined on the sashimi and teriyaki at night, I usually lunched on a chunk of fresh pineapple sold on the street, and for breakfast went very Western indeed – toast, a smear of butter and strawberry jam, and coffee.

My breakfast haunt was the Café 300, so named after the cost of a cup of coffee in yen. If there is a global median in cafés – those well enough run, serving acceptable food, keeping the customers happy enough – then the 300 was right on the middle line. The coffee itself was not very good, American-style, percolated, with a cheap bitter finish, but the place was always packed, mostly with blue-suited salarymen off to their corporate citadels. There were also a few *gaigin*, usually young Americans, Canadians or Britons teaching English, making enough for next year's Chinese bicycle trip or swing through Thailand. Once I even met a fellow Australian.

The morning was grey, warm and rainy, steam misting the big windows onto the street. The café was crowded, and overhung with a thick cigarette smoke pall. A teenage waitress scanned for a place, and directed me to a table by the window where a large Western woman was in the process of polishing off a plate of bacon and eggs. She was in later middle age, in a blue floral sackdress. Her short hair was dyed a bright chemical orange, and permed hard into her head.

'Another cup of coffee thanks dear,' the woman said abruptly to the waitress. 'And another bun.'

I ordered my coffee, toast and jam, and the waitress nodded and went. The woman watched her go. 'Attractive little people aren't they? Such hard workers too. That little girl was here last night when I came in for my tea.'

'Really?'

'Yes. I don't care what anyone says, it's a very nice country. And very nice people. I work in a jeweller's in Collins Street – I'm from Melbourne – and we sell lots of beautiful opals. Get a lot of Japanese in of course. They love our opals. Very well mannered people. They dress so beautifully too, always so polite. Never had any trouble with them. Such *honest* people too. That's what impressed me. What made me want to come here really. I wanted to see them, where they live.'

Her voice was soft and confiding, her s's highly sibilant, particularly at the ends of words. She also had that habit of poking one's arm to ensure full attention. 'Just look at them,' she said, covering the crowded café with a sweep of her hand. 'Look at the way the women do their hair – it's beautiful. Elegant handbags, elegant shoes, beautiful watches, and cameras. Lovely video cameras too.'

'They do seem to like their cameras,' I concurred.

'And they take beautiful pictures too. I've seen them,' she said. 'You're Australian aren't you.'

'Yes, I am.'

'Thought so, right from when you came in the door, before you even said a word.' She nodded. 'I've got a sixth sense about that sort of thing.' She leaned across the table as if to confide a secret. I saw tiny particles of white foundation powder clinging to her neck. I smelt lavender, Anticol, fried egg. The whites of her bulbous blue eyes were wide as if she had just sat on a pin.

'I'm Betty.'

'Nice to meet you, Betty.' I introduced myself and we shook hands.

'Do you know, my friends just couldn't believe it when I said I was coming here to Japan alone.' She prodded my elbow again across the table. 'My kids were the worst though. My daughter's at uni, and she's always carrying on about things, you know, women's this and women's that, and then she's just worried sick when I come here by myself. But I said *no*, this is *my* trip. No kids, no dogs, no husband. I just wanted to enjoy myself this time. Not that *he'd* want to come anyway. He'd just sit around in the hotel and watch the TV. That's what he did when we went to America. All the way to Los Angeles, and he didn't even want to go to Disneyland.'

My breakfast arrived with Betty's extra coffee and roll. 'I just wish it wasn't so expensive here,' she confided. 'You get so few yen for your dollars, it's a wonder we can afford to eat at all.' She laughed. 'My daughter calls us the poor white trash of Asia. And I say to her "speak for yourself." '

She glanced at her watch, and finished her roll quickly. Then she fussed in the enormous leather shoulder-bag at her feet. She looked either way before freshening her pale orange lipstick, and pressed a powdered sponge to her nose and cheeks. She peered into a hand mirror, licked some lipstick from her front tooth, then tidied the compact away in her bag. Outside, another warm shower began falling. The metallic hissing of the rain hitting the pavement came through the open door. A line of children scurried by in plastic raincoats, laughing in the wet.

Betty eyed them. 'I must say though, I have seen better children. They're over-fed if you ask me. But they do dress them nicely, beautiful clothes. And they're all very polite.' She rose. 'Well, I'm going back to Melbourne tonight. I'm off to the shops. Nice to meet you dear.'

We shook again. I watched her walk away quickly, a blue blur, a dash of orange in the rain.

A few moments later the waitress scurried over. 'The lady, she did not pay,' she said, worried and surprised in equal measure. 'You know the lady?'

'No,' I said, scanning the grey street.

'She must forget,' the waitress added.

'Yes,' I said, 'she must have.'

.

Café Lune

NOT long after dawn, I was awakened by the cawing of crows in the palm tree in the courtyard. The air in my room was tepid and still, and the sheets damp with perspiration, so I pulled on my shorts and went out onto the balcony, into the morning cool. I was staying at the Seaview, a long-faded colonial guest house on the seafront in the so-called Ville Blanche, the old French quarter of Pondicherry. The guest house was operated by the Sri Aurobindo ashram, principally for its visiting devotees, but could also be stayed in by ordinary travellers, of whom I was one.

I had Room Ten, enormous, a vault of air and light, with white-washed walls, massive roof beams and a broad terracotta-tiled floor. The balcony overlooked the Bay of Bengal. Despite the goodness of the hour, the Bay had already taken on its daytime colouring, a human eye hue somewhere between grey, green and blue, flecked with yellow. The ocean esplanade was empty yet but for a few workers dawdling towards a nearby government office block. I watched a lone cyclist pass. A thin, fine-featured man, he sat very upright in the saddle, a hand of green bananas perched on his head, his sleepy-eyed son up on the handlebars, dressed for school.

Returning indoors, I dressed, picked up the black umbrella I had bought the day before at MummyDaddy's emporium on Nehru Street, and shot back the bolts on the double doors. The landing outside was silent, its walls blackened with neglect, the plaster cracked and falling. As I made my way down the steps, I heard the murmurs of the *ayas* as they awoke on the kitchen's concrete floor.

Arrayed downstairs atop a jumble of chipped rosewood cabinets were framed sepia photographs of life here during the French period: Chanel-suited ladies stepping from Peugeots, an extended hand held out by a bespectacled Sartre in a pinstripe suit; squirming children lined up in the sun, awaiting some dignitary; Parisian families atop garlanded elephants, Gallic maharajas. The French had outstayed even the British in India, and the Alliance Française could still be felt throughout the quarter, in posters for visiting French musicians, in street signs and menus displayed in restaurant windows. The old guard on his rickety wooden chair outside the French Consulate always greeted me with a '*bonjour monsieur*'.

I found only one other guest downstairs, a man sitting at one of the dining tables, browsing a freshly delivered copy of *The Hindu* newspaper. He was dark and small, about forty. A languidly cynical expression was set into an impish face whose deep brown eyes enjoyed the asylum of spectacles, gold wire-framed. I had seen him a few times during my week or so there, down corridors, across a street, once or twice on the landing outside my room, but until now we had not spoken.

'Good morning,' I said.

He glanced up. 'Hi.' His tone gave nothing away, personable enough but uninterested, saying, 'Yes, hello, fine, we don't have to speak.' Even in the early morning, his mode of dress was very formal by the standards of other travellers – dark suit trousers and a pressed white shirt, its top button closed. There was no tie, yet.

'More trouble brewing in the north,' he said, matter-of-fact, almost to himself as he returned to the front page of *The Hindu*. His accent sounded American. 'This time they'll get serious. Not that they'd ever tell you here. You have to read between the lines of a lot of political party infighting. But it's coming.'

'What's coming?'

'Chaos. Like you wouldn't want to know. It'll make them pulling down the Ayodya mosque look like a picnic.'

'Are you part of the ashram?' I asked.

'No. Are you?'

'No, just staying here. It's pleasant though, isn't it?'

'Do you really think so?' he replied, lips twisting as if tasting something nasty. His gaze went to the framed formal portraits of Sri Aurobindo and The Mother on the dining room wall, on virtually every wall in Pondicherry. 'Awful, isn't she? Like one of those horrible rich old New York Jews. And *he* had such pretensions,' he went on, eyes swivelling to Aurobindo. 'The great poet, literary critic. Guru. Activist. Visionary. Genius. The two of them so conceited, self-involved, cult-of-the-personality. All they ever seemed to do was sit around in their expensive robes and pose for portraits with those constipated meaningful looks on their faces.'

His eyes swept back to me, their dark irises glittering with freely uttered contempt, but his moment was interrupted by a barefoot waiter in *lunghi* and cotton shirt wandering into the gloomy room, gilded and crimsoned between the eyes from morning *puja*. 'Breakfast, sir?'

'Yes, yes, I'll have breakfast. Of course I'll have breakfast.' He turned to me. 'What about you?'

'Thanks, but I'm having breakfast out.'

He nodded curtly and said something in Tamil to the waiter, who left. I was ready to leave too, but there was something about the man that prompted me to stay a little longer. His demeanour was so marvellously, appallingly brusque, and his accent intriguing. It was a strange collage to the ear. There was a hint of Italian in the American, and it was occasionally counterpointed with yet another accent, a very pukka English one – the product perhaps of schooling?

'Well, yes, Aurobindo,' I said, attempting to revive the topic. 'But you do have to admit he was something of an intellectual, don't you? An important nationalist too.'

'Excuse me,' the man replied, turning in his chair. He yelled something to the *ayas* out in the kitchen.

'You speak Tamil,' I noted.

'A little.'

'You must have been here a while then.'

'Quite some time, yes.'

'India gets under your skin, doesn't it.'

'Under your nails more like it.'

Lakshmi, a young *aya* who always wore a hot pink sari, emerged from a back room carrying a bundle of washed and ironed clothes, each one tagged with a number.

'Oh, I wish you wouldn't put those damn tags through everything,' he fretted as she started to sort them. 'They leave holes.' But he was interrupted mid-complaint by the waiter returning bearing a tray of toast, and a large teapot, cup, saucer and spoon.

'Looks like there's plenty of tea here for two,' he said. 'Sure you won't join me?'

'No. Thanks anyway. I have to get going.' I moved to the door. 'By the way – forgive my idle curiosity, but what are you doing here?'

'You mean, Pondicherry? Or India?'

'Both.'

'As little as humanly possible.'

As I left, he took a silk claret-coloured tie from a stack of ironing, and started putting it on.

Among other reasons, I had declined to join him for breakfast because I had promised myself a farewell visit to the Café Lune. I had stumbled upon it on my first day in Pondicherry, when I strolled down the esplanade to the big Ghandi monument on the seafront, and then threaded my way back through the French quarter's grid of narrow streets, of neat houses overhung with bushes of mauve bougainvillea.

On Rue Suffren, I had passed a pink-washed shopfront place, Madonna Tailors. Inside, gaudily tinted prints of Marx and Lenin shared wallspace with an equally garish Ganesh with attendant costumed rat, and corner shrine statues of a blue-veiled Madonna and Baby Jesus with lamb. A very catholic establishment, obviously. A little further down I had discovered the Café Lune, charming, pistachio-green with blue shutters. Inside, its few tables were busy. There was some sort of transport registry nearby, around which men clustered like bees. After they had filled out all their forms, they sauntered in for a chat and a coffee. Scattered around the walls were framed prints of Mecca, the Taj, and Arabic volumes bookended on either side with jars of Bournvita. (Could I ever have dreamed of drinking another Bournvita in my life – in India of all places?) Above the copper urn was a dented tin flue, painted with the *tricolore*. Green coconuts lay on the concrete floor with crates of empty Mirinda bottles. Racks of Indian cigarettes sat in a glass case, Scissors and Panamas ('good to the last puff'). When I left, the man at the counter bade me a formal '*à bientôt*'.

On subsequent visits I had become intrigued by an oddity in the café's narrow entranceway. It was a quartz the size of a large mango, tied in an oily rope, and suspended just above head height. One time I had asked a man sitting beside me at one of the bench tables, charcoal-suited with a finely-trimmed black moustache, if he knew what it was. When he merely looked pleasantly puzzled I tried, 'The stone – *qu'est-ce que c'est?*'

He smiled, and replied in well-modulated English, 'I'm sorry, I do not have the time to talk now.' He left with his newspaper under his arm, two single rupee coins resting beside his empty steel coffee cup.

I tried asking other patrons, but while happy enough to chat about anything else, they always had to go just then. If I asked the man making coffees at the ancient urn – dramatically shooting a long tan jet of steaming coffee from one steel cup above his head to another held almost at knee height – he would smile and say, 'No time to talk now sir.'

The Mystery of the Quartz of the Café Lune – I admired it for its very implausibility, the apparent improbability of solving it. My curiosity grew with each daily visit.

Over the course of a week or so, I noticed that all the men who came in lacked red *puja* spots on their foreheads. They must all be Muslims, I realised – thus the name of the café, stupid. Perhaps, then, the stone marked the direction of Mecca. I asked another patron about that, but he too lacked the time to talk. I began thinking about Mecca and the *haj*, the thousands of *hajis* swirling around the big black stone in that huge courtyard – the number of circuits, so I had been told, contingent upon how evil one had been in life. More prosaically, a different informant had said everyone did seven. I asked another petit and dapper patron about that big black stone in Mecca, and this time I did receive a clear answer.

'It is called the *kaaba*, sir.'

'Yes, but what's inside it? Is it solid, like a Buddhist stupa, or hollow?'

'Perhaps, yes,' he said. 'Pardon me.'

And then he too had to go.

It was like the quartz, I thought, settling back into my seat, happy there was no Britannica here instantly to dispel the pleasure of enquiry. It was watercolour wash I savoured here, in place of the definite line and cross-hatching of my familiar world.

On this, my final morning in Pondicherry, I had a detail to attend to – a request of the guest house Manager – before I could go out to the Café Lune.

His office stood at the apex of the guest house's clearly defined hierarchy. At the bottom were the *ayas*, who cooked, cleared and cleaned. A step up were the waiters, young men from rural parts mostly. Then there was the Stern & Silent One at the front desk, the heir-apparent. Above them all, cloaked in mystery, presided the Manager, a man who worked to a timetable so obscure that only he knew the hours during which he would actually be seated behind his desk.

He was rarely mentioned, and then only by position, never by name. Even these mentions were rated by rank. The *ayas*, who spoke little English anyway, had to the best of my memory never even uttered the word 'Manager' to me. One of the waiting staff had once in passing noted the existence of the Manager, but nothing beyond. Only the Stern & Silent One had spoken the word on more than one occasion, breaching his retreat to declare 'Manager demands' and 'Manager's directive' when insisting on some refinement of form-filling pedantry.

During my time at the Seaview, in straying past the Manager's office – its door always slightly ajar – I had rarely noticed him in attendance. But on this morning, and needing to speak with him, I stopped by the door and peered inside. In the dimness I discerned a rounded shape silhouetted against a curtained window. Powerful fans blew, and upon the broad managerial desk there was an autumnal flurry of yellowing papers and forms, each anchored down by its own glass weight, here a pink one, there a blue or amber, round, oblong, spherical. The Manager himself appeared absorbed in some important work, but at that moment happened to look up. I saw a man of sixty, white hair meticulously combed back from an ingenuous-looking face fronted by spectacles in grey plastic frames. His brown irises were magnified by the thickness of the lenses, and I saw big soft Lord Krishna eyes, contented cow eyes. He gave me a quizzical look, and beckoned me to enter. When I sat down in one of the pair of green wicker chairs before his desk, he did not utter a word but smiled reassuringly while continuing to write in a massive leatherbound ledger with a bulbous blue fountain pen.

'I hope I'm not interrupting,' I said, 'but I was wondering if I could use your telephone, to ring the railway station for a reservation. The phone at the front desk isn't working.'

He took in a slow, deep breath as his eyes came back to me. 'Your room number, sir?'

'Room Ten.'

He scratched another line with his pen, then, not looking up, enunciated clearly, 'Tell me, what is your opinion of the new troubles threatening in the north?'

Unsure of the etiquette of a foreigner commenting on Indian politics, I hesitated. 'It's difficult for me, not being Indian.'

'And what is your good country?' he asked, voicing the eternal query of India, of infant boys on the street and pushy businessmen from their shopfronts, of well-to-do ladies in hotel foyers and countless official forms I had filled out, the most recent of these doubtless pinned beneath a paperweight in the colour maze before the Manager.

'Australia.'

'Ah, yes, Australia,' he nodded thoughtfully. 'Let me first say that I have always greatly admired your Mr Allan Border.' He went back to writing a moment. Then his brow furrowed. 'Let me then say to you, sir, that although I am a Hindu I have nothing against the Muslims. They are my brothers. But you see, there is a problem.' He looked up at me again. 'Their religion, it is young. Like a wine. It is too sharp. It has not yet had the time to mature. That is why they are so fierce, that youth, that immaturity. And the women, they have it the worst. Don't imagine they have any freedom. Do not judge them from the privileged likes of Mrs Bhutto. They have no freedom. Not like your Christian women. You are a Christian, sir, are you not?'

'Well, no, not really. Not personally anyway. I mean, I come from a Christian culture, yes . . . well, agnostic actually . . . atheistic . . . hedonistic, to tell you the truth . . .' My words trailed off.

Eyes fully adjusted to the gloom now, I looked around his office at the adjoining desks with worn green leather tops and brass fittings, at the perfectly geometrical arrangement of pens, paperweights, ledgers, forms. From here the influence of the Manager spread throughout the guest house, into every room, corridor and cupboard. Everything had its correct timing, form, fee, as fixed and noted by the Manager, the human hub from whom all spokes ran away to the turning guest house wheel. Yet here, at its precise centre, was an enigma.

'Hinduism has had many thousands of years,' his deep voice recommenced abruptly, making me start slightly in my chair. 'It is one of the oldest religions in the world. If not the oldest. Perhaps in another few hundred years or so the religion of the Muslims will evolve. But for now . . .'

He was staring at me again. Then he capped his pen and set it down by the side of the ledger before him, precisely parallel.

'Please, sir,' he said.

'Yes?'

'Please stand.'

'What for?'

But I did so, and he came out from behind his desk. He was one of the taller South Indians I had met, strong-looking for his years, his white hair still thick. He stopped some two metres from me, still staring intently. I had no idea what to expect next.

The Manager crumpled, fell, prostrating himself on the carpet before me, the joined tips of his fingers coming to rest upon the toes of my shoes. His lips moved rapidly, words low, in prayer. He's blessing me, I realised with wonderment and relief. I am being blessed by the guest house Manager.

It was all over in a few seconds, and when he stood back up I saw the faint remnant of a red *puja* spot on his forehead. He stood there, waiting, and realising what was required, I prostrated myself onto the threadbare green carpet before him, murmuring, 'I bless you guest house Manager, I bless you sir,' my outward stretched fingers creating an apex which came to rest upon the dust thinly coating his brown Bata lace-ups.

When I regained my feet he smiled a moment longer, then with a single stride returned to his seat behind the desk. 'Now sir,' he said decisively, 'your request.' He indicated the telephone.

I secured a reservation, thanked him and rose to leave. With a small, world-weary smile, as if he bore that global weight upon his own shoulders, the Manager nodded and recommenced writing in the leatherbound ledger.

The Still & Silent One moved not so much as a facial muscle as I deposited my room key onto the Reception desk. The security guard was stretched on the moulded concrete bench outside the front gate, snoring loudly. I raised my black umbrella against the glare and started walking towards the Café Lune. As I did, I pondered the chasm between Islam and Hinduism, between rowdy West and veiled East. The Quartz abided. Mystery lingered here in the dark, exquisite shading of a world not quite explained.

The mid-morning wind was hot and blew strongly, chopping up the waters of the Bay into a grimy brown broth. I was already well acquainted with that wind. It would blow all day while beggars slept outside the temple off Rue de la Marine, blow on into the hazy dusk, when the temple would light up candy-pink, blue and green, and the people would gather to chant. The lepers came out then too, thrusting forth their begging stumps. Someone, they knew, would bless them with one or two rupees; on a lucky night the salving leaf of a green, five-rupee note.

The

Café Bar

THE night before I left London, Tom telephoned from Los Angeles with a special request – could I bring them back an electric kettle? He explained that Americans tend to boil water on a stove, or use a coffee-making or home cappuccino machine, and so electric kettles can be very expensive, if you can find one in the first place.

I departed into a liver-spotted grey October morning, and stopped off at one of those London shops with windows displaying everything from shopsoiled chamber pots to vibrators made in Taiwan. A stooped old man emanated from the shadowy recesses of the shop, and I explained I was flying to America that afternoon and wanted to buy a kettle. After first marvelling with respectful terror upon the miracle of powered flight, this latter-day Steptoe recommended a particular kettle, 'retailing at twenty pahn, guv.' I noticed it lacked a wall plug. For reasons known only to the English – could this, like the long-persisted-with afternoon closing of pubs, be some vestige of the Blitz? – British electrical appliances are sold with cables dangling and bared to their copper wiring. To my mind, this national characteristic is as odd as the American eschewal of the kettle. Of course, for a 'small extra fee, guvnor,' the salesperson will wire on the plug for you on the spot.

On the flight, I sat beside a sixtysomething English couple on their way to San Diego and retirement in a motorised home. They enthused at length on the medicinal properties of papaya seeds. Seven, the man assured me, and precisely that number only, would cure any stomach ailment.

On the other side of me sat a skeletally thin young woman with seawater cold blue eyes, punching in fits and starts into a laptop computer. Her hair was crewcut bleach-blonde, her bared tiny arms bore an orchestration of tattoos. Her elfin face showcased a metallurgy of lip, nose, eyebrow and ear rings and pins. Her body language translated readily as 'Don't Even Think About Talking To Me', and I didn't. But several hours into the flight she spoke up, addressing me in heartfelt complaint. 'Shit, why don't the fucking bastards let you smoke any more? Cunts.'

The accent and vocabulary revealed a fellow Australian. Her tone was bitter, an aerospatial whine. She proceeded directly from the conditions of air travel to the conditions of her grant.

'After California they expect me to go to Orlando fucking Florida. Who am I – Snow fucking White?'

I asked about the grant she had mentioned.

'I'm a rider,' she moaned, and trotted out a paperback book which she tossed into my lap. 'Po-mo rodiga.'

'I'm sorry?'

'Po-mo female rodiga,' she said.

I struggled for comprehension, but the back cover notes explained it all. There, a former university classmate in Sydney, now a self-declared international leader in ficto-criticism, described my fellow passenger as one of Australia's leading exponents of post-modern female erotica.

'Ah, erotica,' I said.

'Yeah. What I basically said to myself when I decided to start out riding was, "I'm gunna write pornography – from a woman's point of view of course – and I'm gunna market myself like a packet of cornflakes." '

I flicked through the pages of what quickly revealed itself as a volume of soft pore corn, the chapter I scanned climaxing in a prolix passage detailing the patterns created by menstrual blood spattering a whitewashed wall during lively intercourse.

'My stuff's just so threatening,' she said, managing a grim little smile. Her bared teeth were a brittle yellow, amazingly tiny. I wondered if she could safely eat an apple. 'Strayan cridics are basically terrified. My colleagues just fucking adore it. So does my editor. My publisher . . .'

I browsed a few minutes longer. When I went to return the book I realised she was dozing in her seat. Her eyes blinked open urgently.

'Oh, sorry,' she said, yawning luxuriously. 'Just my CFS. You know, Chronic Fatigue Syndrome.'

'Oh,' I said. 'Is it serious?'

'Pretty horny disease actually,' she said. 'To me, all disease is basically rodig.' She yawned again. 'Christ, I'd kill for a smoke. Cunts.'

Tom and Alison picked me up at LAX and sped me back to their West Hollywood apartment, eager to try out their new kettle. But then, disappointment. It took some twenty minutes for the water to boil. Their patented US adaptor did not work properly with the British plug. We looked at each other and sighed. There was nothing for it – we would have to pay for expert help.

Americans have enormous problems understanding English spoken by non-Americans. The differences go far deeper than mere accent and idiom, into stress, intonation, rhythm. Americans often sing-song in time-worn patterns, typically 'Hello, how are you. I'm fine, how are you?' Outsiders who do not have the hang of this sing-song may be misunderstood, even if they are speaking the very same words as the locals. Then there is the simple ignorance that many Americans have of anything which lies beyond the Valley, the Hudson, the lower forty, the end of the block. This was highlighted by a telephone contact Tom had with a journalist on a national magazine in New York.

'You're from . . . now where'd you say you're from?' she asked.

'England,' Tom replied.

'Enga-land?'

'Yes. England.'

'Cool.' Beat. 'Say, do they speak English there?'

Seeking a new adaptor for the English kettle, we encountered some fairly predictable linguistic hurdles. There is now, for instance, an entire generation of Americans who cannot utter a sentence without a liberal sprinkling of the word 'like', commared on either side, throughout it. This is the so-called Generation X – from, like, hell. (The same generation has also managed to reduce English's generous palate of opprobrious adjectives to just one, 'cool'.)

A representative of Generation X sat behind a counter before us now, in jeans, T-shirt, blond pony-tail and (reversed) baseball cap. This young man was an Electrical Appliance Services Consultant, a role better known outside the United States as a shop assistant.

'You need a wha for wha?' he drawled up from the rock pages of the *LA Weekly*, his consciousness lost in space somewhere between Wayne's World and Nirvana.

'An adaptor for my English kettle', Tom repeated, very slowly, but too English altogether. *Foreign.*

'Keddle?' the young man tried.

'*Kettle*,' Tom said. 'For boiling water.'

'You mean a, like, pot?'

'Yes. Only it's electric. You don't put it on the stove.'

'Stove?'

'Hob.'

'Oh, I geddit. You mean, for, like, coffee or somethin'?'

'For tea.'

'Oh. Tea.' His eyes emitted a blue, triumphant gleam. He finally had a fix on us and our weird English ways. *Tea.* It was all about tea. 'So, wassa problem?' he asked, finger still on his place in the newspaper.

'England has a different voltage to America,' Tom explained. 'I need an adaptor for the kettle's wall plug.' He produced the British plug, that solid, sizeable lump of government-regulated, welfare society plastic and brass, its three prongs stoutly protruding.

The young man's eyes widened slightly. 'That's a plug from, like, Enga-land?' We nodded. It was indeed a plug from, like, Enga-land. 'Cool,' he said. 'But I ain't seen nothin' like it before,' he sighed. 'Sorry, can't help you.' He was already back into the *LA Weekly*.

'Can you suggest another shop where I might be able to find an adaptor?' Tom tried. The assistant gave us a little shrug and a 'well-lemme-see-now-you-might-just-try' and dispatched us to the first of what became a succession of electrical goods places. We actually did find adaptors in some of them – but only for Americans travelling overseas, so that they could run their hair-dryers and shavers in Finland, Thailand, and, like, Enga-land. We ended this paper chase at a giant electrical goods warehouse in West LA stacked floor-to-ceiling with fuses, wires, switches, circuits, gadgets and gismos. The ultimate home handyman hang. This had to be the place.

After the inevitable wait of fifteen or so minutes as the counter assistant loudly sorted out his marriage on the phone, we were finally granted an audience when another assistant rose lugubriously from his seat by the Café Bar and sauntered over. This man is perhaps most easily described as a flesh and blood Homer Simpson as played by a terminally depressed African-American actor. His name-tag revealed that his name was Bob. When we outlined our enquiry, his response was very direct:

'No problem, just swap over the plug. Swap it for an American one.'

The ready simplicity of this solution took Tom so much by surprise that he did not manage to reply at all at first. Meanwhile Bob wandered over to a stand which displayed hundreds of different wall plugs in dusty cellophane boxes.

'Any of these will do just fine,' he said, passing one to Tom and almost smiling. 'Just pay on your way out and have a nice day.'

Tom took the plug and looked it over, still dumbfounded at the ease of this solution.

'But,' I asked quickly before Bob could get away, 'isn't it a problem that England is on a different voltage?'

'Wha?' His eyes narrowed as he sensed an annoying hitch in getting us out of his hair and getting back to his seat by the Café Bar.

'Different voltage,' I repeated, madly over-articulating. 'America is on 110 volts. England is on 220, or 240.'

'Tha' so?' Bob said, genuinely surprised.

'Mightn't the kettle blow up with too much voltage?' I persisted.

He pushed back an imaginary baseball cap and gave his front bald patch a scratch. 'Well, now,' he sighed, 'that may just be so.'

It was a hot day, and, like his English kettle, Tom was on a slow boil. 'Just a minute, you work here, can we or can't we just change over the plug?'

Bob's eyes searched the stained white polystyrene and asbestos ceiling panels for something. 'Guess better not,' he muttered, voice falling on the last word. He had realised, poor bastard, that he would have to fix us. It would take time. His large eyes flicked back yearningly to his seat by the Café Bar, the *National Enquirer* spread out before it, the cigarette smoking in the ashtray, coffee ready and just waiting to be poured and sipped. Would he never get back there?

Twenty minutes later we were at the check-out with, not an adaptor, but a full-scale transformer the size of a shoebox. It was heavy as a pair of dumb-bells, cost twenty-five dollars, and was made in the People's Republic of China.

'Can I return it if it's not right?' Tom asked.

'Sure,' Bob said breezily, sensing escape from us at last. 'You got five days to bring it back.'

We departed into the smoggy late afternoon sun and loaded the transformer into Tom's vintage silver Corolla, running sweetly after being serviced by a pair of overalled mechanics name-tagged Jesus at the local Chevron gas station on Sunset Boulevard. We dropped the kettle off at an electrical goods repair place recommended by Bob, where the English plug wired on by the greyed man in the grimy shop in Kentish Town Road for one pound was to be re-wired with an American plug to fit the transformer, by a guy name-tagged Dwight (baseball cap front on, blond pony-tail pulled down through the back of it) for five dollars.

Ten minutes later we pulled up outside the apartment's basement electric security gate, with a real sense of achievement. We were on our first beer when Alison got home from work. She had spent the past eleven hours dressing a 'medium tech kinda funky' (the director's brief to her) dentist's surgery set for a TV toothpaste commercial. Tom proudly showed her the electric transformer from the People's Republic, but she cast a critically chilly eye over the big orange lump of metal resting in its cardboard box.

'Tom, really . . .'

'What?' he said defensively.

'I just wanted a kettle. A kettle we could use here, and take away on holiday, and I could take on assignment. I can't take that. It's too big and heavy. And is it safe to use?'

Tom cleared his throat. 'It should be, yes.'

'But is it?'

'I don't know.'

'Have you tried it?'

Tom and I looked at each other. 'Not yet.'

'Then I suggest we don't. Who knows what will happen? I think you should just take it back.'

Tom looked at the orange thing a moment longer, opened his mouth to reply, but said nothing.

'We should really have just paid the ninety dollars for a kettle after all,' Alison sighed.

'They won't take it back,' Tom stated glumly.

'What? Why do you say that?'

'I know them. They won't. I know they won't.'

'But Tom, the guy said . . .' I began.

'I know what the guy said. But they won't. They never do. They say they will but they never do.'

'Of course they will,' Alison soothed. 'This is America. If they don't honour their customers, they go bankrupt.'

'This is America alright,' Tom replied grimly. 'And it's already bankrupt. By the trillions.'

The next day we were back at the service counter with the transformer. The only person serving was a neat and compact Hispanic man who studiously ignored us while staring down at a circuit board through spectacles cut from the bottom of a Coke bottle. We looked around for Bob, but his place by the Café Bar was empty, the scene somehow bleak. It looked like he wasn't coming in today.

The Hispanic man, Xavier, continued to ignore us. Tom finally spoke up loudly. 'Excuse me, may I have some service please?'

Xavier did not look up. 'What is it?'

'I'd like a refund on the transformer I bought here yesterday.' Tom took out the receipt and put it on the counter.

'No refund on that item.'

I was surprised by this, but Tom, who had been expecting it all along, indeed psyching himself up with muttered obscenities at the wheel all the way there, did not miss a beat. 'Why not?' he snapped.

'It's the law.'

'What law? Federal law? State law?'

'Just the law,' Xavier said, with a renewed frown of interest in his circuit board.

A sardonic smile slid across Tom's face. He stood well away from the counter now, and started moving about, loping. In that moment he reminded me of a beast I had once seen in a wretched resort in Mexico, on the polluted Baja coast just south of Ensenada – a lion, an old gold, lop-eared, shaggy lion, somehow brought to that blighted place and kept in a barred box for the idle amusement of tourists, pacing.

'What law?' Tom repeated, hard.

'The law that says we can't take back transformers once

they've been sold. No electrical goods store can. We all have to post the regulation in the store.'

He made a vague gesture behind him, to a bare wall which utterly lacked such a posted regulation – in its very American way, it lacked any regulation at all.

Tom stared at the wall in bewilderment. 'But there's *nothing* there!' he cried out.

'Well there should be,' said Xavier, turning some tiny screw. 'It's the law.'

Too stunned to go on for the time being, Tom lapsed into an exasperated silence. At the same moment, my nose irritated by the LA smog, I happened to sneeze mightily. The man looked up over his spectacles. 'God bless you sir,' he said, in a totally unexpected instance of human compassion.

'Thank you,' I said, wiping my reddened nose with a handkerchief. 'But when we bought this thing yesterday the man who served us said we had five days to return it.'

'No one would have said that,' the little man said calmly.

'Well, he did.'

'Who did?' His eyes did not budge from the board.

'The black guy,' Tom said, recovering his momentum now, loping about again. 'A black guy served us here yesterday.'

At this the small Hispanic man shot a mischievous glance across to a second counter assistant, a white flour sack of a man name-tagged Jed, who was doing his own fair share of ignoring a queue of grumbling complainants. 'The black guy, he says . . .' Xavier grinned. The white guy grinned back.

'He *does* work here, doesn't he?' Tom pressed on, but sensing difficulty from some hitherto unexpected quarter.

'He works here,' Xavier said. 'Only all he does is *sit*. At the Café Bar.'

'What?'

'That's all he does,' the white guy agreed. 'He don't know shit.'

'You're telling me,' Tom said slowly, 'that all this guy, Bob, that was his name, Bob . . . that all he does is sit over there by the Café Bar.'

'That's right,' said Xavier. 'Drinking coffee, reading the papers. Only today he's not.'

'How come?' Tom asked suspiciously.

'He's absent,' said Xavier, and the white guy further down the counter let out a little hoot of laughter.

'*Always* absent if you ask me,' said Jed.

'But he *works* here, in this store,' Tom attempted.

'Yes, he does. But he's not, you know, quite right in the head. I don't know why they keep him on, but they do. It's not my business, I just work here. But he just sits over there by that Café Bar, doesn't do nothing, doesn't know shit,' Xavier said.

'Just comes in here, drinks his coffee, dunks his donuts, reads his paper right there by the Café Bar,' Jed agreed. 'Lord, how he loves that Café Bar. Lives for that damn thing, he does.'

'So you can't believe anything he told you,' Xavier said. 'If you did, you'd probably end up with an electric shock. You can't listen to him, he doesn't know anything, and if he gave you the wrong idea, it's too bad. That's just how it is.'

'I want to see the manager,' Tom said with an angry tremble.

'He ain't in today.'

'When will he be in then?'

'Tomorrow, maybe,' Xavier said.

'This is utterly preposterous, and you know it. I'll have to report you to the consumer affairs people.'

The little man's eyes came up for a moment from the circuit board and engaged with Tom's silently, the drama of the moment punctuated with another staggering sneeze from me.

'God bless you sir,' Xavier said again.

I idly wondered if he was born here, or how he'd come into America – whether he was one of those people a Texas State Trooper once searched my car for: 'Sorry sir, we're jes' lookin' fer *wetbacks*.'

Xavier stared a moment at Tom, then returned his attention to the circuit. I could tell he was weighing up the aggravation he was getting from us against the aggravation he would get from his boss if it was found out he was getting soft on all the bums queuing up to get good money back for all the useless bits of junk they'd bought here. But he sensed he had to do something in our case. We were strange. *Foreign.*

'Okay,' Xavier said. 'This is what we do. I'll give you a twenty-five dollar credit on the transformer. You can take your pick from the store.'

Tom replied with another of his sardonic smiles. 'And what about the law? That law you were talking about. The government regulation that's meant to be posted on the wall but isn't? What about that?'

The little man didn't even look up. 'What about it?'

Tom got twenty-five dollars in light bulbs and we left. Driving home we passed the repair shop where the kettle was having its plug re-wired by Dwight – the one with the blond pony-tail pushed back through his (not reversed) baseball cap. And there, on a dusty shelf out back, is where that English kettle will no doubt end its days, a stranger in a strange land.

The black woman behind the check-in counter for the Sydney flight seemed jumpy. Her mind was not altogether on the job. As she took my passport and ticket she was continually glancing around as if looking out for a friend, or a snooping supervisor. Her fingers leafed automatically to some old US airport tax stamps in my ticket.

'Paid your airport tax yet sir?' she said tersely, still not looking at me. I saw her name-tag: Loretta.

'Not yet.'

'What are all these then?'

'They're old ones,' I said, feeling somehow guilty.

'You'll have to pay some tax then.'

'Okay. How much is it?' I felt for my wallet.

Her seriously efficient eyes came to rest on mine. 'Well, where you bin?'

'Er . . . I flew from LA to London. That's when these stamps are from. And then I came back here, went down to Mexico . . . and now . . .'

'Mexico . . .' Loretta's purpled eyelids gave a little flutter, her fingers no longer dog-earing my passport. 'You like it down there?'

'Very much.'

'Mexico,' she repeated to herself, as if recalling some sultry, long lost weekend. As she looked up at me again she noticed a cinema magazine in the crook of my elbow, with Spike Lee on the cover. 'Do you like him?'

'Yes,' I said. 'How about you?'

'He's okay.'

'I liked *Do The Right Thing*.'

'Oh yeah, now that was real good,' Loretta agreed. 'But some of his other stuff is like, you know, just too sexist. Like that one *She's Gotta Have It*. Now that was sexist shit.' She paused a moment. 'But *Malcolm X* was good. Long. But good.' She smiled, a flash of brilliant white teeth. 'I'm Loretta by the way.'

We shook hands. 'Nice to meet you, Loretta.'

'There's no tax payable, sir.'

'Really? Why, thank you.'

'I like your hat,' she said, handing me my boarding pass. 'And you have a nice flight, won't you?'

the
Air
Bar

Okay,

Here's the Deal

IT was mid November when the first snowfall dusted New York. I was crossing Park Avenue on the Upper East Side as a big flake fluttered down out of the gloom. I watched it melt into the pavement while women in furs marched by grimly, small dogs clutched beneath their arms.

Eighteen months had passed since my curious lost week in Accra. In my pocket was an airline ticket I had just purchased – another ticket for West Africa – from a bucket shop down on 42nd Street, a broom closet just big enough to get the computers in and the mouldering pizza cartons out. During those eighteen months Kathryn and I had lived together and apart, both had been involved with other people, both had given up on 'us' more than once. When she left her voice-teaching job in Sydney and took off for Europe, we did not know what would happen next. A month later I left too, on an Australian Film Commission screenwriting fellowship in New York. I lived in a tiny walk-up apartment on First Avenue and East 86th Street, in a 'fancy' neighbourhood of pugs and poodles, borscht and boredom.

We exchanged a string of telephone calls as Kathryn travelled through Italy, Portugal and Spain, while she flatted in Paris and crashed with our old friend Dirk in London. When she went to Athens to visit Manolis, the Greek composer she had met two years before in Paris, I thought they might become lovers once more – perversely almost encouraged her to do it.

I myself did not become involved during my time in New York, although I did undergo a rather Woody Allenesque dalliance with a film company executive.

'Okay, here's the deal,' she would telephone from her office downtown. 'I don't get out of here till ten tonight, ten tomorrow night, then I'm in LA for three days for the MTV awards, then I go upstate for that shoot, then I'm back for a day before London for a week.'

'Quite a schedule,' I would say, marvelling at that phrase, 'okay here's the deal' – the 'deal' not a deal at all but a *fait accompli*.

At this point she would speak to someone in her office, and I would hear trenchant orders being issued.

'Sounds like you're pretty busy,' I would say, as a prelude to signing off.

'Uh huh, yeah – but do it *now*, okay?' I would hear her ordering her minions; then, resuming her train of thought, coming back to me on the phone: 'Sorry, things are just a little crazy here right now.'

'That's okay,' I would say.

Then she would pause. 'How about coming round for a glass of wine later tonight. I'll be tired, but . . .'

It went on like this for a few weeks, before fading to black in a succession of heartfelt apologies from both parties.

Not long after, as I worked at my computer screen one evening, Kathryn telephoned from Athens.

'I'm coming to New York!'

'What? How?'

'I've got a voice-over job in Toronto. And they say I can stop off in New York.'

'That's fantastic. So when are you coming?'

'Tomorrow.'

'Tomorrow?' I looked at my computer, and the screenplay upon the screen, just a few days short of completion.

She sensed my hesitation. 'Why, is that a problem?'

'No. Not at all. It's just I've got a lot of work to finish up before Africa. But I can do it. I'll meet you at the airport.'

The following night I took the subway out to JFK Airport where wilder, wiser, somehow even more beautiful despite the months of travel, she suddenly was.

Over the following week, in a series of cafés and bars, prompted by much too much red wine, it came out, the days and nights of love in a half-built house in Athens. She was as candid as I had been secretive about the fine print of my involvement with Susan eighteen months before. The truth of it was she loved him. The topsy-turviness of it, the neatness of the reversal, hit me. Now she held the cards. She could go back to Athens, to a lover I had arrogantly discounted – and many times during our chaotic, wine-soaked week together I declared she should do just that, go, fuck off, get out of my life, leave me alone. But no, she said, she had come to New York because she believed the future lay with us, if we wanted it enough. As she talked, I tried not to picture her in another man's arms. Yet I could not complain, because of the times I had been in another woman's arms, and how she had borne that with dignity.

Then there was Africa. Mali. Our trip there together had been long mooted, but now she wasn't so sure. She was tired, exhausted. For a number of reasons she had to return to London too, before any possible departure – it was all very complex and difficult. Again Mali shimmered, to vanishing point.

Discord prevailed in nightly bars where we argued across bottomless glasses while techno music simpered around us and pill-hazed nightclubbers pumped out self-importance.

'Why the big thing with Mali anyway?' Kathryn shouted over the din. 'You just want to go so you can say you've been to Timbuktu.'

'You just want to go back to Athens.'

'No, but I'm tired out emotionally *from* Athens. And I'm worn out. I want to go somewhere and get some peace and quiet. Why don't we go to India? Bodysurf at Kovalum, stay in a white room with a view, live on papaya juice and kingfish?'

It was a tempting picture. Mali shimmered a little more. 'So, you don't want to come to Mali.'

'I'm not saying that,' she said. 'But it'll be so hot, and dusty, repressive like Morocco.'

185

'It won't be like Morocco.'

'I know what it'll be like.'

'No you don't!'

'I do!'

'So, you don't want to come. That's what you're saying.'

'No, I'm not saying that.' She paused. 'My passport's full anyway.'

'What??'

She pulled it out of her leather jacket and dropped it in front of me. The navy blue booklet with its gilded coat of arms rested primly on the bar. On second thought, it looked very much at home there.

'Look, there's not one whole empty page left. And I've been travelling so quickly, there hasn't been time to apply for a new passport. It takes weeks to get one.'

I strained my blurring eyes in the half-light. A fellow drunk bashed into my elbow and my drink spilled onto the bar, the vermilion plume just missing the passport.

'That'd look great in a Muslim country,' I said, snatching it up. 'A claret-stained passport.' I grinned at my own dumb joke, saw the posts of my wine-dark teeth in the bar mirror. Around my shoulders hung a smoky gloom. 'Want some more red?'

'Just a finger or I'll get pissed.'

'You're already pissed,' I said. 'We both are. And the wine's so fucking undrinkable.' I flicked through the pages of her passport. It did look very full. 'Wait on, look, see here, you've got a nearly empty page. Just one little tiny stamp on it.'

'They don't like other little tiny stamps on pages as a rule. They want empty pages,' she said as the barman mooched up and slopped us out more wine. 'Where do we apply for the Mali visas anyway?'

'In Dakar. When we get to Senegal.'

'And what if they won't give me the visa there?'

'They will.'

'They might not.'

'Oh, they will. Why wouldn't they? We're tourists. Don't they want fucking tourists?' I raised my newly refilled glass. 'To Mali.'

She raised her glass, clinked, and drank down her wine. 'Let's get out of here,' she said.

Luridly hungover the following morning, I tried to recall the name of the travel agency in London where I'd bought my ticket for Accra the previous year. I got their number and telephoned. Despite it being high season, they had one London–Dakar seat available, on the day after my own arrival in Dakar from New York. Kathryn nodded a final confirmation to me, and I went ahead with her booking.

Next we visited the medical centre where the week before I had updated the long list of inoculations mandatory for travel in West Africa. After administering the yellow fever and cholera injections, and stamping Kathryn's health certificates, the perky young doctor asked what she intended to do about malaria. 'There are a few possible drugs,' she said breezily. 'I suggest you take X. You only have to take it once a week, and it works damn fine.'

'That was the one I took in Ghana last year,' I said. 'I think I had an allergic reaction to it.'

The doctor flicked back her bangs and smiled. 'Oh, I've taken X and felt okay. In Guatemala.' She thought a moment. 'Did feel a little funky the first night after taking it, but it was cool after that.'

She rummaged up a booklet produced for travellers by the medical centre, and I scanned the section on malaria. I saw X mentioned, and in the column under possible side-effects, the words 'neurological' and 'psychiatric'.

I blinked. 'Hang on,' I said, 'it says here you can get psychiatric side-effects to this stuff.'

'Uh-huh,' she said.

'Is that common?'

She shrugged. 'Ish.'

'Then maybe I did have an allergic reaction to it.'

'Maybe. There's, like, you know, support groups of people

187

who've suffered problems with it. A site on the Net. Stuff like that.' She turned to Kathryn. 'Wanna hep shot too, babe?'

Kathryn looked up with a grimace. 'I don't even really want to go to West Africa in the first place.'

'No? How come you're going then?' the doctor looked from Kathryn to me and back again. Then she smiled. 'Oh, I geddit. Love,' she cooed. 'You know, I just love love . . .' She smiled sweetly. 'Now how 'bout the hep shot?'

Kathryn shook her head. 'I'll eat carefully.'

'It's your funeral,' she said, retiring the drawn syringe to a drawer. 'And the X for malaria?'

Kathryn looked at me hard. 'Will it be green in Africa?'

'Of course it will.'

'You're sure.'

'Of course it'll be green,' I repeated. 'It's Africa.'

Kathryn thought a moment, then nodded to the doctor to write the prescription. My eyes returned to the printed page, to the words 'neurological' and 'psychiatric'. Was this the explanation for what happened to me in Accra? Or just a part of the story?

'And how will you be paying for all this?' the doctor chirruped.

'My poor aching Visa card,' Kathryn said.

So we were really going to Mali. But as usual it was all confused and difficult. What would it be like to travel there with her now? Would we be able to cope with a whole month together, down dusty red African roads? Would I arrive in Dakar to a telegram of sincere apologies sent from Athens?

When Kathryn left the next day, I felt like a whirlwind had passed through my life. I expected her to telephone from Canada, but when I only received one call from her in the two days she was there, I found myself agonising over how many calls she might have made to Athens. 'Jealous fuckwit,' I told myself.

Threes

The night before I left New York I walked out of a Broadway show into the crowds milling round Times Square. It was very cold. An illuminated sign on a building said it was thirty-two degrees, freezing point. My jacket was barely up to it. I was taking a sidestreet back towards Lexington Avenue and the subway home, when a beggar on crutches crossed the road and came swinging himself my way. He begged from a man in front of me, then his eyes implored my way, his polystyrene cup extended. I gave him a quarter. He looked disappointedly into the cup, where my coin rested alone.

'Just enough for a hot dog, please sir.'

I shivered, felt for another quarter and put it into his cup, then walked on. But as I did, it played on my mind, that he wanted money to eat, that he was a cripple and the night freezing, in this, one of the richest cities on earth.

He knew I would turn around even before I knew it. He saw the dollar bill in my hand.

'Oh, thank you sir. God bless you.'

'Can you get something healthier than a hot dog?'

'With more money I could,' he said hopefully.

I found another dollar and gave him that too. Walking away, I found myself shoulder to shoulder with a bearded man with a thick Eastern European accent. No doubt he wanted something too.

'You know what the Bible says, don't you, about those who give to the poor?' he said.

'No,' I replied, quickening my pace, 'what?'

'They will be rewarded.'

He smiled with very un-American teeth. He went to say something more, but fearing he was a conman I gave him the slip at the corner. As I walked away I sensed his disappointment. Then I felt disappointed too.

The following evening I ate an Indian takeaway meal in my apartment, did a check of tickets, passport and money, locked up, dropped the keys into the letter box, and dumped a final bag of garbage on the pavement before shouldering my backpack and heading off towards the subway station on Lexington Avenue.

Up ahead on 86th Street, I saw the black woman who sat each night by the warm air vent out in front of the Republic Bank at Third Avenue, smiling at the passing parade: the Zen of panhandling. I'd kept the change from my dressing table for her, and she grinned broadly.

'Hey, thank you! What's with the bag?'

'I'm leaving town,' I said.

'Where to?'

'Africa.'

'You're kiddin' me. When?'

'Tonight. I'll be there in the morning.'

'Africa,' she sighed, far-away. 'You know, I always wanted to go t' Africa. Uh-huh. Sure did.' She averted her gaze a moment. Then she looked up solemnly from her plastic stool on the wet, shiny concrete. Her eyes were alive, her skin warm, face virtually unlined. 'God will bless you.'

'Oh, I don't know about that,' I laughed. I put out my hand and she squeezed it.

'No, believe me,' she said. 'God will bless you.'

I took the Number 4 Express down to Fulton Street, and changed for the 'A' train out to JFK. But when the train arrived I was on the platform telephone saying goodbye to a friend, and did not realise until I had boarded and the doors had closed that it was the wrong 'A' Train.

It rumbled out under the East River, and when it stopped at the first stop over in Brooklyn, at High Street, I stepped out with my luggage and waited on the platform for the correct 'A' train, the one to Far Rockaway. I realised with a prickle of mild discomfort that I was on the near-deserted platform of a station I did not know, on a miserably cold Sunday night. How unfortunate that would be, to get mugged on my last night in New York. I looked around uneasily, and found I was standing beside a gangly black teenage girl who had also got off the train. She wore a pink jump-suit and had a child's backpack with a giant Minnie Mouse on it.

'I'm goin' to Far Rockaway,' she enthused. 'Seein' my sister. I love to see my sister! I don't like my mom.' She paused and looked me over. 'Goin' t' the airport ain't you, with that bag 'n all.'

'Yes, I'm going to the airport.'

'I'm Charlene,' she said, and we smiled at each other, side by side in the silent subway station.

But then we realised there was somebody else. We heard him first, rather than saw him. He was sitting on a piss-stinking flight of steps, gorging himself with long slow chews on a slice of a pizza and drinking down a can of Pepsi, grunting occasionally before slurping down another mouthful of the drink. He was young and white, no more than twenty-five, and he looked like the actor Matt Dillon, only overweight and busted up, as if the Drugstore Cowboy had been broken in, fattened up and put out to pasture.

'Rock rock, Rockaway Beach,' he muttered low and guttural, just on the point of singing the old Ramones song. 'We can hitch a ride t' Rockaway Beach . . .'

Neither of us looked at him, but he wasn't deterred.

'Tryin' to get to the airport, huh? Jesus Christ, I know all about the trains in New York. Every fuckin' train. I'm from fuckin' Brooklyn. Why wouldn't I fuckin' know?'

He finished chewing, belched, drew himself up to his feet, and sidled down the stairs towards us.

'You gotta get the train to Far Rockaway,' he said.

'I know, thanks,' I said.

'Yeah.' He looked wearily up and down the hushed tracks. We were the only three people on the platform now. 'Y' know, my cousin got himself killed the other week. Hit by a car and a truck at the same time. Real fuckin' mess. So now I'm tryin' to get out to my aunt's place on Long Island . . . She's got a spare bed out there now, y' see . . .' He smiled at me bleakly. 'Fare's three dollars.'

His manner wasn't threatening, but he was sizeable and the situation unpredictable. I had some quarters I'd been saving for a final call from the airport to some friends upstate, but there probably wouldn't be time to call them now anyway, so I gave them to him. It was about three dollars' worth. He peered down at the silver pieces resting in his hand, then looked up and beamed like a giant child. Despite the pummelled, panel-beaten quality of his face, his dark eyes were soft, with long lashes. His lips were full, the ends tweaked with humour. His voice was low, enigmatically engaging. I thought he was probably a shy man forced by circumstance to beggary. His jumper was threadbare, and his old sheepskin-lined denim jacket smelled like boiled offal.

'Some guy just bought me the pizza,' he chuckled, tongue running round the inside of his mouth, recalling the taste. 'Just some guy up on the street. I hadn't eaten in two whole days. I'm a homeless person,' he added, the term sounding very technical and demographic.

All this time Charlene had been quiet, just watching and listening. 'Too bad, huh?' she said.

'Yeah,' he said.

The train arrived in a shriek of metal brakes and chugging of engine, and we clambered on board. The homeless man, who introduced himself as Joe, got on too and the three of us sat together in an otherwise empty car.

'So where're y' goin' tonight, from th' airport?' Charlene asked.

'Africa,' I said.

'Woa,' she said, excitedly turning to Joe. 'Say, he's goin' t' Africa! How'd you like that? Africa!' Her plump young lips curved around the word and held its shape a moment as her thoughts raced on. 'How long does it take you to get there, t' Africa?'

'Actually, I think it's only about seven hours.'

'Seven hours!!' the pair of them chorused. I couldn't work out whether they thought that a surprisingly long or short space of time to shift worlds.

'Seven hours, shit man, I can't even sit on a bus, not even jus' for a fuckin' hour,' Joe said.

Charlene had never been on an aircraft. When I mentioned I was from Australia, she thought it was in Europe. The one place she really wanted to go to was Mecca.

'My dad went down t' Washington for that, you know, Million Man March,' she said. 'Minister Farrakhand, Nation of Islam 'n all.'

'So what you think of America, and us Americans?' Joe asked me. 'Pretty fuckin' crazy . . . not such great, like, manners 'n all, uh?'

'Oh, I don't know,' I said. 'Actually, I think Americans are very polite. Unless they're actually shooting you, that is.'

He laughed and Charlene joined in. I asked Joe about his family.

'My dad's French. My mawm's dead. I'm French, Russian, Irish, bastard, every damn thing!' he laughed.

'Does your dad live in New York?'

'Uh-huh. With my step-mawm.'

'You don't live with them?'

'Naw. She hates me, see.' A cloud passed over him. 'No place to live, no job.' Then suddenly he brightened. 'Finished high school tho'. I got my fuckin' health. And I know the subway like the back of my hand.'

He showed me the back of the big white hand he knew as well as the subway, and its prominent veins and blotches did indeed have the appearance of lines and stations.

The train rattled and banged at speed through a station. 'East New York,' Joe announced. 'Now that's a *bad* stop.'

'Amen,' Charlene intoned, Gospel-style.

'And Bedford-Stuyvesant. That's another *bad* stop. Lotta bad stops on this line. Lotta bad stops.'

'Amen,' Charlene intoned again. 'Man, I just can't wait to get to Far Rockaway. My sister's place. You should see it! She's got this real pretty balcony, stickin' way out. You can see the sea from it . . .'

We were interrupted by a deep voice from behind us, very loud. 'Alright you people! This is NOT a robbery! I repeat, this is NOT a robbery!!'

I jerked around in my seat and saw a very big, bald black man in an orange parka standing powerfully erect, centrestage in the empty subway car.

'Now I could rob you all! Easy! But I won't, 'cos that's not my way! That's not what I'm doing here,' he proclaimed. 'I'm collecting money for the needy!'

I saw one of those indefinable charity-style name-tags on him, the kind worn by people who panhandled cash from subway commuters while at the same time asking the hungry to come forward for food. He delivered his spiel in a booming voice, his eyes scanning left to right as if addressing a full car, even though it was actually just the three of us there, huddled together on a single bench seat. 'If you got money, give now!' he barked. 'And if you're hungry, speak up!'

I had never heard anyone take up this offer, but to my surprise, and the black guy's, someone did – Joe.

'Hey, you got an apple, man . . . little juice maybe?' he asked. 'See, I just had pizza, but I'd really like an apple. Gotta get your fruit.'

The black guy sized him up with undisguised suspicion, hesitated, then rummaged in a filthy old crew bag and produced a sachet of cheese popcorn, the words 'Artificially Flavoured' printed in bold type on it. Joe took it without a word, ripped it open and started stuffing popcorn into his mouth. 'Man, I'm hungry,' he said.

I handed the black guy a dollar bill. He looked at it disdainfully, and at me with equal disdain, his look riding the delicate line between encouragement to donate more and robbery with menace. Then he picked up his bag and swaggered on into the next car. Through the lit-up doorway we saw him announce to the passengers in there that this was not a robbery.

Watching him, Joe shook his head and grinned. 'Man, I was scared. Real scared.'

'Me too,' I said. I had just imagined myself robbed of my French franc traveller's cheques, my US dollars in cash, and my credit card – the money for the entire African trip.

'I thought he had a gun,' Joe said.

Charlene misheard. 'You thought he had a donut?'

'No, a gun,' he grinned. Because of the thickness of his Brooklyn Irish accent, and the gun sounding like '*gon*', it might really have sounded like '*donut*'.

'He acted like he had a gun,' I said.

'Yeah, he pulled a whole lotta focus,' Joe said.

'Donut,' Charlene cackled.

The train stopped, and a neat-looking young black guy got on and sat down beside Charlene.

'Hey, Jay Jay,' she giggled to him, 'imagine, robbin' a subway train with a friggin' Dunkin Donut!'

Jay Jay laughed a pleasant, if restrained chuckle.

'Jay Jay, this guy's goin' to Africa tonight,' she announced, proudly proprietorial. 'Say, I bet you speak French,' she said. '*Bonjour, merci*, that kinda stuff?'

I said a few words and she giggled again. Joe grinned happily and Jay Jay nodded politely. Then Joe turned towards me and made significant eye contact, and I knew what was coming. The fare to his aunt's place had just risen to eight dollars.

'Okay,' I said, 'I'll give you some more before I get off the train.'

He nodded thanks. I saw crumbs of scoffed popcorn in his lap.

'Do you get cold at night?' I asked him.

'What?'

'Do you ever get cold at night, sleeping out?'

'Sure.'

I was wearing an old jumper against the cold which I wouldn't need once I got to the airport, and certainly wouldn't need in Africa. I asked Joe if he wanted it. He looked at me curiously, as if not quite taking in what I was saying.

195

'This sweater,' I repeated. 'Do you want it?'

He nodded, and I took it off, a white windcheater, and gave it to him.

He put it on. 'Charlene, Jay Jay, look!' he announced with disbelief. 'He's givin' me the shirt off his fuckin' back!'

They smiled.

'God will bless you,' Jay Jay said.

'So people keep telling me. In fact, you're the third one in twenty-four hours,' I said. 'But I'm still waiting.'

The three of them burst out laughing, and I joined in.

'You must be blessed if you can just up and fly off to Africa like this,' Jay Jay said.

'No, you're right,' I conceded. 'I am.'

The train pulled up at Howard Beach, where I was to connect with the airport shuttle bus to the terminal. I gave Joe another five dollars, said goodbye to the three of them, and got off. As I walked down the platform and the train pulled away, I saw the flash of my white windcheater on Joe, and Jay Jay leaning across saying something to Charlene, on her way to Far Rockaway.

Dez-air-tif-ication

The Air Afrique airbus banked around over a sparkling blue Atlantic, and began its approach into Dakar. I saw the profile of a modern city in concrete towers. The country around looked yellow and dry. I remembered promising Kathryn it would be green. 'She'll kill me,' I thought. 'Why can't Senegal be fucking green? It's tropical, isn't it?'

We swept in low across the khaki of Cape Vert, the most westerly point on the mainland of Africa. I saw whitewalled seafront houses with blue backyard pools, and funky sixties apartment blocks with old Peugeots mired in dust up to the axles. The plane's wheels kissed the tarmac, we bounced and jolted, the wheels touched again and we thundered down the

runway, braking for dear life. The passengers burst into spontaneous applause, and I recalled that ritual of acclamation, for the
pilot who delivers you safely out of those big blue African skies.

I found a good enough room in a good enough hotel, the Al
Baraka. I pushed the two single beds together, wondered if I
really needed to do that, switched on the TV and dozed. Given the
right circumstances, CNN can be a very restful channel, the news
equivalent of processed cheese, with an occult obsession with the
weather. A few minutes before a live cross to the signing of a
Bosnian peace accord, I was sleeping peacefully. I awoke hungry
at sunset and unearthed a pizza place in an ill-lit sidestreet.

The *al funghi* wasn't too bad as pizza goes, but as I chewed on
the carbonised crust I ruminated on something else – why had I
really wanted to go to Mali so badly? It was a fair enough question, considering that Mali is one of the remotest places on earth.
Partly the explanation resided in the photographs of Djenne and
Timbuktu I had seen in the Mali Café in Sydney many years
before. But my fascination stemmed more directly from a night
two years previously in Paris, when a friend and I attended a concert of Malian music.

We took the Metro to a seedy neighbourhood near Sacré Coeur,
and arrived at a darkened hall which bore no clue that an event was
to be staged that night. This was because many Malians were in
France illegally, and could be carted off directly from the concert
to the airport if the Fortress Europa authorities got wind of it.

The Malians pulled up in occasional beaten up little cars,
furtively looking this way and that as they stepped onto the pavement and approached the darkened front doors. But their caution
had not translated into dress. Certainly some of the men had
eschewed traditional African robes for tight, neat, sixties-style
suits that looked left over from a Godard film. But the women
were extraordinary, big women for the most part, exuding a wild
joie de vivre, a truly feline sexuality. They were swathed in volu-
minous shimmering violet, pink or amber silk, gold-embroidered,
their luxuriant black hair braided up fantastically, all resplendent
with jewellery – heavy gold bangles and arm bracelets, shining

197

metal head-bands, massive earrings and nose-rings, necklaces threaded with amber chunks the size of crab-apples.

Inside, the cavernous old theatre rang with excitement. Children – African fauntleroys in lavish miniatures of their mothers' outfits – rollicked in the aisles or sat laughing in rows at the comic turns on stage. The music was intoxicating, frenzied drumming, intricate *kora* – the twenty-one string West African instrument played like a harp, its sound truly celestial – and twanking thumb piano. A story-telling *griote*, or wise woman, and a chorus of women sang heads back, full-throated, and danced with an atavistic energy amazing to behold. It was a celebration of human sexuality, but not our own televisual sexuality, exploited, abused, spastically twisted in rock-hooker freezeframes. This spouted up through the hard bodies of the women as if they were divining rods, ran up through the taut-ness of their spines from the bare soles of their feet, from the very earth upon which those feet – even separated by the boards of a Parisian stage – danced. This was the soul of a vibrant, living cul-ture.

I read all I could about Mali after that concert. The highpoints and extravagances were remarkable. When the fourteenth century Malian Emperor Kankan Moussa made his pilgrimage to Mecca, he took an entourage of 60,000 followers, as well as 150 kilo-grams of solid gold – the generosity of his gift-giving causing chaos with the currencies of countries he visited along his route. This was also a time when one of the world's most startlingly individual architectural styles, Sudanese, which attained its finest form in the mosque of Djenne, was born. And all of it only to be shattered by Berber invasion, by European maritime trade down the African coast that out-competed the trans-Saharan caravans, by rampant slaving for the Americas that left whole regions depopulated, and by the final indignity of colonisation. This was the fatal combination of woes which had reduced Mali to the sta-tus of a 'Third World' country, one of the world's poorest. Yet once its borders had stretched as far west as the Atlantic Ocean, and its zenith had lasted nearly a millennium, from Europe's Dark Age until well beyond its Renaissance.

And now, here, a year and a half after my first abortive attempt, more than 520 days after I had stood before that sign in Zagora, Morocco, which teased '*Tombouctou 52 jours*', I finally was. Well, almost. Actually I was just in a pizza place in Dakar. But Mali beckoned strongly now. I chewed on.

The following day, the Senegalese capital revealed itself as a lively, if edgy town of narrow streets, good food, rows of souvenir shops, and an endless cavalcade of street-sellers badgering with everything from music cassettes to African rag-dolls and Christmas tinsel. Even the tea-towel sellers wouldn't leave me alone.

At the hotel bar that night I downed a quick succession of vodkas before taking a taxi out to the airport. I sat upstairs in the café, watching the white Air France 737 taxi to a halt. I strained my eyes to see if Kathryn was among the passengers coming down the stairs and onto the shuttle buses, but did not see her. Downstairs I waited amid a hot, pressing throng of relatives, taxi drivers and hotel touts that pressed ever further forward as the first passengers emerged. The flow started in fitful dribs and drabs, then a torrent came forth. I had begun to wonder just how many people could fit into a 737, when, in pale blue denim jacket with bag slung over her shoulder, she emerged. It struck me I was forever meeting her in faraway airports.

'Kathryn!' I called out. 'You did come!'

'Of course I did,' she said. 'You didn't really think I wouldn't, did you?'

We dropped her things off and took our taxi on to Pompidou Avenue, to the Ponty Bar, the best known nightspot in Dakar. The pavement outside was crowded with hawkers, spruikers, beggars and pickpockets. Little yellow taxis honked and shunted by in the dusty amber streetlight. Inside, sullen prostitutes sat scattered in

199

ones and twos at tables. Open doors revealed red lights down long corridors.

We shared a pichet of wine at a table, then moved on to the adjoining cabaret room where Mr Sam, a burly man sweating in an African shirt, fronted his hi-life band. He danced over to us, pausing between sung lines to ask our names and then insert them into his song:

> *Monsieur Larry, il aime sa chère Kath-a-ryn,*
> *Mais Kath-a-ryn, elle aime seulement Mr Sam!*
>
> ('Larry loves his dear Kathryn
> But Kathryn only loves Mr Sam!')

In between verses he flung his arms around the pair of us and laughed while Abadou, his diminutive saxophone player, jived around blasting out a solo.

We found ourselves dancing with two girls from Mali, pretty teenagers who had picked up their mark for the night, a tubby, pink, grey-haired Englishman attending a conference at one of the big hotels down on the foreshore. Before long the five of us were sharing more pichets of wine. Then we jammed into a taxi, the girls giggling all the way, and found ourselves in an absurdly expensive steel and chromium disco, where French businessmen shed their jackets and ties for their karaoke *My Way*.

The taller of the girls, Rose, wore batwing spectacles and a long, body-hugging green crêpe dress that clung tightly to her magnificently muscular buttocks. She was instantly, magnetically attracted to Kathryn, and spent the next hour or so out on the dance-floor pumping and gyrating outrageously with her. The music was drekky Madonna and Michael Jackson – the kind one could only ever abide with a belly full of wine in a far-off land, but Rose was effervescent, charismatic, wildly sexy, and Kathryn gave back as good as she got. All the while the Englishman sagged into a sofa watching, drinking, saying nothing to Rose's friend, Oumou.

'Where are you from in England?' I asked him when I took a break from the dance-floor.

'Bluckpool,' he muttered. He felt compulsively for his wallet, hiccupped loudly, and followed it up with a lion-sized yawn. I wondered whether the Malian girls might fall below their projected income tonight if Rose stayed out on the floor much longer.

'What's your conference about?' I asked.

'Desertification,' he replied, dragging the word out glumly. 'Dez-air-tif-ication of the fookin' desert. Then, you'd know all about that, Mr Crocodile Fookin' Dundee,' he said, with a nasty little growl.

We had consumed quite an amount of very expensive alcohol by now, and would have to pay dearly. I presumed the Englishman would be paying for the two girls' drinks, but he seemed utterly uninterested in the bill when it came. His little eyes went back towards the floor. Finally Rose noticed him, and she came over, sweating, arm slung around Kathryn's waist. The Englishman got up abruptly, dragging Oumou to her feet. 'That's it for me for tonight,' he announced, dropping a few thousand CFA (Central African franc, the currency of many of the former French possessions in Africa) onto the table – a fraction of the bill. 'Enough?' he enquired tartly of us. But Rose grinned and whispered something in his ear, and he irritably dragged a few more notes from his wallet before walking off with Oumou. Rose gestured to her to wait outside, and lingered a moment with us. As the Englishman went out the door we both pleaded with her to make sure she was 'careful' – then, baldly, to use condoms.

'*Bien sur,*' she laughed happily, '*toujours, toujours . . . A demain, j'espère!*' ('Of course, always . . . See you tomorrow I hope!') She kissed us both on the cheek, and with a final look back disappeared into the smoke of the disco.

Two more beers appeared at the table just then, so we relaxed and drank them and watched a group of terminally pissed French and Senegalese combine in a karaoke cats chorus of *We are the World*. It felt deliciously strange to be alone together after our months apart and all that had happened. New York had been a rush of half-formed moments, but this was to be an entire month, for better or worse.

We stayed on and drank more wine, ever cheaper wine, wine that eats holes in old shoes, and left the bar arms around each other like a pair of bare-knuckle fighters. We finally slept as dawn came, only to be awakened at 8.30 by the rude jangle of the bedside telephone. I thought it might be Rose calling for Kathryn, but it was the taxi driver from the night before. Kathryn had left her denim jacket in the back seat.

I shambled downstairs into the foyer in my hangover and unlaced sandshoes, accepted the jacket, thanked the driver and paid him a reward. He smiled, bowed and went.

'Senegal very honest country,' the desk clerk muttered disdainfully behind me as I wandered back upstairs.

We lunched, badly, at the Café de Paris: watery *soupe de légumes*, packet Continental. The old Frenchwoman who ran the place sat at a long rustic table behind bowls of heaped limes, scowling into her account book. There were faded paintings of the Seine, the Eiffel Tower, the Arc de Triomphe on the walls. A popular singer rasped away in full tar Gauloise on the stereo. Street-sellers continually materialised in the entranceway hustling *Paris Match* and the *Herald Tribune*, and were chased off by the snarls of the Frenchwoman's six-pack of revolting poodles.

Over coffee, we drafted the plans for our trip. I had already booked two onward tickets to Bamako, the capital of Mali. Kathryn suggested we apply for our Malian visas straight away, in case the fullness of her passport delayed things.

We walked down Rue Mohammed the Fifth, dodging little Renault taxis in the narrow streets of central Dakar, to the Boulevard de la Republique, and the Malian Embassy opposite the Cathedral. The visa section occupied a corridor in the rear of the building. We found two women on duty, both of them in brightly coloured African robes. The elder had lowered her forehead onto her desktop, and appeared to be asleep. The younger one, the whites of her eyes wild and flashing, looked up with a taut half-smile as we entered. I had already heard about this woman: she was said to be 'difficult'. My French suddenly far less than fluent, I explained that we wished to apply for Malian tourist visas.

'*Mardi*,' she said, the single word hard and clipped. I looked uncertainly at Kathryn, then asked the woman whether she meant we had to wait five days until Tuesday to lodge our applications.

'Passport!' she commanded.

'Pardon?'

'Your passport, your passport. What is your passport?'

'Oh, Australian.'

She scowled, and released a very French 'pfff' from her lips. Then she laughed with a disconcerting abruptness while relating something in what I took to be a Malian language to her co-worker, who dozed on, forehead on desk.

I repeated the question. 'Well, may we make our application?'

She looked up at me contemptuously. 'Why not?'

'Today?'

At this she opened her mouth very wide and released a prodigiously bored yawn, before lowering her forehead to her desk like her friend, and appeared ready to sleep.

We looked at each other, amazed. Then Kathryn spoke up. 'It's just that I have a . . . little problem with my passport . . . which we need to discuss with you.' The woman did not look up. 'You see, I am running out of space, and I need to know how big your visa will be.'

'Big,' the woman muttered, head on desk.

Kathryn got out her passport, and placed it on the desk before her. She looked up, yawned again, then flicked through the book-let with long, disdainful fingers.

'Not possible,' she said.

'Pardon?' My stomach did a quick churn.

She tossed Kathryn's passport back. 'It is full. A visa is not possible. You must get a new passport.'

'But that is not possible here. There is no Australian embassy or consulate in Dakar.'

'That is not my problem.'

'And there *is* room,' Kathryn insisted. 'Look, see, there's a half-page here, two thirds here . . .'

'You must have a *full* page,' the woman declared flatly.

'But look, see, this page has got just one tiny stamp on it,' I tried.

'It is not possible.'

Kathryn and I looked at each other despairingly, and back at her, but she just yawned and lowered her head to the desk again.

I peered around the office, at the yellowed tourist posters on the wall, the dusty old typewriters. It all felt desolate and hopeless.

'Any ideas?' I asked Kathryn.

Just then the woman got up decisively and strode out of the room without a word. I thought she might have gone out to lunch, but she returned moments later with a polite, very correct-looking young man, cool in a grey woollen suit. He flicked through Kathryn's passport.

'No, it is not possible,' he confirmed.

'You see?' the woman said to us.

'But . . . but Mali was the entire reason for us coming to Africa.'

'Sorry,' the young man said.

'Perhaps we can pay a little more, a *supplémentaire* . . .' I tried.

'Not possible.'

'Quite a large *supplémentaire*.'

'Not possible,' he repeated. He glanced at his watch and turned to go. We looked at each other: sunk. But then Kathryn, seized with a renewed resolve, bent far forward over the desk, close to the woman's face.

'*S'il . . . vous . . . plaît, madame,*' she said, very slowly and determinedly. 'There is no reason why I cannot have my visa. And I simply must, must have that visa.'

The woman stared back up sternly, and I feared for a moment Kathryn had gone too far. But to my astonishment a big smile swept across her face, she trilled with a girlish laugh and batted her eyelids coquettishly at Kathryn. She turned to the young man and said something in Malian to him, and he looked across at Kathryn quite shyly, said something in reply, and they laughed together.

'Let me see your passport again,' the woman said with a click of her fingers, and flicked through it until she reached the space Kathryn had mentioned earlier.

'*Ici,*' she indicated to the young man. He studied the space intently, then slowly nodded to her, and she nodded to us.

'You mean, it's possible . . .' I said breathlessly, almost unable to believe the alacrity of the transformation.

The woman fluttered her eyelids at Kathryn again, and replied to her, not me. 'Of course.'

The young man opened a desk drawer and took out a stamp and pad. As we held our breath, he manoeuvred the stamp over the page, stopped, tried a different angle, hesitated a moment, then finally brought the stamp down hard onto the page. We actually applauded the inked image.

'Oh thank you, thank you very much,' Kathryn said.

'*Du rien,*' ('Forget it') the woman said, with a toss of her head. She laughed, and embraced Kathryn. '*Du rien.*'

My passport was also stamped, and with warm farewells we made our way back out towards the street.

'What is it with these Malian women and you?' I asked.

A few moments later we encountered Rose, with the man from Bluckpool. She rushed up to Kathryn and kissed her on each cheek.

'Until tonight,' she breathed, 'at the Ponty Bar.' She slipped her hand through the man's arm, and they walked on. We watched them go.

'Mali should be interesting,' Kathryn said.

Pathetic White Bastards

We decided to visit the old French capital of Saint-Louis up near the Mauritanian border during the few days before our flight to Bamako. We boarded a toy-sized train at Dakar Station and found seats in the front carriage, which was fitted with a pleasantly shabby bar selling coffee, Coca-Cola and Sprite. (No alcohol.) The train ventured out through sprawling suburbs, then picked up speed north through a long khaki dust-plain of baobab trees, bare limbs thrust mournfully skyward. The track was a very narrow gauge and the ride decidedly bumpy, the little train lurching violently from side to side as it hit the joins between rails, constantly seeming on the point of derailment. To make matters worse, the carriage filled up at each stop, the air warmed uncomfortably and leg-room gained a premium.

We talked away the afternoon with the other passengers, most of them Senegalese business people. As night fell I drifted in and out of a light doze, and woke mildly irritable in the hot and stuffy carriage as we neared Saint-Louis. When Kathryn happened to mention something about a bar she had gone to in Athens, I felt a nasty current surge through me.

'You haven't stopped talking about Athens since you left it,' I said.

'What?'

'I'm surprised you're even here. You love him, don't you?' I suddenly snapped.

She looked out the window where the white skeletons of baobabs floated by in the darkness. 'No, I don't love him.' Then she smiled. 'I wouldn't mind having a bit more sex with him sometime, but I don't love him.'

Again the neatness of the reversal astounded me. Now it was her pining after the great sex had with the other, and me raising the 'but what about us?'

'Are you still going on to India after this?' I asked.

'Just for a while. Then I'm coming back to Sydney.'

'Is he going to India too?'

She hesitated. 'I did actually mention to him that we might link up for a little while at the end of my trip . . .'

'I see.'

'It was just a passing comment. He won't come. He's got too many commitments in Athens.'

'But you want him to come, don't you.'

'I wouldn't mind it,' she said. 'As a friend.'

'A friend you fuck.'

'Shhhh, you'll wake people up!'

I glanced around at our sleeping fellow passengers, wondering if any of them spoke English and what they'd make of all this if they did.

Sorry,' I said. 'It's just, you have to realise that if you keep seeing him, you'll just get more involved. And if you do, I'll have to reconsider my own position.'

The train hit a huge bump, and the woman opposite me, with whom I had been carefully negotiating foot-space in the demilitarised zone between us, blinked awake and looked up blearily before drifting back to sleep.

'I know that,' Kathryn said quietly.

'So are you going to meet him in India?'

'Actually, I'd prefer to travel by myself.'

'But are you?'

'He won't come.'

'But are you?' I hissed. 'Come on, tell me.'

She looked away. 'I don't know.'

And so there they were, my own words, my own convenient opt-out, served up back to me.

We lapsed into silence as the train found a footing on the first of the long, steel-framed bridges that cross the Senegal River out to the Isle Saint-Louis. I stood up and looked out the window as the train crawled across the black river. In the still and heavy air I heard the tranquil aria of swarming insects. The ambient light disclosed the white contours of fish, rising to feed.

We took a room at the Hotel de la Poste, a French colonial place where early aviators stopped over on the southern mail route from Paris, before continuing on the long and perilous final leg across the Atlantic to South America. The Isle is the centre of the old capital, with more recent settlements on either bank, the most distant of these being the Langue Barbarie, the sandy spit fronting the Atlantic.

On our first afternoon in town, we crossed the pungent Senegal River to the Langue Barbarie, and the sea. The landscape transformed instantly as we crossed, from rundown French colonial to a squalid shanty town, broken streets and pavements caked in filth, the stench of gutted fish and open sewers inescapable, the people in the thrall of a desperate poverty.

We continued on to the seafront where we found, tightly packed together for a kilometre or so along the Atlantic shore, a vast armada of fishing pirogues, long and sleek, hauled up onto the sand. Beyond the breakers we saw an equally large fleet at work fishing. We were instantly surrounded by a cheering throng of infants in rags, begging for '*un Bic*' and '*cent francs*' (the equivalent of one French franc, approximately twenty-five Australian cents). Some were quite aggressive, grabbing for our bags. Others splashed us with seawater and ran off shrieking. One older boy approached us wildly swinging a stick of driftwood.

We walked on through this hand-made flotilla, past circles of African women gutting piles of rays, the lewd pink intestines dumped in mounds on the stained sand, piebald goats gorging on the offal. The wind was cool and stiff but the air remained heavy with the stink of rotten fish and shit. We saw people squatting on the sand all around us, and the excrement they walked away from, making no attempt to bury or cover it. I tripped on the severed head of a grey hammerhead, and looking down more carefully after that, realised the beach was no longer truly sand, but a collage of bones and scales, shells and fishing line and hooks, shards of broken glass, fish gut and faeces.

We passed a drab grey concrete mosque and cemetery, each gravesite marked by a stake and the dead fisher's net cast over it. At last we cleared the line of boats, the crowds thinned and the beach whitened beneath our feet, and we sat in the dunes out of the wind. Returning near sunset, we found the beach wild with hundreds of teenage boys, some hauling up the returning pirogues and casting their catch writhing onto the sand, others playing soccer with small rubber balls, shouting at us with gleeful pugnacity as we passed. One boy executed a strange shaking dance in front of Kathryn. When she stopped to watch a moment, he asked courteously if he could touch her breast. When she said *'non'* and we walked on, he pursued with demented cries of *'arrête, arrête!'* ('stop, stop!')

The bedside telephone rang before dawn. We had signed on to visit the Djoudj National Bird Sanctuary, sixty or so kilometres northeast of Saint-Louis on the Senegal River delta, reputedly one of the most important sanctuaries in the world for stork and flamingo. We dressed, grabbed a coffee downstairs, and emerging outside found a big four-wheel drive truck idling and people huddled on bench seats in the back beneath a canvas awning, waiting for us. We chugged off over the bridge to the mainland in the chilly morning air, and through the sleeping town. A few kilometres out of Saint-Louis the roads worsened, and soon we were being thoroughly bumped into our fellows – two salt 'n pepper crewcut couples of gay Frenchmen in plastic sandals, an inanimate foursome family of Rolexed Singaporeans, and three thirty-something serious young men, Euro-economists on time out from a conference in Dakar.

As the sun strengthened we passed tiny villages of concrete walls and thatched roofs, adolescent barefoot goatherds and lone donkeys braying. The landscape changed swiftly, one moment all bare sparseness and dust, then baked red mud and spinifex, then finally the tendril waterways of the Senegal River delta, luxuriant with grasses, towering reeds and lilies.

We halted at a dock where a motorised pirogue awaited, and for the next couple of hours drifted through a wild waterworld of white egrets and black African cormorants, storks newly arrived from the European winter, and a profusion of pelicans flying in long, lethargic lines to the horizon.

We continued up the delta, and entered a dense carpet of what looked like floating cabbages, through which the pirogue forced a path like an icebreaker. The air was alive with dragonflies and ladybirds, and tiger fish leapt into our boat. The trip reached its climax on the crest of a remote island in the river, from which we observed acres of the nests of pelicans and cormorants convened in their calm multitudes, an avian kingdom from prehistory, somehow still extant in the late twentieth century. But it felt so precarious, threatened.

We both felt out of sorts on our return. We found ourselves arguing about nothing in particular over lunch, and kicked around the listless streets of Saint-Louis for the rest of the day. We drank heavily at dinner.

'We're becoming a pair of alcoholics,' Kathryn said. 'Pathetic white bastards in Africa.'

'Bullshit. We're just drinking with dinner.'

I ordered another bottle.

That night was hot in our little room. The window was open to the river but the stilled air was heavy and sultry, and we lay sleepless side by side.

The Red Tricycle

I was robbed the day we returned to Dakar. We were crossing the Place d'Independence, a wide and desolate square of battered colonnades with a glaring white gravel park and dried-up fountain at its centre, when we were approached by two young men hawking the kind of brass and copper bracelets sold in public spaces the world over. When we responded with '*non merci*', they pursued us between a pair of parked cars, jostling us as we walked. It was only when we sat down for lunch and I felt for the prescription spectacles in my day pack that I realised the rear zippered compartment was open, and my glasses were gone. As acts of theft go, it was very petty, and utterly futile. Fitted with lenses crucial to me but useless to anyone else, the only thing the thieves could do was smash out the glass and sell the frames. But it left me with just my sunglasses with my day prescription, and my reading glasses, which were useless beyond two or three metres. Worse still, I realised that to claim on my travel insurance I would have to report the incident to the police, and theirs is a rock beneath which one does not readily place one's hand.

Police headquarters was a grubby yellow colonial building in a street near the Place. Entering, we were challenged by a tall man in a Chicago Bulls T-shirt, New York baseball cap, tight blue Levis and white Reeboks. It turned out that he was a senior detective. I explained my problem, and he directed us towards an office upstairs. 'After that you will come back to my office,' he directed, 'and give me telephone numbers for girls in Australia.'

The main detective office was crowded and chaotic. Ten teenage boys stood handcuffed together before a table covered with official papers, a heavy black baton as a paperweight. An ample, surly man sat behind the desk, barking orders into a black bakelite telephone. The boys were clearly afraid of him, and cowered in a corner while other detectives, also à la Miami Vice in jeans, baseball caps and Reeboks, swaggered about joking and laughing. About a dozen car tyres were piled incongruously in a corner: I deduced the teenagers were accused of stealing them.

We were told to sit down while the senior officer conducted a quick, irritable interrogation of the boys. Their only response was to hang their heads and not dare look up. When his humourless eyes jerked my way, I tried to outline the theft as briefly as I could, but found myself in difficulty as his questions came rapid-fire in heavily-accented French. All the while the boys shifted about uncomfortably in a clanking of chains. This only heightened the bristling irritation of the big man. After barely a minute listening to me, he wiped his brow, picked up his telephone and started shouting down it. To complicate matters further, three young blond dreadlocked Germans walked in just then, declaring they had been robbed of everything – money, passports, traveller's cheques – at machete-point by a gang down on the seafront. The policeman sighed testily, looked at me and the boys in chains, sighed again and said something to one of his junior detectives, who conducted us out into another office.

Here a young man in a short-sleeved business shirt worked with enormous concentration on an old Facit typewriter. He was typing an account being dictated by a woman in a matronly dress and Muslim headscarf of the theft of her handbag. It too had been snatched out in the Place, the equivalent of US$100 taken – an enormous sum for the average Senegalese. The clerk laboured on conscientiously, stopping every now and then with a pained mutter to white out a typographical error. All the while the woman struggled to maintain her composure, the occasional tear escaping nonetheless.

'*Excusez-moi,*' I said. The clerk looked up and nodded curtly towards a spare seat. I suggested to Kathryn that she go back to the hotel on the off chance the glasses had been handed in there, while I waited here to give my details. One of the denim detectives watched her go, all the way down the corridor. Then he twirled his baton in the air, and thwacked it hard into his palm before opening a door and disappearing into a side-room. It appeared he was about to question the ten boys further.

The reading glasses I now wore gave proximate things a bizarre, microscopically detailed quality, while everything else faded into a background blur. While the woman continued with her account, I peered through bug eyes around the room, at a pair of desks where older men sat. One of them was reading the Koran, mouthing the words. When he finished, he opened a desk drawer, put the book away and took out a disposable razor which he dragged across his face in short, rapid strokes. This completed, he picked up the big office blotter from his desk, flexed it into a funnel, and deposited his shavings in a fine soot-like deposit beneath his desk. Then he lowered his head to his desktop and instantly fell asleep, snoring gently.

The man at the other desk sat engrossed in a French paperback novel, oblivious to the angry shouts which now could be clearly heard coming from the adjoining interrogation room. Heavy fist-slapping sounds and pained cries followed.

A trim, neat man in an olive-green safari suit and black suede Hush Puppies wandered in and glanced bored around the office. He had one hand behind his back, the other held a cigarette in a studied pose. Seeing the sleeping man, he complained queru-lously to the one reading the French novel, who seemed to ignore him. The Hush Puppy man drifted on then, trailing a white wisp of cigarette smoke.

The moment he had gone, the reader urgently woke the sleeper, and the pair of them quit the room and returned with a pair of beaten-up Facit typewriters. It was then I realised that they, like the young man still labouring over the woman's account in his typewriter carriage, were clerks – only they, perhaps because of seniority, had not until this moment needed to work. Now they rummaged lickety-split in a rusted filing cabinet for paper and carbons, then sat down at their machines, ready to re-type piles of handwritten reports. But they had not got in a single keystroke before two officers in uniform khaki marched in and commandeered both machines and left without a word of expla-nation. The response of the two clerks to this turn of events was for the sleepy one to go back to sleep and the reader to his French novel. It was bureaucracy at its finest.

So engrossed had I become in all these reading-lensed minutiae, that it came as a surprise that I had lost contact with my left leg. As I stamped around to restore circulation, the young clerk peered up apologetically from his page and promised he would be onto my case 'within minutes'. I decided to stretch out my legs with a stroll.

Out in the corridor, straining my eyes, I could just make out a watchhouse of dark cells below. The barred windows were tiny, and I imagined what it must be like for the men huddled down in there, with the rats and roaches. Then my eye was drawn to something on the prison roof, a soft blur of red. Removing my reading glasses and squinting, I could just make out a red child's tricycle up there, broken, lying on its side, wheels gone. How had it gotten there, I wondered? To whom had it belonged? Had someone tossed it up there in a fit of rage? But my thoughts were interrupted by more shouts, frightened cries, thumps and groans, and I realised I was standing right outside the room where the interrogation was proceeding. The door opened and one of the young cops swaggered down the corridor. Not long after, the ten teenage boys emerged, heads down, shackled together two-by-two, a uniformed cop prodding them on with his nightstick. The boys went downstairs, and disappeared into the cells beneath the broken red tricycle.

Then, astoundingly, the young clerk was standing before me, saying it was time for me to come and detail the account of the crime to which I had been victim.

I found myself mildly depressed on the way back to the hotel. The late afternoon streets felt fervid and dirty. I passed a bar and saw half a dozen drunks lined up on stools, then a row of lepers in the dust no longer even bothering to beg. A trio of teenage prostitutes flounced by, heads back laughing in their bright, tight tube dresses and heels.

I saw the Al Baraka up ahead, but didn't feel ready to go in right away. Instead I stepped into a streetside place and ordered a coffee. It came quickly, steaming in a stainless steel cup. As I watched the condensed milk swirl in with the motion of my spoon, I wondered if Kathryn and I would ever, ever be content. Sex, love, being together – the key to it seemed to be in some alchemical equation to which human beings are not privy, to the whimsy of molecules which may bond this time, but next time, despite heating and reagents and all the right conditions, will do nothing but spin off past each other. Was that, finally, what was going to happen to us? Were we to spin off after our few years of shared orbit? Is that all there is – a space–time continuum, a mish-mash of matter and anti-matter? Or was all this rationalising bullshit, and our only problem that I was suffering from that most venal, most stupid, most utterly human of failings, jealousy?

I drank my coffee and ordered a second. The Al Baraka Hotel sign blinked on. High overhead, thousands of wedgetail eagles were adrift in their daily lazy circling of the dusky Dakar skies. Evening impended. I left my money on the table, got up and walked towards the hotel.

We drank a good deal at dinner that night. We made love and then we talked and then argued. The quarrel heated up, red into white. Finally it plunged into something deadly cold.

'It's over,' Kathryn said. 'We just have to face it, it's over. It really is.'

The next day we flew to Mali.

A Wonderful Couple

8.15 a.m. Awake in Room 232, Le Grand Hotel de Bamako. Fresh lime and mineral water. Shower. Dress.

10.00 a.m. Leave hotel, walk to main street of town, Rue du Fleuve and the Grande Marché.

10.15 a.m. Three young touts attach themselves to us, and are not easily shaken. However they do assist in discovery of optician. New spectacles are ordered.

10.50 a.m. Purchase a large papaya, five mangos and seven bananas from a fruit vendor in the market.

11.00 a.m. Guides direct us to the Salon du Thé La Phoenicia, on Rue Gouraud. Breakfast on fruit, baguette and jam, coffee.

11.45 a.m. Taxi back to the hotel, deposit remaining fruit in mini-bar fridge.

1.00 p.m. Take taxi to Air Afrique to reconfirm return reservation to Dakar for following month.

1.20 p.m. Take taxi on to see Grand Mosque. Find barbers' market. Request to photograph a barber giving a young man a sharp 'Boeing 707' cut. The barber agrees, but we are driven off by a seemingly crazed old man with a stick.

2.00 p.m. Visit National Museum. Unfortunately, permanent collection is closed.

3.00 p.m. Walk from Museum back to hotel. Rest.

4.00 p.m. Taxi to Le Salon du Thé La Phoenicia for lunch. Riz Cantonese, Vegetarian Pizza à la Reine, haricot beans, red wine, mineral water, coffee.

5.00 p.m. Walk through the Grande Marché once more. Almost buy mosquito net. Pick up new spectacles. Look like newsreader on public access TV.

5.30 p.m. Taxi back to hotel.

5.45 p.m. Frisbee by hotel pool. Swim. Shower.

6.30 p.m. Sunset gin and tonics on the terrace at invitation of hotel management, to mark presentation of the hotel's 'Employee Of The Month' award.

7.00 p.m. Return to room. Watch CNN. Doze.

8.30 p.m. Taxi to Bar Bozo, reputedly a good place to hear Malian music live.

12.30 a.m. Taxi back to hotel. Sleep.

A cosily dating couple drank beers at a plastic table outside Bar Bozo. Beside them, a line of women sold oily-looking cooked catfish from large tin bowls. The street was dimly lit and quiet, the passing trade minimal beyond the rattle of an unlit bicycle or trundle of a car, halogen headlights like sulphurous flares in the fine suspension of desert dust.

Inside Bar Bozo – the name from one of the ethnic populations of Mali, the river-dwelling Bozo fisherpeople – was small and very dark, so dark in fact that the woman behind the bar counted out change by torchlight. We found half a dozen tables where a few patrons chatted quietly over beers, a tiny stage with a cracked glass fish-tank behind it, and glimpsed a rose-lit side room where prostitutes lounged. A big poster of Martin Luther King commanded one wall, captioned 'I Have A Dream'.

We drank beers while the band – we learned it was to be a band tonight, sadly not Malian music – tuned up and sound-checked, '*un-deux, un-deux*'. When ten o'clock came and went with no action, we wandered out for a stroll, and took a quiet dirt side-street past rows of red earth houses where people sat out front together talking in low voices, or listened to cassettes of *kora* music. There were no streetlights, merely the flicker of candles in open doorways, and the moon which marbled the undersides of tall wavy clouds. The feeling, in this capital of one of the world's poorest nations, was of a deep and abiding peace, however snap a judgement that might be: here one experienced arrival into a harmonious world. People occasionally greeted us with a '*bonsoir*', but no one badgered, no one begged. Babies laughed, waving stubby fingers. Dogs sniffed and slept. A group of teenagers playing a battered old arcade soccer game on a dark street asked us to join in, 'Mali against Australia', and defeated us with a politely smiling effortlessness.

We returned to Bar Bozo, but there was still no action on stage. We had a last drink, and were paying at the bar when a woman loomed up in the murky light and asked us to stay a while. She was in her thirties, in a smoothly flowing, iridescent green African dress. Her smile gleamed white in the darkness, her eyes were intelligent and lively. She introduced herself as Issiya.

'Please,' she said, 'have another drink, and let us talk.'

We took a pavement table and drank more beers under the stars in the clean dry Bamako night. The band finally came on. They were good, strong and passionate, the tight reggae formations punctuated here and there with anti-racist diatribes in proximate

English, but amplified to near distortion so that outside was the best place to hear them.

Issiya said she was a Malian princess, related to the royal family of the famed albino singer Salif Keita, but that now she lived down in Abidjan because Côte d'Ivoire was more modern and socially progressive. She reached across the table and clutched Kathryn's hand as she denounced the barbaric practice of female circumcision in Mali, and declared her defiance of Islam.

'I will never marry,' she declared with bitterness, 'because in Mali the man can take two, three, four wives – so there is no real love.' She looked away, shaking. Then she turned back, shrugged and smiled. When we finally got up to leave, Issiya kissed us both warmly on the cheek. 'You two . . . such a wonderful couple,' she said.

It was only in the taxi back to the hotel, picking over the events of our first crowded day in Mali, that we realised that Issiya too was probably a prostitute. The thought was saddening, and we sat in silence after that as the taxi slipped through the midnight cool.

Bambara Blues

We boarded a bus for the overnight trip northeast, the road following the Niger River up to Mopti, which was to be our base for reaching the most famous places in Mali – Djenne, the Dogon Country, Timbuktu. As overnight bus-rides go, it wasn't too bad. The bus was modern and verged on comfortable, the ride smooth enough. After a number of delays – upon departure we drove straight to a petrol station where we waited half an hour while they filled the bus up – we finally cleared the outer suburbs as the sun sank low in the sky. We soon found ourselves in a pale orange, dusty landscape jutted through with rocky ridges and occasional stands of eucalypt, much like South Australia.

The bus was nearly full. The only other Europeans were a silent German couple, a rather unhappy-looking woman in a white cotton shift dress, and a skinny, balding man in jeans. They were travelling with a Malian guide who introduced himself across the aisle as Omar. The Germans fell asleep almost immediately we left Bamako, and Omar leant over and informed me with a wink that the woman was seeing a musician friend of his who lived in Mopti, and that her man didn't know.

'He think he's back going there for the sights,' Omar whispered cheekily. 'She know better.'

Just as the headlights began to bore into the solidifying darkness, we pulled up abruptly. The men on board silently filed out onto the rocky ground to pray, the Islamic sunset observance. I noticed two or three men, Christians or animists perhaps, did not join the others. We got off too, and walked up the road. From where I stood I could see the men kneeling bent over on their prayer mats, facing Mecca from beside this bus out in the Sahel. I wondered how many other buses were halted at this moment, all across Africa, across the entire Islamic world.

Kathryn came up and we watched the men together. Then the horn sounded, and we walked back along the asphalt road as the men dusted off and folded their prayer rugs, and began to board. I realised that not a single vehicle had come by in the fifteen minutes we had been stopped, and this was a major highway.

'Roads are quiet in Mali,' I said.

'And the drivers don't drink. So we might live to tell the tale yet,' Kathryn said.

Security was tight on the roads. Insurgency had been a problem in Mali for years, particularly up in Timbuktu where the Tuaregs were active. White forty-four gallon drums blocked the road at regular checkpoints where uniformed shadows milled around campfires. At each stop the driver trooped off with his papers and came back with a lightened wallet.

After four hours we reached Segou, a river town of fine colonial and Sudanese architecture. The bus pulled up outside a hole-in-the-wall café where we were dispensed fleshy white Niger catfish and boiled rice in plastic bowls. The only beer was religiously de-alcoholised.

When we resumed, Kathryn and I took sleeping pills for the long haul through the night, and started to doze as the bus nosed ever deeper into the flat horizon of the Sahel. It was a magical night, all softness of air and starry skies. The bus driver played Malian music, very loud, starting off with Salif Keita's *Africa*, a national anthem of sorts, which got everyone jiving in their seats. Then came more Salif Keita, Ali Farka Touré, Ina Baba Coulibaly, Lobi's *Bambara Blues*, *kora*, guitar, thumb piano, drum . . . a music 'classical' yet popular, drawing one into its sweet and sublime complexities. Here were the roots of the blues, the roots in fact of virtually all popular twentieth century music from jazz to rock 'n roll, soul, reggae, rap . . . the astonishing creative energy of Africa unleashed in the Americas. What, I wondered, was twentieth century musical innovation without Africa: Stockhausen? Boulez? Cage? Glass? But not a great deal to dance to, drink to, make love to. And what was twentieth century art without Cubism – and where had that come from, but Africa? And language. Groovy. Hip. Uptight. Chill. And, yes, 'cool' – an entire vocabulary that has transformed modern English . . . And Africans among the foremost ranks of contemporary writers . . . Achebe, Okri, Ngugi, Walker . . . Curious, I thought, this has been very much an African century, only no one seems to realise it – certainly not the international media, which only takes an interest in coups, wars, starvation, murder and dictators. Yet Africa is *funky* – funky to its truck-tread sandals.

After a couple of hours we realised the music would play all through the night, but it was so subtle, delicate, the rhythms so satisfying to the ear, that the prospect was not unpleasant, even on a couple of sleeping pills. We stopped resisting, trying to sleep, and as we lightly dozed the music permeated us, transported us, worked a gentle spell so that we drifted far out over the desert, with all the bumps and stops and hot airless irritation soothed away.

Towards the end of the journey we crossed a long viaduct, with fields of young rice waving in the river overflow on either side of us. The bus slowed repeatedly while barefoot teenage cowboys in ragged shirts herded their mobs of cattle out of harm's way. It was still night when we pulled up at the waterfront of a soundly sleeping Mopti. The music was switched off at last, and most passengers slept. Omar told us the bus would not be unloaded until dawn, still two or three hours away. As we got down to stretch our legs, he told us he knew a place where we could sleep, and took us into a café on the river bank where we shared a concrete floor with the German couple, who snored stentorianly, and with Omar. We awoke with the sunrise, retrieved our bags and moved into the nearby Campement Hotel. Our room smelt of urine long-trapped in a drain, but the bed had a mosquito net, so we took it. We dozed until midday, when we rose to deal with the formality of registering our presence here with the police.

Percy in Djenne

Mopti is a busy little port at the junction of the Niger and Bani rivers. It is sometimes called the 'Venice of West Africa' for the delta formed where these two powerful rivers meet, and for the town's fleet of arched and pointed, black-hulled pirogues, which do resemble Venetian gondolas down to the poling boatman. The bigger pirogues, powered by truck engines, carry up to thirty passengers and a considerable tonnage of freight. They transport rice and maize downriver to Timbuktu, and return laden with the tombstone-shaped slabs of salt mined in the remote Sahara. The port is alive with people selling everything from bottled water and foodstuffs to Kleenex and aspirin, for the three-day journey to Timbuktu. There are dozens of vendors hawking black, dried fish piled up in pyramids on tarpaulins in the dust, the pungent smell permeating the entire port. Men strip down boat engines in the sun on the river bank while goats graze meditatively on banana peels and cigarette packets.

The Campement is the only hotel right in town, and each day a jostle of touts, carvers, souvenir shopkeepers and would-be guides hung around outside. Upon our venturing outside the gates, we found ourselves hotly pursued. Inevitably, one of these young men feigned anger at our refusal of his services, and we allowed the least pushy of them to walk with us – we knew the game by now. His name was Moussa, and over the course of days this quiet, measured young man installed himself as our 'official' guide.

On our first afternoon, we hired a small pirogue and visited Kakalodaga, a Bozo settlement on the far side of the river, where people live a traditional village life. The tiny earth-floored houses were built of hand-moulded *banco* (a mixture of clay and straw, bonded together with pebbles and shells) with millet stalk roofs. As we made our way between houses, communal courtyards opened before us where fish were being smoked in earth ovens, and two or three women pounded millet into flour in time together, clapping their hands between strokes as they let the wooden pounder fly high into the air, then catching it again and slamming it down into the grain with their next stroke. Here again was that African beat – perhaps, even, a source of it – in the very rhythm of village life. We passed men mending fishing nets, and babies lolling luxuriantly on straw mats while their siblings sucked at the teat of women rolling millet into balls for hotcakes. The coals of evening cooking fires glowed orange in each mud hearth. A teenage girl flourished her breasts at us and laughed with a long, pink tongue: 'Photo, one photo!'

After dinner back in Mopti, we strolled down the aisle of mango trees that line the river dyke out to the old Komoguel quarter of town. The air was balmy, the way tranquil. People drifted by, chatting in twos and threes. Night draws down a silken veil over Africa, vacuum-cleans dirty streets, smooths off the scarred façades of buildings, soothes tempers, cures leprosy.

We came to the famous old Mopti mosque, electric blue under moonlight, its earthen works so eerily strange as almost to give credence to the speculation that aliens had visited Mali. Its tall mud buttresses looked like missiles topped with rounded warheads, the high sandy *banco* walls latticed with timber planks for climbing and patching with fresh mud after each rainy season, the knobby minarets topped with white ostrich eggs.

A young man in a pressed white shirt stood motionless on the corner outside, arm lazily round a light pole, staring raptly up at the walls and minarets. We walked past him down a sidestreet and into the silent alley behind the mosque, by a row of neat two-storey houses. Here again I experienced that overwhelming sense of harmony I had felt in Bamako. People sitting in doorways greeted us as we passed. There was no sound of discord or argument. Occasional strings of *kora* caressed the air.

We encountered a beautiful woman in a richly patterned, gold-embroidered robe, as she left one of the houses. Her hair was newly oiled and braided. This was her nightly salon visit, she said. She asked whether Kathryn was my wife, and when I shook my head and said no, she smiled, said, 'This is a pity,' and wandered off. When we arrived back onto the main street the young man was still there, hanging off the light pole, staring up dreamily at the mosque.

As we walked back towards the hotel we shared a new contentment, neither wishing to speak and risk breaking the spell.

We sat on a smooth log in a wicker enclosure, awaiting word of the departure of our bush taxi. It was to be the last taxi to go to Djenne that market day. Three others had already left, and the word was it might take another hour or so until all eight seats were sold in this last Peugeot. 'Of course, you may hire a taxi,' the man sitting beside me on the log suggested. 'And sell seats to people along the way. I myself would be happy to be your client.'

It was not cheap to hire the car – but, then, it might be our only chance to see Djenne. We agreed, and moments later a ramshackle white Peugeot station wagon pulled up in the red dust. The man who had sat beside me on the log climbed into the rear seat with a shy young woman in an iridescent violet robe, and an entirely toothless old man, his weathered rags drawn around so skilfully as to achieve an acceptable covering. We had the central bench seat behind the driver to ourselves. As he cajoled the old car into gear, I could see the road surface through the myriad of rust-holes in the floor beneath my feet. But then the entire car was a mobile miracle – seats patched together with string, roof and door trim non-existent, door handles snapped off, winders gone. Yet it was nothing more nor less than a standard vehicle in Mali, and we trusted it, and it went.

We drove down a main road for two hours, picking up and dropping off people: small men with goat staves who got out and strode off without a backward glance into a sun-baked plain of thorn and stone; women who climbed in clutching impossible amounts of fruits, nuts, roots, dried fish, drinking-water in thin plastic bags like balloons, sticks of firewood, stones for building, babies tied to their backs in old cotton wraps; and young men, woollen beanies pulled down over their ears against the 'winter chill', who stared equably at the flat horizon, the quinine stalk protruding from their mouths their leisurely toothbrush.

Finally we turned off down a dirt side road towards Djenne, and arrived on the banks of the muddy brown Bani. We saw that the ferry was on the far side, and did not look like returning for some time. As the midday sun strengthened uncomfortably, we were surrounded by an excited throng of children selling toys hand-made from recycled metals – bush taxis, fire engines, tractors and bulldozers from condensed milk tins; Airbuses and Concordes from red and yellow insecticide cans printed with mosquitoes; even a tin model of the ferry we hoped soon to board. Each one was ingeniously clever, with moving parts and wheels.

After the crossing, the driver drove on quickly, and minutes later we crossed a small bridge onto an island in the Bani River, where, pursued by the eager shouts of children, we entered the 1,000 year old red mud walls of Djenne. We came to a halt before the Grand Mosque itself – the biggest earth structure in the world, and undeniably one of its wonders. It was entrancing at first sight.

It towered, drawing the eye heavenward like a Gothic cathedral, shimmered in the heat haze like an giant sandcastle in the sky. Disappointingly, there was a sign at each major entrance, '*Entrée Interdit Aux Non-Musselmans*' ('Entry Forbidden to Non-Muslims') so that all we two Western agnostics could do was gaze upon the mosque from various vantage points around the square, and across the flat mud roofs of the town, topped with television aerials.

It being market day, the Great Mosque square was crowded with shoppers from far off towns and villages. The air was bright with the electricity of commerce, heavy with its grime. Here and there tendrils probed the nostrils with the stench of tanned hides. Buyers pushed down narrow aisles between tall pyramids of pigments and spices on mats, raw cotton and bales of fibre, sacks of rice and cement, slabs of rock salt, dried onions in rounds and tomato and chilli pounded into scarlet powders, stalls of embroidered woollen rugs and Fulani blankets, ostrich feathers and velvet Moroccan slippers, transistor radios and batteries, hair-combs and toothbrushes and endless racks of cheap baby clothes – this last item confirmation, if ever it were needed, of Mali's population explosion.

Djenne is a city of artisans, and we spent the hottest part of the afternoon within the cool of mud walls, drinking mint tea with sculptors, painters and wood carvers. Kathryn bought two masks, primal, satisfyingly creepy. Down its twisting streets and alleys Djenne exuded an oddly European ambience, like a medieval Italian city. We passed Koranic schools where children memorised verses inscribed in chalk on wooden tablets, arabesque *jalousies* in pink wash and lime-green, and *banco* houses amber-yellow against the azure sky, their façades jutting out with clay pipes. A wide courtyard opened out before us, a spreading paper-bark splashing shade across a sandy floor, a chicken pecking, a child working a water pump pausing to smile while all around him an immaculate tranquillity abided.

In the late afternoon we returned to the taxi for the trip back to Mopti. While we waited for the driver to show up, a group of children edged forward curiously. One older child offered Kathryn a yellowed textbook which turned out, of all things, to be a school anthology of English poetry. She took it and flicked through until she came to *The Cloud*. The crowd quietened as she began reading, her voice clear, unusually deep to the listening ears.

> *I bring fresh showers for the thirsting flowers,*
> *From the seas and the streams;*
> *I bear light shade for the leaves when laid*
> *In their noonday dreams . . .*

At the end of each couplet, the children soundlessly mouthed or murmured the rhyme . . . '*streams . . . dreams.*' As Kathryn read on, their voices gained in confidence, so that soon they joined her in the well-drilled pattern of the verse. I tried to envisage the classroom, the young teacher posted up from Bamako to the dust of Djenne, halted in an aisle between desks by a daydream of a sweetheart left behind, all the while drilling the drowsy class with a foreign poem called 'The Cloud', by some long-departed Englishman called Percy Bysshe Shelley.

> *I am the daughter of Earth and Water,*
> *And the nursling of the Sky;*
> *I pass through the pores of the oceans and shores;*
> *I change, but I cannot die.*

The children were silent, held in deep attention, when she finished reading. Without a word Kathryn returned the book, stooped and picked up three stones. To the delight of the children, and the adults watching them, she began juggling, high tosses, slow loops, trick catches. The children were still clapping when our driver returned and started up the Peugeot engine, and as we got in they surrounded the bush taxi, laughing, farewelling her.

We found ourselves sharing the ride back with an American photographer, a taciturn man I remembered from a few days previously when he had accidentally locked himself in his room at the Campement Hotel. From the banging on his door I realised he was in difficulty and summoned the manager, and we spent ten minutes working on the lock until we finally got the door open. When we did so, the American emerged with barely a word of thanks, and walked off. Now he sat in the seat before us, bossing around his Malian guide. Our only other travel companion was a pony-tailed thirtysomething French hippie, who maintained the conspicuously silent self-absorption of the hipper-than-thou all the way back to Mopti.

As night fell Kathryn dozed, her head bumping gently against my shoulder. 'We'll have a full moon in the Dogon,' I said when she woke and stared up into the sky, the Milky Way clear across it.

'Of course we will,' she said.

Grace & Abandon

Some days later, another hired bush taxi crawled along a rocky track beyond the frontier town of Bandiagara. We were journeying into the Sahel at the start of a five-day walking trip through the *Pays Dogon* – the Dogon Country.

The Dogon People live in a string of villages nestled along the hundred or so kilometre length of the Falaise de Bandiagara, a tall sandstone escarpment that drops off into a vast, orange sandy semi-desert called the Gondo Plain. They have no centralised form of government or administration, and some of the villages do not even speak the same language, although there is a Dogon *lingua franca* that can be spoken by all.

The Dogon have spiritual leadership as a people in the form of the *hogon*, who lives alone high up in the cliffs. They have a complex religious and metaphysical system – as well as a keen interest in astronomy. All these coincide in a rite called the *sigui*, held every sixty years when the dog star Sirius in Canis Major – the brightest star in the terrestrial sky – appears between two mountain peaks. The ceremony is based on a Dogon belief that 3,000 years ago beings from Sirius visited them – cherchez Erik von Daniken. Fieldwork by French anthropologists in the 1950s and some astronomical diagrams drawn in the sand by the Dogon led to the theory that somehow the Dogon knew of Sirius B, a white dwarf star, before Western astronomy. The existence of Sirius B was deduced by Western astronomers in the nineteenth century because of the irregular behaviour of Sirius, but it was not actually photographed until 1970. How the Dogon could have known of the existence of a tiny star light years from earth without the use of telescopes has mystified Western thinkers for a generation. The Dogon themselves say they learnt of Sirius B from the *Nommos*, a race of reptilian-amphibious aliens who visited them, and whom they call *The Teachers*. The Dogon also believe there is actually a third star in the Sirius group: this has yet to be confirmed by western astronomy.

The origin of the Dogon as a people is equally intriguing. One Dogon man told me they came from what is now Saudi Arabia, chased all the way across the Sahara by Muslims to their current home in the cliffs where they made their stand, and found a new life. I also heard it suggested that they are the lost crew of the Argo, who intermarried with Africans – or perhaps they are just a lost tribe of Israel. Whatever, they are a singular people, with a quiet determination to hold onto their culture, their values and their way of life. Their villages have no running water, no electricity, telephone, two-way radio, certainly no television. Here one quits the world wide web.

We went in with Moussa, our guide from Mopti. We had by now come to know him quite well as a courteous, trustworthy and resourceful person. At just twenty-one years of age he was one of the most respected guides in Mopti. Everyone we spoke to said, '*Ah, oui, Moussa – très bon, très honnête.*' His two greatest enjoyments seemed to be illuminating the fine points of Dogon culture, and playing frisbee at dusk.

The bush taxi stopped abruptly, and I thought for a moment we had a flat tyre, but Moussa said, 'We are here.' I scanned an arid, unprepossessing landscape, and wondered precisely what he meant by 'here'. We got out and shouldered our packs, and started walking up a steep, boulder-strewn path. Gradually a human habitation revealed itself on the crest of the hill, the village of Djijuibombo ('Ji-ji-bombo'). Although Moussa's father was a Bambara living in Bamako, his mother was Dogon, and he had relatives and friends scattered all through the Dogon Country. He was greeted affectionately as we went down meandering alleys of flat-roofed *banco* houses, and squat mud-brick granaries with thatchroofs of grey millet stalks. We were directed to a courtyard between buildings, and a shelter where we put down our bags. This turned out to be the chief's enclosure. The chief himself was there to greet us, a circumspect man of about forty, dressed in an old brown pinstripe suit jacket and baggy pants. Straw mats were pulled out for us, and we rested out of the sun while children gathered around, watching us curiously.

We were offered warm soft drinks and Flag beer carried in from Bandiagara, and a calabash of the local millet beer, still fermenting. I drank, and found it very bitter but quite palatable, if strangely active. Next lunch was brought out – all food and sleeping arrangements were included in our handwritten, signed contract with Moussa – of braised, freshly-killed chicken and a plastic bucket full of steaming sweet potato, deliciously herbed. This was followed by slabs of watermelon, which we ate as best we could before Moussa nodded to the young children hanging around, and they descended upon the remnants with glee.

After lunch the chief discreetly directed us to a mud-floored room off his enclosure, where we were treated to a Dogon art show – elaborate masks, bronze pendants and ancestral figurines, intricately carved slingshots, and a Dogon 'pop-gun' fashioned from a single dried millet stalk and wooden trigger. There was no pressure to buy, but we did purchase one or two bronze figurines.

Moussa next asked if we would like an overview of the village from the roof of the chief's house. The ladder turned out to be a notched pole, extremely challenging for novices such as ourselves – myself in particular, having washed down lunch with a warm Flag beer as well as the calabash of (albeit quite weak) millet beer. From the vantage point Moussa pointed out the various parts of the village – the Muslim quarter, with its tiny *banco* mosque, the Christian quarter with its equally tiny church, and the animist quarter, still the biggest despite the incursions of the two exotic religions over recent years. The geographical divisions not-with-standing, everyone got on well in the village, Moussa assured us. If there were problems they were worked out in the *togu na*, or talking house.

The *togu na* was a shelter of a thick, low roof of millet stalks supported by eight poles carved to represent the eight ancestral figures, four female, four male, of Dogon lore. Here the men spend the day chatting, chewing over problems, and consulting the witch doctor. Although women are excluded, this did not extend to visitors, and Kathryn accompanied me inside to meet the village's one hundred year old witch doctor. He lounged in the hollow of a boulder, his lean face faceted like a Cubist bronze. Dust adhered to his legs, arms and leathery feet. He smiled and chatted with us in French as bad as our own, but would not shake our hands. Moussa had warned us about this. He never shook hands with anybody because he did not allow outside influences to enter his body. As we left, Moussa pointed out 'fetish points', mounds of dried spilt blood and milk, built up over Dogon generations into sacred 'power points' in the earth.

We left the village around mid-afternoon, hiking first down a track through arid country past grazing goats and donkeys, until we started to descend into a hard landscape of red rock hills – again reminiscent of Australia – with a horizon-wide vista of the Gondo below, the sandy, tree-scattered plain that extended all the way into Burkina Faso, and beyond.

A group of four teenage boys with big, hand-carved slingshots joined us and scampered on ahead down the warm, rounded plain of stone. We descended a steep staircase of boulders, clambering down into a delightful green gorge, past a cold spring sprouting with ferns. The climb was hard, exacting with a heavy backpack in the sun, and soon I perspired freely. I realised that coming down out of the thousand metre tall Falaise, we had well and truly left the modern world behind. There were no rescue helicopters, certainly not back in Bandiagara or Mopti, perhaps not even in Bamako for all I knew, to come and pick up any injured hikers.

'Do people find the going hard?' I called forward to Moussa.

'Some, yes.'

'Do they ever slip and fall?'

'Sometimes.'

'What happens?'

'I wait. They feel better. We walk again.'

'But what happens if they take a really bad fall, and can't go on?'

'It has never happened.'

'But if it did?'

'It has never happened,' he said. 'I choose my tourists too wisely,' he added, with a cheeky grin.

We arrived in the village of Kani-Koboli, where we were to spend our first night. Here we did encounter the influence of the outside world, in that several of the village elders wandered around with 1960s transistor radios strapped around their necks, blasting out music from the single station that could be picked up out here, one in nearby Bankass that played wall-to-wall Dogon music. The radios played on through much of the night, a wild, impassioned talking blues, very loud, while we tried to sleep on straw mats on the hard ground, wrapped against the chill in a pair of Fulani blankets. Around three o'clock we heard drumming from a nearby village and the screams of laughter of children who ran by our walled enclosure, playing almost until dawn. It being just after millet harvest time, we encountered similar revelries all the way through the Dogon Country. Visitors would turn up in a village at three or four in the morning, play music, sit around talking loudly and laughing. If they were animist or Christian, they would drink millet beer, litres of it, and leave after dawn, rollicking homewards.

I got up and wandered out of the enclosure, and watched the first light play in filmy reds and golds high in the sandstone bluffs of the Falaise. The air was soft, the dust beneath my feet powdery fine. All the way to the horizon I saw fields dotted with dry humps like ant nests: these were the mounds from which the millet had been harvested. Women met on the pathway to the well, massive water gourds balanced on their heads, exchanging the highly formal Dogon greetings, chanting back and forth as they wandered off in either direction. The sun's rays probed down, gently warming my face. I basked a few moments, then returned and awoke Kathryn with a cup of boiled water and squeezed fresh lime.

We left the village after breakfast, and hiked in file down a sandy path along the shaded base of the Falaise. Before too long we encountered a tall German, fifty-ish, grey pony-tailed, patrician – the first other visitor we had met in the Dogon. Stopping to unscrew his canteen, he noted our guide and mentioned disdainfully that he himself had dispensed with guides many visits ago. He much preferred to travel alone now – it was so much less of a mere tourist experience that way. With that he turned his back and marched on in his Birkenstocks.

When we continued, I mentioned to Moussa that I had thought visits to the region were forbidden without guides. He said this was true, but that this man was a professional, a buyer for ethnic-antique shops back in Germany. He and others like him, Moussa said, had stripped the Dogon granaries of nearly all their precious carved wooden doors, Creation images of the eight Dogon ancestors. The dealers had paid the people next to nothing for their doors, and sold them back in Europe at vastly inflated prices – cocktail party talking points in Frankfurt, study accessories in Berlin. Now the Dogon granaries had reproduction doors, Moussa said. And thus threatened are all the tribal peoples of the world, threatened with being left with a mere reproduction of their own culture after the pony-tail vultures from the ethnic chic boutiques have picked their way through.

Moussa announced, 'Telli!', and there, in a long, deep cleft high up the Falaise, was our first 'classic' Dogon village. All we could do was gape at that mud town perched up so high in the side of a cliff. It was like seeing the Cathedral of the Sagrada Familia, or Venice, or New York for the first time. Indeed, the profile was Manhattan-like, a range of smooth, beautiful earthen towers running the length of the cleft in the sandstone escarpment. The fragile mud structures were sheltered from the rain and wind by the massive overhang of rock, just as for hundreds of years the cliffs had sheltered the Dogon villagers from the aggressors on the sandy plain below.

Moussa pointed out other houses honeycombed into the sandstone, higher and ever higher, places one could never imagine humans being able to climb. These were the houses of the Tellem people, pygmies, he said, extraordinary climbers who lived along this escarpment long before the arrival of the Dogon several hundred years ago, and who had been pushed out by them, migrating south to a new homeland down in Cameroon.

We lunched in the chief's enclosure at the foot of the cliff-face, then began the sharp ascent over mighty boulders. As we came up into the shade of the overhang and reached the lowest of the mud buildings, about five hundred feet up into the cliff-face, I realised this part of Telli was now deserted. The walls were cracked and scabrous, the ceilings tumbled in, the mud floors crumbled away to the rows of tree branches underpinning them. There was a poignant neglect about it all, and I wondered how much longer even this remnant would remain.

'People stop living here years ago now,' Moussa said. 'They moved down below.' This had been when they had decided to stop resisting Islam. Now a considerable proportion were Muslim. 'Now the Falaise is like this,' he said, pointing high up the mountainside. 'Christians up top of the cliffs, animists in the cliffs, Musselmans down on the plain.'

We walked along further, and came to the end of 'town', where the gash in the cliff-face ended. Down below stretched a forest of conical buildings jutting up out of stone, and beyond that the current settlement on the khaki plain. We sat down to rest on a log bench, and noticed a strange bowl-shape cut into the mud at our feet.

'This circumcision place,' Moussa said.

Kathryn grimaced. 'For boys, girls?'

'Many girls brought here.'

We moved uncomfortably at the realisation of what had been perpetrated in this place. Female circumcision involves the excision of the clitoris, perhaps the labia too. In the most extreme of cases, infibulation, the vagina is sewn closed. One couldn't help but wonder what bizarre human impulse – male jealousy, desire for control of female sexuality, sexual-political hegemony – had caused this practice to come into being and flourish. And so integral to the culture was it that women carried out the mutilation themselves, upon the young of their own sex, without surgical instruments or anaesthetic.

Kathryn had previously told me she could tell which women had undergone it and which ones remained intact, and as I had looked at the faces of the women and girls in Mopti and Djenne, I had to agree. There was something dull about the eyes of the women and girls who had been 'done'.

'They've been lobotomised, so that they're beasts of burden, servile workers. So they'll pound the millet and bring up the children and not rebel,' Kathryn said. 'Their souls have been cut out of them.'

Now Moussa pointed to the bowl shape carved in the hard clay at our feet. 'Blood go here,' he stated.

I saw Kathryn shudder. 'What do you think of it,' she asked him carefully, 'female circumcision?'

'I think it is a good thing.'

'Good thing?'

'It is part of our tradition.' He looked at us both, thought a moment, then added: 'Boys have it, why not the girls? It is only fifteen days to get better.'

I looked at Kathryn, and knew what she was thinking – whether to point out that there is an inestimable difference between removing the penile foreskin and the clitoris. But, perhaps uncomfortable at this exchange, Moussa got up and walked off a few paces, and in the end nothing more was said.

'He's very young. He may even be a virgin,' she said quietly. 'He might not even know what a clitoris is.'

Moussa went on ahead and we followed him down a dank and narrow, debris-strewn path between the tumbledown rows of houses, up notched climbing poles, and precariously along crumbling walls until we reached a house in relatively good repair, with a padlocked hatch-door. This had belonged to the last witch doctor of the upper town, Moussa said. When he died, he locked all his magical tools inside, where they had remained undisturbed for years. A pair of buffalo horns guarded the front wall, and beside it, set into the cliff-face, was a fetish point, the blanched skulls of sheep, goats, monkeys and dogs fixed on to the rock with dried blood, milk and mud, breaking away now and falling back into the dust.

As we began our descent back down to the plain, Moussa mentioned there had been a French plan to build a five-star hotel near the village so that tourists could come in numbers to see this world historic site. The villagers had vetoed the plan however, saying they did not want the intrusion of electricity, piped water, cars and chaos, into their lives. If tourists wanted to come and see their world, the villagers had said, they would have to walk in here just as we had, and sleep on the earth as the Dogon did.

'I bet they offered a lot of money,' I said.

'Yes. But the people did not want it.'

'Not even the young people?' Kathryn asked. 'Don't they want hamburgers and Madonna and all that rubbish?'

'Not yet,' Moussa said.

We stayed the night at Ende, where the village girls performed a vibrant impromptu dance in the moonlight. They formed a circle and chanted exuberantly while each girl took her turn in the middle, whirling around in her wild signature dance. The words were translated for us as:

If you go to Côte d'Ivoire / If you go to Abidjan / Don't forget your people / Don't forget your home.

Kathryn was urged into the circle, and danced her turn with grace and abandon to the cheers of the girls. Later we lay on a straw mat up on the roof of the chief's house, bathing in blue moonlight. We made love for the first time since Dakar, then stretched on our backs staring up the host of hard white stars just out of reach, drifting up into the softly curving blackness of space, and away into our dreams.

The next day we reached Begnimato, a predominantly Christian village perched on a rocky shelf high above the Gondo Plain, surrounded by sandstone peaks weathered into fantastic, Arizona mesa-like formations. The night was chilly up here, and we slept inside a house, but were awakened before dawn by another millet drinking party.

We departed in the early morning, the air still heavy and cool, marching up through the wind fissures in the sandstone and ironstone ranges, past villagers tending terraces of tomatoes and green onions, carrying water in calabashes from a nearby well. We climbed through gorges tangled with morning glory and fragrant with jasmine, past a spring-fed lake in a rock fissure that bloomed with water lilies. As we traversed the top of the escarpment we looked down onto a line of swells out in the Sahel, rolling pinky-gold dunes spiked with spinifex. The day remained overcast, perfect for walking, and we made the next village, Dourou, in a couple of hours.

We rested there, then, leaving our bags behind, began a hard, precipitous descent of a staircase of boulders and rocks, passing through more mesa-like formations, to the Gondo Plain again, where, under escort from a throng of '*ça va, cent francs? ça va bonbon?*' chanting children, we ended our hike resting in a wicker enclosure out of the sweltering midday heat. A chicken pecking at our feet was grabbed and hustled off, there was a rustle of feathers and a sharp cry. Lunch was on its way.

A calabash of millet beer was handed to me by one of the village men, and even though this time I wasn't quite sure about it, I was thirsty enough to drink it all down. Later, as we climbed through the upper cliff part of Nombori – another extraordinary site, another Telli, more crazy avenues of conical mud houses – I began to feel that I had seen enough. But perhaps there was something else at play: I experienced a mild queasiness. I thought it might just be the lack of variation in the diet – it felt like we had eaten enough millet and chicken here for several lifetimes – but from then on I could not help but see the grime encrusting my fingers and nails, notice the dirt on the children's hands ever extended to shake, notice every goat, dog, human turd on the path we traversed.

We returned to Dourou in the late afternoon and found a pair of other visitors there. These young men, Quebecois, had just spent three months over the border in Burkina Faso working on the construction of a remote hospital. We conversed as best we could – they had limited English and we found their heavily-accented French difficult. Later, feeling better, I went off and played frisbee with them and Moussa, while Kathryn indulged in the luxury of a bucket shower.

We played beneath tall, spreading trees on a dusty field in an arid valley below the village. The air was still and golden, swifts darted and circled. The Quebecois were skilled frisbee players, and the four of us formed a big square and threw hard – great, long throws that swooped, curved and dipped in the twilight.

Word spread through the village, and soon all the children, about a hundred of them, had assembled on either side of the valley and atop towering boulders, to watch this strange rite. Some gathered behind each of us, running shouting after each stray throw, tackling one another hard for the disc and the chance to try their own hand. Others stayed up where they were, applauding good catches, falling about laughing when one of us tripped over a dried millet-mound and sprawled in the dust.

We played for about an hour, and with each darkening gradation in the pink sky, each fresh nuance of cool in the air and the ever deepening still of the coming night, the game attained a new perfection. None of us wanted it to end, and we continued until all that could be seen in the gathering darkness was the glint of the yellow disc and the white teeth of the children laughing all about.

Despite the hard walking and climbing of the day, and the long game of frisbee, I had little appetite at dinner. We retired early, up to a roof to sleep out under another purple–black, star-filled sky. But later on a wind sprang up, the *Hamrattan* out of the Sahara, hard and cold, bristling with stinging dust, and we half-froze, tossing sleeplessly all night up on the hard clay roof.

The next morning I had no appetite at all. A feeling of nausea came and went in waves. We were to be picked up that day, and after washing we shouldered our bags and walked out of the village, pursued by most of the children from the night before. The Quebecois asked for a lift back to Mopti, and the five of us stopped and sat on our packs where something of a broken road began, waiting for the car to arrive. I was just beginning to wonder what would happen if it failed to turn up – after all, there was no way of telephoning and requesting another – when we saw a red dust cloud coming up through the stony ranges.

Son et Lumière

I had bought our Malitas airline tickets for Timbuktu a week or so previously across a dented steel desk in a room at the Campement

Hotel where a Lebanese man called Monsieur Raymond ran a small travel agency. As his assistant hand-wrote our air tickets on small, blank pieces of paper, I asked what kind of aircraft would be flying up to Timbuktu.

'It could be the small áeroplane, but then again it could be the big one,' Monsieur Raymond replied.

'What kind of planes are they?'

He stretched and yawned. '*Russe.*'

'Russian. I see. And . . . are they well serviced? Safe?'

'In all the time I have worked here there has been no problem,' he said, then repeated the phrase with well-practised emphasis, '*Pas problème.*'

'And how long is that, that you have worked here?'

'Oh, a very long time,' he said. '*Three* years. Three entire years and not one crash.' He handed me the newly-inscribed pair of tickets. '*Trois ans. Et pas problème.*'

'I . . . I see. And . . . are we assured of a place on the return flight, when the plane flies back from Gao?' I asked.

'Yes. No problem. No problem at all,' he said, then cleared his throat abruptly. 'If that is, it is the big plane that comes.'

'And if it is the small plane?'

'If it is the small plane, well . . .'and he shook his head with a 'maybe'. He smiled generously in parting. '*Eh bien, bon voyage, inshalla*' – *inshalla* the Arabic expression, universal in the Islamic world, for 'if God wills'.

As we waited on the tarmac at Mopti Airport, I wondered if it was to be the big or the small plane. Timbuktu was still a hard place to get to, but no doubt even harder to get out of if we didn't manage seats on the return flight. Planes flew only three times a week. Bookings were heavy.

Mopti Airport was curious, in that it almost totally lacked aircraft. There was only one on the ground when we arrived, a small business jet with a European crew in starched white, its engines shrieking as final checks were made. The word was it had flown in from Paris to fetch a sick French tourist. A very rich one. Chocks away, the jet taxied fast to the end of the runway, turned sharply and took off, seemingly wanting to get out of here as fast as possible.

Then the airport was quiet, utterly devoid of aircraft, the only sound the swishing gusts of the *Hamrattan* and the sales pitching of the vendors circulating through the smattering of passengers-to-be with their carvings, necklaces, dolls in national costume and menacing-looking Tuareg swords. Those swords looked danger-ous enough to be of use to a hijacker. We had been through no baggage or personal security searches here, even though, until rel-atively recent times, Timbuktu had been a hotbed of insurgency. This promised to be an interesting trip, I thought, particularly if it was the small plane that came up from Bamako.

But then an old twin-engined Antonov lumbered down out of the clouds. About the same size as a Fokker Friendship, this was obviously the big plane. After a delay, we were finally called on board, and it was time to say goodbye to Moussa. He had been acting strangely all day, and now that the moment came for us to part we saw big tears tumble from his eyes. Kathryn embraced and kissed him on the cheek, and then he embraced me, fiercely, so that I felt the damp heat of his tears against my cheek. Then he turned, waved once, stepped onto the back of a friend's mobylette and sped off.

The Antonov was sixties vintage. Its interior was stained pale blue and off-white. The seats were battered. Roaches crept in the luggage racks. But as we entered, a Fasten Seat Belts sign duti-fully illuminated red in Russian and English, and the belts worked. Through the open door into the cockpit, I saw what looked like a crew of Russians doing take-off checks, and out the porthole window I saw a technician, another Russian by the look of him, perusing the landing gear. It looked like the plane had been leased lock, stock and barrel from Aeroflot.

The pilot gunned the engines, and the aircraft began to vibrate alarmingly. The take-off was smooth enough however, and we climbed steadily out over the khaki expanse of the Sahel. After we levelled off, an African stewardess in a tropical print uniform arrived with the in-flight service – a plastic cup of mineral water and a tray of cellophane-wrapped sweets. Kathryn took one. It turned out to be a cough drop. Later I ventured back to the lavatory, yellowed bakelite and steel: sputnik deco. The luggage lay all chucked in a heap in the cargo bay beyond.

The plane laboured north, engines emitting the bored drone of a World War Two bomber. We wrote cards to post from Timbuktu. Glancing over, I happened to notice that Kathryn had ended one with a long row of kisses.

'I thought I'd send Manolis this one,' she said, flipping it over. It was the Mopti Mosque.

I said nothing. We had not mentioned Manolis, or her trip to India with or without him, since Senegal.

'Well, I can't just not write to him, can I?'

'Of course you can't,' I said.

I looked out the window. Below, the Niger overflowed into a chain of silver lakes fringed with green. We passed over intensively cultivated islands and river towns alive with black-hulled pirogues. Beyond lay all the whiteness of the Sahara.

'How does your stomach feel?' Kathryn asked.

'Better,' I said.

The plane droned on.

I had half-expected to be blasted by hot desert air when we descended the steel ladder onto the tarmac at Timbuktu, but the day was mildly sunny, midwinter cool. Things did hot up however, when we entered the terminal building to be greeted by troops in combat fatigues armed with AK-47s. An officer demanded our passports, and cast a cursory eye over them before turning and starting to walk off with them.

'*Excusez-moi monsieur,*' I said. '*Nos passeports?*'

He turned, shrugged, and tossed them to a subordinate, a lumbering grizzly of a man, AK-47 dangling casually over his shoulder, who shepherded us into a side-room with a sharp nod of his head. Inside, crates were stacked high in a corner, and what appeared to be a snapped-off aircraft nose-wheel lay in another. The man divested himself of his weapon with a metal clunk, sat down on a box and located a leatherbound ledger. Then, wordlessly, painstakingly, he transcribed our names, ages, sexes, professions, passport numbers, visa numbers, the date and place of issue of the visas back in Dakar, the date and place of issue of each passport back in Sydney, into the ledger. The big ugly gun rested easily by him all the while, entirely familiar. At last he finished writing, grunted something, handed back the passports, got up with a casual sling of the gun over his shoulder and escorted us back out into the crowded terminal. We had passed our final rite of entry.

Timbuktu began most humbly around a thousand years ago as a Tuareg seasonal camp – its name taken from the slave woman Tombouctou, 'the mother with the big navel', whom the tribes left in charge whenever they went back out into the desert. Under successive Malian empires, it established itself as the crossroads of the trans-Saharan trade routes – 'where the desert caravan meets the Niger canoe'. From here camels went north laden with gold, ivory, slaves for Morocco, for the Middle East, for the rich salons of Europe. At the same time the desperate demand for salt in the south meant rock salt from the Saharan mines was shipped from Timbuktu up the Niger to Mopti, to be traded for gold. At its zenith in the fifteenth and sixteenth centuries, Timbuktu was a thriving city of one hundred thousand people. Its universities, libraries, its judges, doctors and intellectual elite were famed across the Islamic world. But all this came to an abrupt end in 1591 with the arrival of a Moroccan expeditionary force under the command of an ambitious eunuch called Judar. Timbuktu's

Songhai troops were routed, its merchants and scholars massacred or exiled, books burned, treasures pillaged. At the same time, the sea trade routes down the West African coast pioneered by the Portuguese eclipsed the privileged position of Timbuktu, ensuring its decline. European explorers attempting to reach this most inaccessible of inaccessible places often paid with their lives, until a young Frenchman, René Caillié, reached Timbuktu (or Tombouctou as the French call it) in 1828, and got back alive to France to tell the tale. By then the mystique of Timbuktu had gripped the European imagination:

> *Then I raised*
> *My voice and cried, 'Wide Afric, doth thy Sun*
> *Lighten, thy hills enfold a city as fair*
> *As those which starr'd the night o' the elder World?*
> *Or is the rumour of thy Timbuctoo*
> *A dream as frail as those of ancient Time?'*
>
> Tennyson, 'Timbuctoo'

Effectively, today Timbuktu is a phantom, a crumbling remnant. Just a few thousand people subsist now in a city so fallen from earthly grandeur that many outsiders believe its existence to be a myth, and 'Timbuktu' merely a metaphor for 'the end of the earth'. There is no 'road' here as such. You must come by four-wheel drive, pirogue, the big or small plane. When visitors do get here, some find Timbuktu disappointing, a relic, little more than a dried-up ruin. But I liked it from the first for its austere beauty and its profound, trance-like tranquillity – a tranquillity I had experienced in other 'fallen' great places: Luxor, Knossos, the Parthenon, the Foro Romano, Avebury, Glastonbury, Vijayanagar, Borobudur.

The taxi sped down a narrow tarred road, its edges lacy with white drifting sand. Ahead was the first line of houses, straw-grey in the sun. We entered a wide sandy boulevard, and continued on

243

until it narrowed and snaked about in the old part of town, in shuttered alleys of two-storeyed houses of mud and stone.

The taxi wheeled down a side alley and suddenly headed out of town, across a river of white sand. I wondered if we would make it through, but we did, just. We climbed a low, tree-studded hill on the far side and came to rest outside a modern hotel built in the Sudanese style. It felt a little neglected, but the grounds were leafy, and there was a central courtyard bordered with flowers and crowned with a towering ghost gumtree.

The hotel was very quiet, and it was not long before we realised that only three rooms were occupied, by two American couples on retiree grand tours, and ourselves. Our room smelt of urine, just as old and strong as back in the Campement. A new wave of queasiness swelled in my stomach.

We were obliged to register at the police station, where our passports were impressed with the 'Tombouctou' stamp (said to be the entry requirement to the legendary Timbuktu Club in New York – later on I tried to find out if this place really existed, without success) and went on to the post office. I had expected to find mail waiting at *Poste Restante*, but because we had arrived a few days before planned, nothing had yet come. The visit was rewarded, however, by four letters being kept from my first attempted visit here, eighteen months before. Two were dog-eared Australia Post aerograms from my mother – news of my aunt's health and a mooted visit to Melbourne by train – there was a postcard from Dirk in London, of Picabia's 'Fig Leaf', and another from London, a letter from an old friend called Pete, who usually wrote jauntily about cricket, but in this case reflected movingly upon the deaths of the British Labour leader John Smith, and his own father.

Kathryn bought stamps. I saw the postcard of the Mopti Mosque with the Athens address among the cards in her hand.

'How many stamps would you like?' she asked.

'Three will do me,' I said. The old gum tasted bitter. I slipped my cards in the posting box, and hers followed.

'What did Dirk have to say from last year?' she asked as we walked out.

'Angst,' I said.
'Anything special?'
'No. Just the usual angst.'

We wandered down the empty, dun-coloured streets in the sun, past cracked old mosques and clustered houses that looked like sets from a cowboy movie but for their carved, Moroccan-style studded wooden doors. I had half-expected a harsh and unwelcoming atmosphere in this frontier town, but Timbuktu defeated expectation. There was no paranoia here. One had no sense of tight security, of watching eyes. The pan-Malian harmony abided here too, perhaps even more strongly so. There was a welcome absence of street hustlers and the eternal '*ça va cent francs?*' begging children. The town felt organic, cellular: it was like strolling inside a spiral seashell. But there was a palpable presence here too, an uncompromising one. Timbuktu retained its power and its secrets, its desert Torah, but this was not revealed, certainly not to the casual visitor anyway. We sleepwalked through the sandy maze while Timbuktu brooded within a hard shell of mud.

When we returned to the hotel in the late afternoon, a blue-robed and turbaned Tuareg stood at the bar soliciting camel rides out into the sunset. He was a lean, sun-dried man, and he bargained very hard. I wasn't even sure I felt up to riding camels over dunes, but a price was reached and we agreed to go.

We went with him to the first line of sandhills outside the hotel enclosure, mounted the camels, and set off with his two young sons leading with leashes. Along the way the man, who introduced himself as Mr Ibrahim, mentioned how poor the Tuareg people were now, how bad the seasons had been and low the goat numbers, and suggested that for an additional payment the women of the village would sing for us. We negotiated as the

245

camels plodded over the rosy-white Saharan sands, hanging on gamely, our feet cross-braced on the camels' necks.

After a half-hour or so we saw the first signs of a camp up ahead. Boys ranged through the dunes while slender women in blue–black robes carried firewood towards a scattering of tents. Dismounting from the camels – mine bellowing profanities, resolutely refusing to genuflect and release me – Mr Ibrahim directed us past a low, dark tent where a woman of twenty or so breastfed a baby, to a semi-enclosure of desert thorns where goats are usually kraaled, and invited us to sit on a pair of worn mats in the sand.

While one of his sons prepared us mint tea in a tiny blue pot, the women drifted up – three ancient withered ones, the indigo drained from their robes by age to a flat grey, the younger ones supple, bright-eyed, lashes long, noses aquiline, teeth perfect as a graduating drama student's. Lastly came the young woman who had been breastfeeding, and I realised she was Mr Ibrahim's wife, the baby his youngest child. He himself must have been at least fifty. Their five-year-old daughter ran up laughing, skin golden smooth as the dunes, with the elfin features of the Parisian model she one day might well be, while the naked baby pulled incessantly at her mother's bulbous brown nipple swathed in blue. As the last rays of the sun slanted across the dunes and the moonlight was affirmed, the women silently arranged themselves in a semicircle before us on the fine white sand. I sipped my tea. The evening was sublimely serene, and the desert felt a wondrous place to be just then, clean and hospitable.

While Mr Ibrahim refilled our cups, his wife took out a single-stringed instrument and began playing it with a tiny bow, and the Tuareg women clapped in time – but bored, very bored. Subdued, almost embarrassed chanting followed, killing time rather than keeping it. Soon the chanting wavered and started to die away, voice by voice. After all, the rice was on the cooking coals back at their tents, they had children to feed and men to deal with, and they wondered how much longer it would be until they were released from this nightly tourist chore. And so even here, I thought, even here in the sands outside Timbuktu, one felt the dead hand of tourism, of culture as fleeting display, heritage as floorshow. I looked across at Kathryn, and we nodded. We said *'merci'* to Mr Ibrahim, and the women were released.

As we strolled through the dunes before the return journey, I wondered how long the Tuareg would be able to go on like this, living in their camps on the edge of town, scraping together what they could. On the way back, I asked Mr Ibrahim whether he used Western medicines when his children became sick. He said he used traditional ones whenever possible, but with so many plant species dying off in the Sahel, they had to rely more and more on Western drugs and remedies.

As we parted, he said, 'We are poor people, very poor,' and I could not work out what was more disturbing – a people whose home is the wide Sahara considering they are 'poor' in comparison to the junk-fed worker bees of the industrial world, or the warrior founders of Timbuktu reduced to beggary at its verge.

That night we walked from the hotel into town to eat, and came back late. I ate little, but the walk back made me feel better. The night was clear, the sky crowded with stars, the sand silky underfoot. The streets were nearly empty.

We walked outside town into the dunes and stopped near the huts of the Bela tribe – until recent times the slaves of the Tuareg – to look back at Timbuktu's pleasing jigsaw of low, rectangular shapes, each corner and angle outlined with the blue coal of the moon. From here Timbuktu's time did look short. A tide of sand washed up along every wall, crossed every alleyway, huddled at every stoop. We listened to the night sounds, to the barking of dogs and hee-hawing of donkeys, the distant crackle and whine of a short wave radio, the muttering from the Bela tents, a baby's cry; and, from the nomad camps that encircled this palace of mud and moonlight, the drumming and the wild ululations of the Tuareg women, no longer bored and muted, but full-voiced and frenzied.

My stomach felt worse that night. I could still taste the millet beer of Nombori, and for the second night I was unable to sleep. The drains smelt ever more putrid. I shivered as day broke. Finally my alarm clock sounded, and Kathryn woke. 'Are you alright?'

'I've still got that queasy feeling.'

'Could you eat some breakfast?'

'I don't know. I could drink some tea perhaps.'

We got up and packed, and went into the dining room and found it unlit and empty. There was no one on the front desk either, just a security guard sleeping on a couch.

'We'll get something at the airport,' Kathryn said. 'I'll find us a taxi.'

The airport appeared deserted too as the taxi pulled up. Fortunately there was a café inside, the Air Bar, a place of such congenial simplicity that I could not explain why I had not noticed it upon our arrival, beyond the general chaos and a stranger wielding an AK-47.

The bar was constructed from pale Timbuktu stone cut in irregular chunks, each piece outlined in thick, pale blue. The wall behind was washed russet-pink, and watermarked with character lines that nightclub designers work so hard to contrive. Cut into the wall were six small arabesque triangles glowing white with the waxing light, and below them two shelves which bore menu samples in small bottles: Sprite, Fanta, Coke. Above was the sign, 'Air Bar', and the Malian symbol, two parallel lines for the sky and the earth, bisected by a vertical line for humanity.

We took our places on a pair of vinyl and chromium bar stools, and the young man behind the bar served us steaming Nescafés with condensed milk, and fresh baguettes and jam. I found I was hungry at last.

'Feeling better?' Kathryn said.

'I must be. It's strange how it comes and goes in waves.'

After breakfast we sat in the semi-circle of seats – the entire airport was charming, the Malians do good airports – and watched as the fire truck trundled out onto the tarmac. A moment later we heard the drone of the Antonov, and there it was, returning from Gao out of the powderpuff sky for the run back down to Mopti and Bamako.

I noticed some new buildings near the terminal, and asked a Malian man sitting beside me about them. He said an international airport was being built and would begin operating in about a year or so, when a new runway was complete. I pictured it: Jumbos from America, Airbuses of Euro-riche, and Timbuktu's prolonged peace would again be shattered by ruthless hordes from beyond the Sahara. I saw the Tuareg spectaculars in the desert, the *son et lumière* shows, the five-star towers and the touts and the sex trade, and the sweat factories down in Bamako stamping out the authentic Tuareg artefacts by the container load. Timbuktu would die a horrible death then, one more painful than the death it had suffered over the past 400 years – news of which, from my point of view at any rate, had been greatly exaggerated.

Kathryn returned to the bar and came back with more coffees. I wrote in my journal, she in hers. Then she took out something from its pages: I recognised the postcard of the Mopti Mosque.

'I didn't send it to him,' she said.

'Why not?'

'I decided not to. It's over.'

The Antonov taxied towards the terminal with a roar, turned like a squat ungainly duck, and came to a halt. The man beside me rose, picked up his briefcase, and walked purposefully out the doorway towards it. Lingering, we embraced by the Air Bar.

The Dire Circumstance

Blowflies buzzed in thick black clouds while we waited for the Bamako bus in Mopti. Kathryn thought they might have been blown in by the *Hamrattan*. I wasn't sure. All I knew was that I was very tired now, that the waves of queasiness came faster and bordered on nausea, that we were surrounded by shit and offal and fishheads and filth and flies, and we had a whole night on a bus ahead of us.

Finally we boarded, and the bus pulled out of Mopti. We stopped for half an hour in nearby Sevare for no apparent reason, and then, as the sun set over the Sahel, we picked up speed and set course for Bamako. Kathryn sat by the window and had it wide open so that we both felt refreshed by the early evening air. As darkness fell over the flat plains, she asked me for the sleeping pills. I didn't feel up to taking any myself, but she did, hoping this time she would be able to sleep properly. The music was not so loud on this bus, and a few minutes later she began to drift towards sleep. I sat with my shoes off and eyes closed, listening to the music, trying to calm my stomach, a bottle of mineral water wedged between my feet.

About half an hour later, as the bus pulled up at a police checkpoint and village women appeared at the window with oranges and dried fish on trays balanced on their heads, I felt thirsty and groped for the water bottle, dislodging its plastic cap, which rolled away. As I bent forward to feel for it beneath the seat in front of me, the smell of something truly rotten down there reached my nostrils, and my stomach turned in an instant. It was all I could do to hurl myself towards the window past Kathryn, and get my head out. The first plume of vomit just missed a pair of women vendors, who looked up and shouted angrily at me. I saw orange dust rise where the next jet hit.

'*Excusez-moi,*' I gasped out. '*Excusez-moi.*'

Kathryn woke and put her arm around me.

'Are you alright?'

Another bout gripped me before I could answer, and the women below stood back and watched as it kept pumping out of me. While it was happening, I envisaged the scene as observed from outside, saw what the watchers must be seeing, my white face thrust out of the bus window, hapless and helpless, heaving into the red dust.

Other passengers murmured sympathy, but the driver was on a
schedule and we started moving again with my head still out the
window. We sped up quickly, the bus charging through the night,
the wind blowing my hair back towards my mouth, and jet after
jet coming from me, flying back along the side of the bus in a long
smear.

Finally the convulsions slowed, started again, slowed, started
again, then, finally, stopped. I found myself breathless, my
insides bruised. I gasped and gulped in the black desert air which
rushed towards me. Then at last, cautiously, withdrew from the
window and fell back into my seat. My face was filthy, my mouth
worse.

'Okay?' Kathryn said. 'Better?'

'Yes . . . yes, I think so.'

'Good,' she murmured, but I could hear the sleeping pills talking as she struggled to stay awake. 'Sure?'

'Yes. Go back to sleep. I'll be alright now.'

And with that she smiled dreamily and squeezed my hand, and
drifted back off to sleep. I realised then that while my mouth was
very dry, my feet were wet. This was because as I had leapt
towards the open window, I had kicked over the open bottle of
mineral water. It was now empty, the water washing up and down
beneath our seat, our daypack sopping.

'Oh Christ,' I said, fishing things from it, trying to get them to
dry. But I was seized then by yet another bout. When I gasped in
air at the finish this time, my stomach was completely empty –
empty as our water bottle. My mouth felt drier than ever, my
throat burned, my lips like they would crack wide apart. Again I
tasted the bitter beer of Nombori.

But I did feel better. At least that horrible queasiness was gone
now. It was as if I had vomited out my indecision and self-doubt,
the debacle of my first visit to West Africa; that I was purged of
many things. I felt strengthened. Yet as this most unendurable of
nights continued, as the music played ever louder and I did battle
with my adversary the bus seat in every position short of
Missionary, I found myself revisiting doubt. What was I doing

here, on this bus, beyond enduring the lot of a hapless, stupid tourist? Was my body again trying to tell me something – that perhaps I was not cut out for this kind of thing? Was 'travel' just a romantic dream? And what was it anyway, travel? All the world was going the way of the theme-park, even, soon, Timbuktu. It was tourism. Travel was tourism without the trimmings and comforts, but tourism just the same. And why had I put Kathryn through what I had, when I obviously loved her as much as I did, and opened the way for her to put me through what she had? What was the use of any of it? This sort of thing went on for a good couple of hours, at the end of which I realised I was dehydrated and somewhat delirious.

Finally the bus stopped at another police checkpoint, and I got off and asked stallholders selling cigarettes and bags of peanuts if anyone had anything to drink. No one did, but someone pointed to a little village up the road and over a ditch. It was pitch dark, but I saw what looked like a flickering candle or two up there, and made my way towards it, down into the ditch, slithering on the seat of my pants and then struggling up the other side. I discerned the shape of a boy by a hut, and approached, asking for a drink.

'*Vous avez des boissons ici?*' ('You have drinks here?') I asked, looking back up the road at the bus, worried the paperwork would be concluded and the driver would take off.

'Fanta,' the boy said.

'*Seulement Fanta? Pas d'eau minérale?*' ('Only Fanta? No mineral water?')

'*Seulement Fanta.*'

I loathe sugary soft drinks – but even Fanta was better than thirst. The boy led me into a hut, the interior in total darkness. A big man loomed up, and the boy said something to him. In the distance I heard the splutter of the bus engine starting up.

'Christ no,' I muttered, again.

The man handed me something in the darkness. It was indeed a bottle of Fanta. He had a bottle-opener ready, and flipped the top off. I thrust the bottle into my parched mouth, drank it down in two mouthfuls, and involuntarily belched.

'*Excusez-moi,*' I said, rummaging in my pocket for money. To my horror, I had none.

The bus horn sounded: it was leaving. An image flashed through my head: Kathryn waking up in Bamako in five or six hours time, and finding my seat empty.

'*Pardon, pardon, je n'ai pas d'argent.*'

'*Quoi?*' the man said.

'I . . . I thought I had money on me,' I explained in French, 'but I don't, and now I have to go. I really do.' And with that I turned and ran off, out of that village enclosure, down into the ditch and up again, stumbling as I went, scurrying on until I reached the closed doors of the bus just as the driver put it into gear, and hammered on the metal and glass until he relented and opened the door for me, and I climbed in and staggered back down to my seat and collapsed into it as we took off. I looked back and saw the man and the boy had followed, and stood in the middle of the road watching, not so much angry as surprised, miffed, as the bus disappeared from view.

Kathryn opened her eyes.

'Some women came by, and I got us some watermelon,' she said sleepily. 'Would you like some? You must be thirsty.' And she handed me a chunk of the reddest, sweetest, wettest, most watery melon I have ever had the joy to taste.

'Thank you, darling,' I said, sucking on it like an infant a teat.

When I awoke it was still well before dawn, but the bus was already entering the outskirts of Bamako. Minutes later it pulled up in a desolate lot by the side of the highway, outside the shuttered company office, and the engine was switched off. Someone said we had to remain on the bus until the luggage compartment was opened at six o'clock. I looked at my watch – it wasn't yet three-thirty. People snored all around. To make matters worse, the smell that had triggered my nausea earlier was now far stronger, a terrible stench that seemed to seep up from the baggage compartment below.

We struggled towards the front, manoeuvring around poked out legs, and stepping over sleeping bodies in the aisle.

'Why can't we have our bags now?' Kathryn asked the driver.

'You sleep now,' was all he said in reply.

'Then at least let us off please.'

'It is not company policy.'

'Please,' she insisted, and with a hiss of compressed air from the doors, he relented.

We climbed down onto the bare, rocky ground. The air was cold. There was the odd building here and there by the roadside, and we looked about for a café, but the only place that appeared to be open was a police station. There were no taxis either. Unless we intended to walk five or so kilometres into town, and return in two hours' time, we were stuck here – and our blankets and warm clothes were all locked in the luggage compartment.

We wandered around the parking lot searching for a bench or seat, a sheltered place to sit down, but there was nothing: just more hard, rocky ground. We ventured further, and behind the parking area discovered a walled-off building site of dug foundations and half-built walls. We nosed about, and stumbled upon a man sleeping in blankets on a straw mat in the dirt, whom I took to be a security guard or worker who slept on site, or perhaps he was simply homeless. He awoke and asked what we wanted. We explained our situation, and without hesitation, he offered us one of his two blankets. Dog-tired we took him up on it, and lying down in the red earth and rocks, pulled the blanket over us. I looked around at the turds and the rubbish scattered all about us, but soon gave up and just slept.

Intense cold and hip-on-rock ensured I did not sleep beyond dawn, and I woke Kathryn just as the eastern sky was lightening. We got up, dusted and cleaned ourselves off as best we could, and she draped the blanket back over our sleeping benefactor. We returned to the bus just as the other passengers were blearily alighting. As we all stamped our feet in the cold, the luggage compartment was finally opened. An overpowering stench issued from it, and two goats and a sheep came staggering from where they had slept, pissed and shat all night among our bags. Three men unceremoniously grabbed the dazed animals, stuffed them into hessian sacks and bundled them into a waiting van.

A taxi turned up. 'The Grand Hotel, please,' Kathryn said.

'The hotel is full,' the night manager said matter-of-factly, glancing up from something he was writing behind the counter. 'In fact, all hotels are full just now.'

'Why?' I asked weakly.

'A conference. The UN.'

He resumed writing. Kathryn and I looked at each other.

'We stayed here before,' she tried.

'Yes,' the man said. 'Actually, I remember you.'

'Well, could we leave our bags here please?' she asked. 'Perhaps use the pool?'

The man looked us over, seemed to take pity on us.

'Will you eat lunch in the restaurant?'

'With pleasure,' Kathryn said.

We spent the rest of the day by the pool, magically transformed by its cool blue waters from road bums into first class tourists. I swapped my vomit-stained, ground-slept-on T-shirt and jeans for speedos. Staff wheeled out sun lounges and umbrellas, towels were of softest white. We swam, slept, swam, read, slept. We dressed for lunch, later swam and slept again. At dusk we took a shuttle bus out to the airport, sharing it with one other passenger, a French businessman.

'Did you see the international airport they are building at Timbuktu?'

'Yes,' I said.

'Such a gift to the Tuaregs,' he said.

'How do you mean?'

'What better bargaining chip? Give us our independence, what we want, or we blow up the runway when the first big Jumbo comes in. *C'est vrai, n'est-ce pas?*'

We snored through the flight back to Dakar. The next day was my birthday – and our last full day together in Africa. The following afternoon we said our goodbyes. My flight to New York was leaving earlier: Kathryn had to wait another ten hours for hers back to London, but she came out to farewell me. After Christmas in London she was going on to India for two months. And then what? What was there to do, in our dire circumstance of love, but be together, as best we could?

The temperature fell a hundred degrees during the eight-hour flight from Dakar to New York. The worst snowstorm to hit in thirty-five years started blowing as I dragged my bags from a taxi in SoHo and pressed my cousin's buzzer. While I waited, big flakes of snow fluttered down steadily, gathered on my shoulders, in my hair, gently settling on the black asphalt until they covered it in a soft white blanket, white as the sand down the streets of Timbuktu.

The

Cafés of Paris

I wonder why Pinter chose squash for *Betrayal*? Is it really so treacherous? I met a very rich man through playing squash. He owned a big house up on Bellevue Hill, mixed and matched his prestige cars with the occasion.

He was a broker, market operator or some such, it was hard for him to describe. He was a tough squash player, a hunter on the court – doubtless even more a hunter off it.

When he moved his family into their new place up on the Hill, he had a movie critic compile a catalogue of 3,000 video titles for his theatrette. One night after dinner there, we went downstairs to watch *Last Year at Marienbad*. My choice – it was one of those films I had always meant to see. From the portentous opening chords I knew I had made the wrong choice. Wined and dined eyelids drooped, and within ten minutes all four of us were sleeping like babes.

My squash partner used to ask me about books, whether I could recommend something he might like to read. When I suggested Hemingway one day, he went straight out and bought *Fiesta*. At our next game a week or so later, he told me he had enjoyed the book so much he was buying an apartment in Paris. One or two million US dollars, he was flying over next week. When I asked what he had responded to most, he said it was the way Hemingway wrote of the cafés of Paris.

LONELY PLANET JOURNEYS

JOURNEYS is a unique collection of travel writing – published by the company that understands travel better than anyone else.

It is a series for anyone who has ever experienced – or dreamed of – the magical moment when they encountered a strange culture or saw a place for the first time. They are tales to read while you're planning a trip, while you're on the road or while you're in an armchair, in front of a fire.

These outstanding titles explore our planet through the eyes of a diverse group of international writers. JOURNEYS books catch the spirit of a place, illuminate a culture, recount an adventure, or introduce a fascinating way of life. They always entertain, and always enrich the experience of travel.

'Lively, intelligent and varied . . . an important contribution to travel literature' – *Age (Melbourne)*

LOST JAPAN
Alex Kerr

Lost Japan draws on the author's personal experiences of Japan over thirty years. Alex Kerr takes his readers on a backstage tour, exploring different facets of his involvement with the country: friendships with Kabuki actors, buying and selling art, studying calligraphy, exploring rarely visited temples and shrines.

'one of the finest books about Japan written in decades' – *Insight Japan*

A SEASON IN HEAVEN
True Tales from the Road to Kathmandu
David Tomoroy

In Iran and Afghanistan, in Rishikesh and Goa, in ashrams, mountain villages and dubious hotels, a generation of young people got hip, got busted, lost their luggage, and sometimes found themselves. From confusion to contentment, from dope to dysentery, *A Season in Heaven* presents the true stories of travellers who hit the hippie trail in the late 1960s, taking the trip overland from Europe to India, Pakistan and Nepal.

Only available in Canada and the USA

IN RAJASTHAN
Royina Grewal

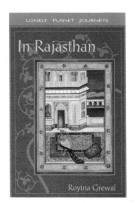

As she writes of her travels through Rajasthan, Indian writer Royina Grewal takes us behind the exotic facade of this fabled destination: here is an insider's perceptive account of India's most colourful state, conveying the excitement and challenges of a region in transition.

'a vibrant portrait of the state of princes, snake charmers and astrologers' – *Tatler*

SONGS TO AN AFRICAN SUNSET
A Zimbabwean Story
Sekai Nzenza-Shand

Returning to her family's village in Zimbabwe after many years in the West, Sekai Nzenza-Shand discovers a world where ancestor worship, polygamy and witchcraft still govern the rhythms of daily life – and where drought, deforestation and AIDS have wrought devastating changes. With insight and affection, she explores a culture torn between respect for the old ways and the irresistible pull of the new.

'Nzenza-Shand offers us a generous gift' – *Canberra Times*

THE RAINBIRD
A Central African Journey
Jan Brokken

(translated by Sam Garrett)

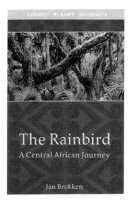

Following in the footsteps of famous Europeans such as Albert Schweitzer and H.M. Stanley, Jan Brokken journeyed to Gabon in central Africa. A kaleidoscope of adventures and anecdotes, *The Rainbird* brilliantly chronicles the encounter between Africa and Europe as it was acted out on a sidestreet of history. It is also the compelling, immensely readable account of the author's own travels in one of the Africa's most remote and mysterious regions.

'travel writing at its most enthralling, meaningful and engaging' – *Sydney Morning Herald*

MALI BLUES
Traveling to an African Beat
Lieve Joris
(translated by Sam Garrett)

Drought, rebel uprisings, ethnic conflict: these are the predominant images of West Africa. But as Lieve Joris travels in Senegal, Mauritania and Mali, she meets survivors, fascinating individuals charting new ways of living between tradition and modernity. With her remarkable gift for drawing out people's stories, Joris brilliantly captures the rhythms of a world that refuses to give in.

THE GATES OF DAMASCUS
Lieve Joris
(translated by Sam Garrett)

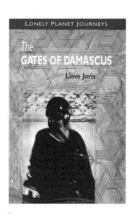

This best-selling book is a beautifully drawn portrait of day-to-day life in modern Syria. Through her intimate contact with local people, Lieve Joris draws us into the fascinating world that lies behind the gates of Damascus. Hala's husband is a political prisoner, jailed for his opposition to the Assad regime; through the author's friendship with Hala we see how Syrian politics impacts on the lives of ordinary people.

'she has expanded the boundaries of travel writing'
– Times Literary Supplement

DRIVE THRU AMERICA
Sean Condon

If you've ever wanted to drive across the US but couldn't find the time (or afford the gas), *Drive Thru America* is perfect for you.

In his search for American myths and realities – along with comfort, cable TV and good, reasonably priced coffee – Sean Condon paints a hilarious road-portrait of the USA.

'entertaining and laugh-out-loud funny'
– Alex Wilber, Travel editor, Amazon.com

SEAN & DAVID'S LONG DRIVE
Sean Condon

Sean and David are young townies who have rarely strayed beyond city limits. One day, for no good reason, they set out to discover their homeland, and what follows is a wildly entertaining adventure that covers half of Australia.

'a hilariously detailed log of two burned out friends' *– Rolling Stone*

'a definitive Generation X road epic ... a wonderful read' *– Globe & Mail*

NOT THE ONLY PLANET
Science Fiction Travel Stories
Compiled by Damien Broderick

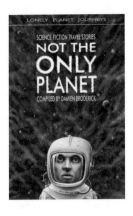

Here is a collection of travel stories with a difference. Not one of them even pretends to take us to a world we know. This international science fiction collection explores both ends of the space–time continuum, taking us back to the Crucifixion, forward to an Earth theme-park for android tourists and through parallel universes. In a world where every inch has been exhaustively explored, analysed and described, *Not the Only Planet* provides a refreshingly new perspective on travel writing.

'a stroke of high-concept brilliance . . . easily the anthology concept of the year' – *Age (Melbourne)*

BRIEF ENCOUNTERS
Stories of Love, Sex and Travel
Edited by Michelle de Kretser

Love affairs on the road, passionate holiday flings, disastrous pick-ups, erotic encounters: in this seductive collection of stories, twenty-two authors from around the world write about travel romances. Combining fiction and reportage, *Brief Encounters* is must-have reading – for everyone who has dreamt of escape with that perfect stranger.

'definitive holiday reading' – *Independent on Sunday*

'sexy tales of hot holidays' – *Elle*

THE LONELY PLANET STORY

Lonely Planet published its first book in 1973 in response to the numerous 'How did you do it?' questions Maureen and Tony Wheeler were asked after driving, busing, hitching, sailing and railing their way from England to Australia.

Written at a kitchen table and hand collated, trimmed and stapled, *Across Asia on the Cheap* became an instant local bestseller, inspiring thoughts of another book.

Eighteen months in South-East Asia resulted in their second guide, *South-East Asia on a shoestring*, which they put together in a backstreet Chinese hotel in Singapore in 1975. The 'yellow bible', as it quickly became known to backpackers around the world, soon became *the* guide to the region. It has sold well over half a million copies and is now in its 9th edition, still retaining its familiar yellow cover.

Today there are over 350 titles, including travel guides, walking guides, language kits and phrasebooks, travel atlases and travel literature. The company is the largest independent travel publisher in the world. Although Lonely Planet initially specialised in guides to Asia, today there are few corners of the globe that have not been covered.

The emphasis continues to be on travel for independent travellers. Tony and Maureen still travel for several months of each year and play an active part in the writing, updating and quality control of Lonely Planet's guides.

They have been joined by over 80 authors and 200 staff at our offices in Melbourne (Australia), Oakland (USA), London (UK) and Paris (France). Travellers themselves also make a valuable contribution to the guides through the feedback we receive in thousands of letters each year and on our web site.

The people at Lonely Planet strongly believe that travellers can make a positive contribution to the countries they visit, both through their appreciation of the countries' culture, wildlife and natural features, and through the money they spend. In addition, the company makes a direct contribution to the countries and regions it covers. Since 1986 a percentage of the income from each book has been donated to ventures such as famine relief in Africa; aid projects in India; agricultural projects in Central America; Greenpeace's efforts to halt French nuclear testing in the Pacific; and Amnesty International.

'I hope we send people out with the right attitude about travel. You realise when you travel that there are so many different perspectives about the world, so we hope these books will make people more interested in what they see.'

– Tony Wheeler